Dialogue and the Interpretation of Illness

EXPLORATIONS IN ANTHROPOLOGY
A University College London Series

Series Editors: Barbara Bender, John Gledhill and Bruce Kapferer

Dialogue and the Interpretation of Illness

Conversations in a Cameroon Village

Robert Pool

BERG

Oxford/Providence, USA

First published in 1994 by
Berg Publishers
150 Cowley Road, Oxford, OX4 1JJ, UK
221 Waterman Street, Providence, RI 02906, USA

Library of Congress Cataloging-in-Publication Data
A CIP catalogue record for this book is available from the Library
of Congress.

British Library Cataloguing in Publication Data
Pool, Robert
  Dialogue and the Interpretation of
  Illness: Conversations in a Cameroon
  Village. – (Explorations in Anthropology
  Series)
  I. Title II. Series
  306. 4
  ISBN 0-85496-873-2

ISBN 0 85496 873 3 (cloth)
     1 85973 016 7 (paper)

Printed in the Kingdom by SRP, Exeter.

**To the memory of
Bob Scholte**

Like verbal communication itself, ethnographic presentation may appear full of redundancy if measured by standards that presuppose an ideal reader, a perfect match of content and form between text and translation, and complete sets of findings covering the, and only the, announced subject of research. Parsimony is a supreme value for those who already know; ethnographers, although some of them can say what they have to say more clearly and succinctly than others, are destined to tell baroque and tortuous tales.

Johannes Fabian, *Power and Performance.*

...all ideas seem equally good to me; the fact of their existence proves that someone is creating. Does it matter whether they are objectively right or wrong? They could never remain so for long.

Lawrence Durrell, *Justine.*

We know now that a text is not a line of words releasing a single 'theological' meaning (the 'message' of the Author-God) but a multidimensional space is which a variety of writing, none of them original, blend and clash. The text is a tissue of quotations drawn from innumerable centres of culture. Similar to Bouvard and Pécuchet, those eternal copyists, at once sublime and comic and whose profound rediculessness indicated precisely the truth of writing, the writer can only imitate a gesture that is always anterior, never original. His only power is to mix writings, to counter the ones with the others, in such a way as never to rest on any one of them.

In the multiplicity of writing, everything is to be *disentangled*, nothing *deciphered*; the structure can be followed (run like the thread of a stocking) at every point and at every level, but there is nothing beneath: the space of writing is to be ranged over, not pierced; writing ceaselessly posits meaning ceaselessly to evaporate it, carrying out a systematic exemption of meaning. In precisely this way literature (it would be better from now to say *writing*), by refusing to assign a 'secret', an ultimate meaning, to the text (and to the world as text), liberated what may be called an anti-theological activity, an activity that is truly revolutionary since to refuse to fix meaning is, in the end, to refuse God and his hypostases – reason, science, law.

Roland Barthes, *Image–Music–Text.*

Contents

Acknowledgements

In announcing the death of the Author, Roland Barthes claimed that the text is nothing but a 'tissue of quotations'; the writer, never original, can only mix and imitate other writings. The author does not exist prior to the text, but is born simultaneously with it. The text only finds unity in its reading.

To a certain extent this is true of the present text. It is a product of my readings of other texts, be they the published texts of other anthropologists, the transcriptions of interviews and conversations from the field, or the spoken discourse of everyday life. Following convention, I will attempt to name the authors of some of these texts.

There are those whom I have never met but whose writings have inspired me: Dennis Tedlock, Michelle Rosaldo, Kevin Dwyer, Stephen Tyler, Paul Friedrich, Clifford Geertz, Richard Bernstein. And there are those who have inspired me both through their work and through personal acquaintance: Bob Scholte, whose untimely death deprived me of an inspiring teacher and friend, and Johannes Fabian, who supervised an earlier version of this book as a dissertation. When it comes to supervising Ph.D. students Johannes's philosophy is 'you either sink or you swim'. Individual tutoring sessions were few and far between, but he read my manuscript thoroughly (it was sometimes quite shocking how thoroughly) and wrote his comments in the margin, or announced them tersely while looking down at me from behind his pipe. But there was also dialogue. In his Tuesday afternoon anthropology seminar at the University of Amsterdam he aired his ideas and reported on work in progress. More importantly, through his maieutic method, he prompted, even forced us to develop and formulate our own ideas, often seeming to assume that we already knew, and that his task was simply to make us aware of this by patiently drawing out our knowledge. His Socratic approach, initially baffling in an academic context still largely dominated by a monological tradition in which knowledge in assumed to be transferred in a one-way process and facts discovered through the application of the proper methodology, has been perhaps my greatest inspiration.

Then there are those in the village of Tabenken who welcomed me in their midst as a guest and a friend and shared their lives with me, and on whose discourse this ethnography largely rests, both those who appear in these pages: Lawrence Banyong, Fai Nga Kontar, Fai Gabriel, Susan and Mathias Tomla, Fred Ngiri, Simon Ngengeh, Pa TaKwi and Pius Kwison, Tobias Ngwang, Pa Andrew Nfor, Francis Kongor, Father Robert Tanto, Pa Manasas Yangsi, Freda Malah; and those who do not appear, though they were no less important: Pa Tanto Ngeh, Yingkvu Cletus Ndamsa and many others.

David Zeitlin's suggestions and comments have contributed to improvements in the later stages of revision and rewriting, and Piet van Reenen and Margo Fransen provided invaluable assistance with the Limbum.

Texts are not born only of other texts, though, they are also shaped by the circumstances of their production. The fieldwork on which this ethnography is based was made possible by various persons and institutions. Professors Mathieu Schoffeleers and Jane Kusin supported my grant application, the Netherlands Organisation for the Advancement of Tropical Research (WOTRO) financed the project generously (grant no. W52-370) and René van Kessel at WOTRO ensured that my interactions with the bureaucratic apparatus proceeded smoothly and efficiently. In Cameroon the Ministry of Higher Education and Scientific Research (MESRES) granted permission for the research and a special word of thanks is due to Dr Paul Nchoji Nkwi.

I am indebted to the Roman Catholic Mission in Cameroon, in particular the Reverend Father Paul Verdzikov, Archbishop of Bamenda, the Reverend Fathers Erwin Hein, John Wilite, Fred ten Horn and Felix Muscat, Sister Rosa in Njinikom and Sister Xaveria and Dr John Dawson in Shisong. Without their assistance and hospitality my stay in Cameroon would have been both less pleasant and less productive. Thanks are also due to Professor Daniel Lantum at CUSS in Yaounde, Mr Enoch Tanfu Ngwani in Nkambe and Dr Obed Fochwang Nana, the Provincial Delegate of Health in Bamenda.

I am also grateful to Sally Chilver and Shirley Ardener for their assistance in getting this book published.

Finally, a special word of thanks to Sjaak van der Geest, without whose constant effort and stimulation this ethnography would never have been conceived.

Chapter 1

First Encounters

A Case of Malnutrition

My neighbour's compound consisted of three buildings, constructed from sun-dried mud bricks. There were two small houses with corrugated zinc roofs and windows with pieces of cardboard for panes, and a separate, windowless kitchen with a high, pointed thatch roof. The buildings formed three sides of a neat courtyard of stamped earth. It was a typical compound in Tabenken village and, indeed, in the rest of the Grassfields of western Cameroon.

My assistant, Lawrence, and I approached along the path through the coffee trees which separated my neighbour's compound from mine. Two women were sitting under the thatch awning of the kitchen roof. One of them, who was in her late teens, was shelling beans. The other, old and grey, had a child on her lap. As we entered the courtyard the old woman looked up and greeted us. The young woman ignored us and continued shelling her beans.

We sat down under the awning and Lawrence exchanged a few words with the old woman in Limbum, the local language. I looked at the child, a girl of about twenty months old. Her face was round and puffy. The dark brown skin was peeling from her cheeks and forehead to reveal pink patches of new skin. Her hair was soft and yellow instead of the usual springy, glossy black. Grossly swollen and discoloured limbs protruded from her ragged clothes, and there were open sores on her shins, on which hordes of flies had settled hungrily. The old woman occasionally swished them away with her hand, but they were persistent and returned as soon as she stopped. It looked like a textbook case of kwashiorkor, a disease described in the medical literature as a form of acute protein–energy malnutrition.

In 1978 a national nutrition survey had shown that the highest percentage of chronically malnourished children in Cameroon were to be found in the western Grassfields, and that the area also had a relatively high degree of acute protein–energy malnutrition (URCNNS 1978). Local health workers considered kwashiorkor to be a major health problem and the Catholic Mission had established a special health centre in Tabenken village for treating kwashiorkor. This was all very surprising, because the western Grassfields were also one of the richest agricultural regions in the country and there was no shortage of protein-rich foods. It was thought that 'cultural factors', and in particular people's ideas about food and the etiology of disease, were responsible. I had come to Tabenken to investigate the cultural factors related to infant malnutrition and illness, to find out how people explained and interpreted illness in general and malnutrition in particular.

Shortly after I had arrived in Tabenken and settled down in my house Francis, a village health worker at the Catholic Mission health centre, had come to inform me that two women from a neighbouring village had brought a child with serious kwashiorkor to him for treatment. He said he had ordered them to remain in Tabenken until the child was better and they were now staying with a relative, who was one of my neighbours.

Lawrence and I had now come to examine the child, whose name was Confidence, and to interview the women. The old women was Confidence's grandmother, the young woman her mother. The grandmother was very worried about Confidence and she answered most of the questions, while the mother seemed unconcerned, gazing sullenly at the beans during the whole interview.

As I did not yet understand a word of Limbum and the women did not speak English, Lawrence acted as interpreter. I asked him to find out how long the child had been sick. The old woman answered, saying that the child had been sick for about five weeks. They had brought her to Tabenken on the advice of the village health worker in their village. I asked what the initial symptoms had been. The old woman said that Confidence's face and feet had become swollen. They had taken her to the village health worker, who had told them to give Confidence eggs, meat and milk. She had also given them medicine for Confidence. I asked whether they had followed this advice. The old woman said that they had followed it exactly, and that the swelling had then reduced. But then it started again very seriously later. In the meantime they had stopped feeding her the eggs, meat and milk. When the swelling started once more they tried to feed her eggs again but she refused. Then they had gone to a traditional medicine man. He had given them medicine, but it did not help. Then they changed to another one, but that did not help either. Then they decided to come to Tabenken. I asked what they thought was causing the disease. The grandmother said that they did not know, but that the medicine man had said that Confidence had *bfaa*.

A Visit to a Traditional Healer

A few days later Lawrence, whom I had instructed to keep his eyes open for children with kwashiorkor or traditional healers who treated the disease, reported that he had been drinking with a man at the market who said that his child had kwashiorkor. The man said his child was being treated by Pa TaKwi, an old medicine man who specialised in the disease. I decided that we should pay the healer a visit as soon as possible and instructed Lawrence to find out where he lived.

That evening Lawrence met the man again and this time he pointed out the son of the medicine man, who was called Pius Kwison. Lawrence spent some time drinking with Pius and arranged to come, together with me, to see the old man the next day.

The following morning we set out to climb the hill up to Pa TaKwi's compound. It was about twenty-five minutes' walk from my own house. After walking along the dusty main road of the village for some ten minutes we branched off to the right along a narrow path. Though the sun had not yet risen the sky was bright blue and the air was crisp and clear. We passed through the cold, damp shade of a raffia-palm grove and then past the coffee bushes separating the scattered compounds before starting to climb the stony slope which led to Pa TaKwi's compound. Once we had cleared the coffee bushes a few houses became visible on the slope below us, their red-brown mud brick walls blending in with the dry grass and soil which the women had worked into mounds in preparation for the planting that would follow the first rains some three months later. Looking up the slope toward where Pa TaKwi's compound was hidden by tall, dark green kola-nut trees, the first rays of the sun reflected off the early morning dew, turning the long grass into a sparkling white sea. In the valley below there was a mass of green foliage: the dark green, caterpillar-like forms of the raffia-palm groves, as they followed the contours of the numerous streams, the light green clusters of banana and plantain trees, the tall, slim blue-green forms of the eucalyptus trees with their white, peeling stems, and the huge, cumulus-like masses of the ancient kola-nut trees, billowing up, high into the air. This green mass was surrounded by the browns of the surrounding hills: dry grass and bare, tilled soil, punctuated by great mildewed rocks, each the size of a house. In the valley there were patches of low-lying mist, which were being fed by wisps of smoke seeping through the thatch roofs of the kitchens as the women prepared breakfast before leaving for their farms. The zinc roofs of some of the houses blinked in the early morning light. There was the strong smell of eucalyptus wood smoke.

After we had climbed the steep hill for another few minutes the path turned to the right and levelled out into a straight, wide drive which led into Pa TaKwi's compound. The drive passed through a well-kept garden before leading into the yard. Various species of flowering plants were arranged in a sort of rockery along the drive and around the house. It reminded me of an English cottage. Later I discovered that there were quite a few houses in Tabenken with gardens and hedges, all resembling English cottages. There were even whole villages nearby which looked like English villages. This is a result of colonial influence because, as soon as you cross from the anglophone to the francophone part of the Grassfields, the English cottage-style houses are replaced by rows of French-style houses with porches and louvre shutters.

At the end of the drive there were four or five stone steps which led into a large, open yard of bare, stamped earth. There was a house on one side of the yard and a separate kitchen on the other. Both buildings were made of sun-dried mud bricks, the universal building material in all Grassfield villages. The kitchen was a cubic structure with no windows, a raffia-bamboo sliding door and a high, pointed, thatch roof through which the smoke of the breakfast fire was seeping. Behind the kitchen was a bamboo enclosure for goats. Along one side there was a raised bamboo platform with cages full of rabbits, the fruit of American Peace Corps volunteers' efforts to increase the protein content of the

1 Tabenken in the dry season

2 A typical compound

(already protein-rich) local diet. The house was built in an L-shape and had a corrugated zinc roof. There were three rooms in one wing, each of which had a window frame boarded up with cardboard, and a single, windowless room in the other wing. This latter was Pa TaKwi's room, where he lived and received his patients. In the past, houses in Tabenken did not have windows, and older people still generally preferred them this way. Younger generations now build Western-style houses with windows, but are usually unable to afford the glass for the panes.

Pius was working in the yard, where the ubiquitous fowls and small children moved about carrying out their respective business. When he saw us coming he stopped and came toward us beaming. He shook our hands and greeted us in the way people do in Tabenken, by translating the more-or-less ritual Limbum sentences of greeting directly into English. 'Good morning. Come good, come good. How did you sleep? You slept fine? Good. What news? How for your skin?' He told us that his father had not yet returned from his palm bush (where he went every morning to tap palm wine) and invited us into the house, telling us to sit down while he fetched a calabash of palm wine, an indispensable part of any social visit in Tabenken, and indeed, as I was to discover, an indispensable part of life in general (newborn infants are often given palm wine before they receive their first breast milk, and it is sprinkled on the ground before social drinking so that the ancestors will not go thirsty). In the meantime I forced myself into a narrow, home-made bamboo chair, which soon began to feel like some fiendish instrument of torture.

Pius returned shortly with the 'calabash', which turned out to be a plastic jerrycan with a label reading 'DANGER, weed killer: this container is not to be used for any other purpose and should be disposed of after use', and three glasses. From the jerrycan he poured himself a full glass of the white, sour smelling liquid and drank it down in one gulp. He then filled our glasses.

All social drinking starts with the host drinking the first glass before offering the wine to his guests. This is a precaution against accusations of poisoning. If the host does not taste the wine first and one of his guests becomes sick then the host will immediately be suspected of having poisoned him. However, if he tastes the wine first in the presence of other guests, no one can accuse him of deliberate poisoning. For the same reason, when you drink beer in a bar in town,

**3 Pius, forcing himself into one of his home-made chairs
for the photograph**

4 Social drinking in Kieku Quarter

the barkeeper always brings the bottles to the table and opens them there, under the eyes of the customers. Customers will promptly refuse any bottle of beer which has been opened behind the counter.

After we had drunk our first glass Pius turned to Lawrence and they exchanged a few sentences in Limbum, which I did not yet understand. Then they switched to English, and the rest of the discussion, except for a few sentences in Limbum, was in English.

[1.1] 1. 'He's telling us about the symptoms of kwashiorkor when it attacks the child,' Lawrence told me. I grabbed my cassette recorder from my bag and turned it on. 'When the child is very young,' Lawrence continued, 'immediately after delivery, you see some rashes on the skin. Then there's something that looks like fire burns on the skin. Sometimes the hair is very soft. These are the symptoms. This shows that when the child gets a bit bigger...'

2. 'When the child is about two years,' Pius interrupted, 'when the mother is going to contact [have intercourse] with the father. After some time you see the eyes swelling, you see the feet swelling. Then you know that it has gone right to the heart, already destroyed. It's easily cured when they are young.'

3. 'So when the child has just been born you can already see whether it's going to get kwashiorkor?' I asked.

4. 'Yes', Pius said. 'My father can see it. Right from when the child is born. So when he gives the medicine, then only three days and the child will be better. If, after three days, it has not been cured that means that it cannot be treated.'

5. 'So if the child can stay three days after he has given the medicine and these signs are not seen then he's not sure of treating the child?' Lawrence asked.

6. Pius took no notice of him. 'And the cause of that disease is pepper,' he said.

7. 'Pepper?' I asked, surprised.

8. 'Yes', Pius replied. 'Pepper, kola nuts, palm wine, young elephant stalk and garden eggs. They all cause the disease. From the mother's womb. If the mother stops then it cannot affect.'

9. 'Did your father learn his medicine from his father?' I asked, changing the subject.

10. 'No, he was born with it.'

11. 'Born with it?'

12. 'Yes.'
13. 'So he's a born doctor?' Lawrence asked.
14. 'Yes.'
15. Lawrence seemed pleased. 'Then he must be a good scientist?'
16. 'Yes,' Pius said. 'He's a good scientist. And a soothsayer, he's a good soothsayer. If there is something, if there is any mistake, he can refer and tell the patient or the mother who comes with a child before he gives medicine. He cannot just give the medicine like that. If there is any sign he will just tell you what happened.'
17. 'Whether sickness has been caused by witch?' Lawrence suggested.
18. 'Yes, by witch.'
19. 'Or by carelessness of not using correct food?'
20. 'He treats twins too,' Pius said.
21. Lawrence leaned forward. 'Now I'm happy with what you are saying, because yesterday I could not believe that you were speaking good things to me. I thought that you were jesting or that you just wanted us to move and drink *sha* [corn beer]. But now I have seen that you are speaking something good. My name is Lawrence,' he said, as though they had just met for the first time.
22. 'You come from where?' Pius asked.
23. 'From Ndu, and this is mister Robert,' he said pointing to me.
24. 'Welcome doctor,' Pius beamed.
25. 'I'm not a doctor,' I said.
26. He raised his eyebrows. 'Not a doctor?'
27. 'He's doing research for the university,' Lawrence explained.
28. 'Oh, research, very good.'
29. 'I'm interested in kwashiorkor,' I said.
30. 'Same as your father,' Lawrence added.
31. 'Kwashiorkor is one of the worst diseases in this environment, especially Tabenken,' Pius said. 'Tabenken is first in Donga-Mantung. Even in the South West Province children are not having it as here. I don't know what is wrong.'
32. 'Maybe they're eating the wrong food,' Lawrence ventured.
33. 'Perhaps, but this thing is caused mostly by prostitution too. That's how it moves.'
34. Lawrence was not to be discouraged in his nutritional hypothesis. 'But do you believe that there is a type of food that if they eat it this kwashiorkor will stop?'
35. 'Well you know, some children take food and just mix it with

water and begin to swell up. They prepare this corn meal and give it to a child with only a little soup. The child takes a whole loaf of food and that will not work.' When people in Tabenken speak about 'food' they usually mean the staple fufu corn which is eaten with vegetables or meat stew, hence the reference to 'loaves of food' and eating 'food' with 'soup'.

36. 'Then it means that they should be eating much soup?' Lawrence asked.

37. 'Yes. More soup than food.'

38. 'I think that when your father is treating he tells them to eat better soup than what they're eating,' Lawrence said.

39. 'Yes, he tells them to mix it with red oil. It's very useful. In Kumba the people don't have kwashiorkor as here because when they prepare their food, they prepare small loaves, just like bread. You take a loaf and I take a loaf. And then you see big dishes of soup. Here we just eat food like that without soup.'

40. 'Made out of what, vegetable or meat?' Lawrence asked.

41. 'Various kinds. Mix it. Vegetables, okra and so on. You know the people there are very rich. We are very poor,' he emphasised, looking at me.

42. 'I think we have a lot of vegetables here,' Lawrence said, 'but we don't eat them.' He was one of the few farmers in the area who grew a large variety of 'European' vegetables.

43. 'They take them to the market to sell them,' Pius explained. 'You know, women are very funny people. They take them to the market to sell them for money. You see fat loaves of food without any soup and that's how these things develop.'

44. 'I think your father gives this advice to many women?' Lawrence suggested.

45. 'Yes, to many.'

46. 'That when they take this medicine they should go and eat better food too.'

47. 'Better food, especially food and vegetables,' Pius confirmed.

48. Here I thought it time to sum up: 'So there are a lot of different things which cause kwashiorkor?'

49. 'Yes,' Pius answered. 'These four main points which I gave you: the elephant stalk, the garden eggs, kola nuts and palm wine,' he said, counting them on his fingers. 'That is what causes it. And also *rra*, that green vegetable.'

50. 'We wish that you should practice this seriously with your father,' Lawrence said benevolently. 'Do the women here sell

crickets? I think that can act like meat.'

51. 'You mean crickets?' They don't sell them, they just eat them.'

52. 'They cut and eat it themselves and sometimes the adults deprive the children of food. I think so?' Lawrence suggested.

53. 'Yes,' Pius agreed. 'It goes like that.'

54. 'Then they are stingy with food for their children,' Lawrence said.

55. Pius sighed. 'My father treats so many diseases.'

56. 'Cough too?' Lawrence asked.

57. 'Yes cough too, diarrhoea, heart pain, stomach trouble and this thing when the legs are swelling. And if somebody has been killed by a stick or killed by anything, then you go there and...'

58. 'Fix the death,' Lawrence interrupted.

59. '...fix the death, where that man is killed,' Pius continued, 'whether in the bush or somewhere, and drive out the devils. You know that when somebody is killed like that those cannibals gather themselves there and begin to trouble the death. So you have to go there and fix it. That one is a very terrible one...'

60. 'Very terrible,' Lawrence agreed.

61. '...because if you don't fix it people will continue dying like that. Then my father gathers the people from that compound and he gives some three different names. When your own falls down in this way, if it's against you he will tell you [i.e. he discovers the cause through divination with cowrie shells]. Then they will bring a goat and kill it and take out the shit, er...' he glanced at me, 'waste matter, and go to the stream and take a small fowl, then kill it and throw it in the stream. Anyone who comes there now, any cannibal who comes and reaches that place will just die.'

62. 'Now you said the sickness of swollen feet happens to old people?' Lawrence asked.

63. 'Yes, old people, and those attacked by cough have it.'

64. 'So when you are attacked by a cough your legs swell up?' Lawrence queried.

65. 'They swell,' Pius confirmed.

66. 'You don't call these swollen feet kwashiorkor?' Lawrence persisted.

67. 'No, it's not kwashiorkor. This is something which only attacks adults, not children.'

68. 'How do you call that kwashiorkor in Limbum?' Lawrence asked.

69. 'Ngang.'
70. Lawrence looked puzzled. 'Then which one do you call *bfaa*?' he wanted to know.
71. '*Bfaa*?'
72. 'Yes.'
73. '*Bfaa* is the first name, it was the first name,' Pius answered.
74. 'The first name they were calling kwashiorkor?' Lawrence asked.
75. 'Yes *bfaa*. In those days people were not knowing anything about kwashiorkor. That was the beginning.'
76. 'But now they call it *ngang*?' Lawrence asked.
77. 'Yes.'
78. 'Don't they call it *bfaa* anymore?' I asked.
79. 'No,' Pius answered.
80. I asked: 'Is kwashiorkor also caused by witchcraft?'
81. 'Yes cannibalism.'
82. 'Cannibalism?' I was surprised.
83. 'Yes,' Pius said, laughing wildly. 'The practice of eating humans.'
84. 'How does that work?' I asked.
85. 'Pardon?'
86. 'How does witchcraft cause kwashiorkor?'
87. 'Well, it's another way of eating human being. When they see a very fat child they will just take a...a...' he stuttered from excitement. 'If it is in the body, and see what they are holding. Anyway, if they go to a native doctor he will cure it. But he will just pretend, take something behind it...cure that child.'
88. I was not sure what to make of this answer and tried to pose the question differently. 'So what kind of people cause kwashiorkor by witchcraft?'
89. 'Eh...sometimes...well I hope so, because this kwashiorkor mostly comes from the mother. And sometimes through prostitution. You know, prostitutes are with diseases. They have diseases and people don't know. You go and contact one and get a disease and give it to your wife. Then she will begin to suffer.'
90. Lawrence intervened. 'Now among the Wimbum people, a man who can cause witchcraft to eat the child and cause kwashiorkor, would this be a relative of the child or someone from a different family?'
91. 'It could be someone who brings human flesh and gives it to your child without you knowing. Not only from the family,' he

paused. 'That flesh is sold in the market...'
92. 'That's man's flesh?' Lawrence seemed surprised.
93. 'Yes.'
94. 'By witchcraft?'
95. 'By witchcraft it's sold in the market. Some have bought it from the market, some trade it.' Pius's eyes gleamed.
96. 'So witch people go to the market and see it?' Lawrence asked.
97. 'They see it.'
98. 'If you are travelling on your own you can't see it?'
99. 'You can't see it.' Lawrence asked.
100. Lawrence chuckled in his characteristic, high-pitched manner. 'That's interesting. Then we have two types of market here?'
101. 'We have two types of market,' Pius confirmed. 'When we are coming back they are entering...'
102. Lawrence chuckled again.
103. 'At the time people in the market are closing they are entering,' Pius continued.
104. 'So sometimes when the people are carrying a pot of meat, selling in the daytime, they mix it...'
105. 'Yes they mix it...' Pius's eyes flashed with excitement.
106. '...with the meat of people...'
107. '...with the meat of people...'
108. '...who are in witchcraft.'
109. '...by witchcraft.'
110. 'When a witchman puts his hands there, he sees the man's meat and takes it out...'
111. 'He takes it out.'
112. '...and he who does not see will only take the ordinary meat?'
113. 'Yes.'
114. 'Ah, that's interesting,' Lawrence sighed.
115. 'At this death celebration there at Tvum,' Pius said, referring to the death celebration of a village sub-chief who died shortly after my arrival in Tabenken, 'if there are no people who can see, then they can mix it and some are eating a different type of meat, and you who doesn't know are eating your own.'
116. 'You eat but the plain meat,' Lawrence said.
117. 'Plain meat,' Pius paused. 'It's sold everywhere at the market.'
118. 'Is it only the witches who eat human meat?' I asked.
119. 'Yes,' Pius replied. 'He who doesn't know cannot eat.'
120. 'So if I go to the market I can't buy it?' I continued.
121. 'You cannot even see it.'

122. 'I can't buy it by accident?'
123. 'No you can't.'
124. 'Can *you* see it?' I asked.
125. Pius raised his eyebrows. 'Myself?'
126. 'Yes.'
127. 'No.' He shook his head emphatically.
128. 'Because he's not a witchman,' Lawrence explained.
129. 'So only witches can see it?'
130. 'Yes.'
131. 'Yes,' Lawrence agreed. 'But a person who sees witchcraft, like Pa who puts *ngambe* [divines], if he goes there can he see them selling?'
132. 'Well,' Pius paused, 'he sees them selling...' He fell silent, and the sounds from outside penetrated the silence. Hens clucking, children laughing, women stamping corn in the distance.
133. 'A good science [seance?] sees but at night,' he resumed. 'Somebody who can see something clear in the night, not only in the daytime.'
134. 'When he sees...' Lawrence attempted to intervene, but Pius ignored him.
135. 'When he sleeps, that's the time he can see things. When he sleeps you don't find any hill. All this environment is plain. You don't find any hill.'
136. 'And action comes to him like dream?'
137. 'Yes, like dreams, and he sees correctly.'
138. 'Anything that they are doing somewhere, it comes in front of him?'
139. 'Yes.'
140. 'As if he's seeing a video?'
141. 'Yes. A correct science [seance?] or soothsayer sees something better in the night, not in the daytime. Because in the daytime they are hiding.' Pius's eyes gleamed again.
142. 'Hiding,' Lawrence repeated.
143. 'Yes.'
144. 'They too are sleeping,' Lawrence said. 'Then at night they start to move.'
145. 'At night they start to move about,' Puis confirmed.
146. 'That's why in Limbum we call it tvu', because they travel...' Lawrence attempted to explain to me.
147. '*Ntaa tvu*" '*ntaa tvu*", Pius interjected excitedly.
148. Lawrence broke into high-pitched laughter and slapped his

hands on his thighs. '*Ntaa tvu*', the witch market.'

149. '*Ntaa bsaa*,' Pius added, 'the gift market.'

150. Lawrence looked puzzled. 'What is a gift market?' he asked in Limbum. Here the conversation switched to the vernacular.

151. 'A gift market is where they go and take things. It's *tvu*'. They go up to *kop bfu*, it's a gift market.'

152. 'Ndu people only say they go to Kaka, where do people here say they go to?' Lawrence asked.

153. 'To *kop bfu*.'

154. '*Kop bfu*, where's that?'

155. 'On that hill,' Pius said, pointing to a mountain which dominates the village's north-eastern horizon.

156. 'Is the forest on that hill big?

157. 'Yes,' Pius answered, 'it's the biggest market in Mbum. The one at Kaka is not as big as this one. This is where the Wimbum go to take their things. If you are there often they may catch you.'

158. 'If you always go and take things can you take something so that other people will die?'

159. 'Sometimes you take and come with sicknesses.'

160. Lawrence turned to me and said, switching back to English, 'He said this hill,' he pointed in the direction of *kop bfu*, 'the witchcraft people go there and carry things and bring them here. Sometimes they go and bring food, sometimes they go and bring sickness.'

161. 'Sickness,' Pius repeated. There was silence as they both stared at the stamped mud floor. Then Pius looked up. 'By the time they are running from death you will find a kind of wind passing. You will see trees and banana stems falling. People beating them,' he said.

162. 'While they have gone to the market. And when they come back they will be running...' Lawrence added.

163. 'The devil will be following them...'

164. '...while they are going back home.'

165. '...while they are going back home.'

166. 'Or while they are collecting things from the market?' Lawrence suggested excitedly. They were both talking fast, their eyes flashing.

167. 'Yes, then start running,' Pius said, smiling.

168. Lawrence laughed. 'When you collect something from the market, you have not been giving.'

169. 'You have not been giving,' Pius agreed.

170. 'It's just your hand that takes it...'

171. 'Yes.'
172. '...and when you take it you start to run.'
173. 'The time you start to run he will come out and start to dance,'
     Pius said. 'He will continue looking how he is dancing. In a short
     time you will find people running, a terrible wind. You know,
     some brothers and sisters die early because they go several times
     in the year or in the month.'
174. 'But why should they go when people have not sent them?'
     Lawrence asked.
175. 'They want to grow a lot of corn, a lot of groundnuts.'
176. 'Oh, for themselves?'
177. 'Yes for themselves. Some want to deliver a lot of children. They
     want to know books better, and so on. So many things are sold
     there.'

Bewilderment

Although I remember this encounter as a frustrating and bewil-
dering experience, when I re-read the transcript after leaving
Cameroon I realised that it was much more than just my clumsy
'entry' into 'the field'. The text of that meeting now stands as a
epitome of my project as a whole. The form which my fieldwork
was to take, the themes which were to prove important and the
epistemological problems which I was to face, were all present in
this first encounter.

   Lawrence and I had gone to meet a renowned medicine man
who specialised in treating the very disease I was interested in. But
on arriving at his compound we were only met by his son, who was
not actually a healer himself. He then got into a discussion with my
assistant, about subjects which did not seem to have much to do
with kwashiorkor at all and which at times seemed very inconsistent. What was more, they did not involve me in the discussion.

   At first Pius's discussion of the kinds of food traditionally
thought to cause kwashiorkor and his descriptions of the early
symptoms of the disease seemed to be the only parts which were
relevant for me. Later, though, I discovered that the other topics
which had initially seemed interesting but not relevant were really important to the people themselves. The question of the translation of illness terms seemed relatively straightforward:
kwashiorkor used to be called *bfaa* in Limbum, nowadays it was

called *ngang*. There did not seem to be any problem there. Later, however, the meanings of the words "bfaa" and "ngang"[1] were to become the central focus of my research and I was to devote hours of discussion to trying to sort out their complex and inter-linked meanings. I was also to discover that the overlap between the meaning of these terms and that of kwashiorkor was only very partial. This led to a gradual shift of my attention away from kwashiorkor and toward *bfaa* and *ngang*.

It was a shift that brought me into contact with a number of other central themes that were touched on in this initial discus-sion between Pius and Lawrence, and which at the time had seemed interesting, but marginal to my main topic: witchcraft, witch markets, cannibalism, divination, bad death and abomina-tions.

Also present in this first confrontation were the indetermina-cy, fragmentation and even outright contradiction characteristic of many later conversations. After describing the symptoms of kwashiorkor Pius went on to explain that it is caused by the mother eating certain kinds of food. Lawrence tried to force him to admit that it is caused by a lack of certain foods (the biomed-ical view with which he was familiar) but Pius insisted that it is a venereal disease spread by prostitution. He then gave in and went along with Lawrence's suggestion, only to switch back to his original explanation when I ventured to conclude that there seemed to be a lot of different causes.

Later on, in response to my question about witchcraft, he attributed kwashiorkor to cannibalism. In the end I was not sure what he thought was the cause. Was it a nutritional disorder, a venereal disease or the result of witchcraft, or was it caused by a combination of all three? Or maybe he was just talking along and saying whatever came into his head to keep us happy? Or per-haps he was out for gain, as Lawrence had suspected during their first meeting (a motive which was to crop up occasionally throughout the research, particularly in our dealings with Pius).

The discussion also highlights the complete lack of fit between the dominant Western biomedical theories of kwashiorkor and indigenous conceptions. The existence of at least two discrete dis-courses on what is putatively the same physical phenomenon,

---

1. Vernacular terms are printed in italics. I use double quotation marks for the word when I want to distinguish it from that to which it refers. So "ngang" is the word which refers to the illness *ngang* and "malaria" is the word that refers to the illness malaria.

and the direction in which power is being exerted in the relationship between these discourses, is epitomised in the part of the discussion where Lawrence, the self-styled researcher and representative of Western medical science, tried to extract the dominant biomedical explanation of kwashiorkor from Pius, the representative of traditional medicine. Lawrence was posing as the medical expert, with me, the 'white doctor', backing him up and legitimising this status. Pius did not resist and even went along with him; he never tried to convince Lawrence of the validity of his own ideas.

However, the relations of power are not as straightforward as they may seem. It is usually assumed that the anthropologist, as a representative of Western culture, is in a position of power *vis-à-vis* the members of the society he is studying. But the exercise of power is usually two way. I had money and status and could intrude on people and ask them questions if I wanted, but if they wanted to fool around and amuse themselves (perhaps in collusion with Lawrence) by telling me cock-and-bull stories about cannibals causing kwashiorkor I would not even have noticed.

The discussion also epitomises the process of fieldwork as a creative relationship between anthropologist and informants.

The relative absence of the anthropologist in this encounter is also striking. It is largely a discussion between an assistant and an informant, with the anthropologist only putting in the odd question. This deviates significantly from the conventional set-up described (or usually only implied) in much anthropological writing in which the anthropologist converses directly and fluently with native informants in the vernacular and is fully in control of the situation throughout. Usually no mention is made of assistants or interpreters, even during first field trips to areas where languages are spoken which the anthropologist could never have learned at home before departure. Anthropologists often give the impression that a couple of months of language-learning was sufficient to enable them to converse directly and fluently with the natives on even the most complex issues. In a provocative article Maxwell Owusu (1978) criticises this assumption, claiming that many of the classic ethnographers of Africa were, in fact, not competent in the language of the people they studied and that they worked mostly through interpreters.

In such accounts, when interpreters are mentioned it is with some embarrassment and the reader is given the impression that the anthropologist was totally in charge throughout and the interpreter was merely a neutral instrument of translation, transforming the anthropologist's questions into the vernacular and the informant's answers back into the language of the anthropologist, without affecting the meaning or adding to or subtracting from the content. Crapanzano (1980), for example, is quite open about his use of a 'field assistant', but claimed that he was 'invisible' during interviews. Of course, the odd ethnographer has discussed the way in which interpreters influence the image of the anthropologist and the kind of information he received (Berreman 1972). But any contribution by the interpreter seems to be regarded negatively as a contamination of the 'data' being collected from the informant and which should be avoided as much as possible.

In the above encounter with Pius not only did the assistant take the initiative in questioning the informant, but this questioning, and in fact almost the whole discussion, was carried out in English, the native language of the anthropologist. The conventional set-up was completely reversed. Instead of me struggling to interview them in their language, they were interviewing each other quite fluently in my language.

This encounter suggests two things. Firstly, the role of the interpreter, when one is used (and I did not use one in all interviews), must be acknowledged in the final ethnography, not merely an unfortunate but necessary evil distorting reality and contaminating data that is recognised by the anthropologist only in order to put the reader in a better position to minimise these distortions. The interpreter should be credited with making a creative contribution to the joint product which the anthropologist ends up taking home: the interview texts. Second, the whole question of proficiency in the vernacular needs to be made more explicit. The extent of competence in the vernacular determines access to sources of information and influences the process in which information is produced. On the other hand, lack of competence may also open new areas of enquiry, and the discussion of misunderstandings with interpreters may lead to new understandings. This is quite apart from the important psychological and practical aspects of the interpreter's mediation between the ethnographer and the culture being studied, particularly at the beginning (see Crapanzano 1980).

Another factor which must be recognised is that the people

whom anthropologists usually study are increasingly becoming fluent in the anthropologist's native language. This is illustrated in the preceding discussion. Both Pius and Lawrence were quite fluent in English, as were many of my other informants. Thus the question was raised: Should I stumble along in broken Limbum trying to speak to locals who have grown up as almost bilingual speakers of English?

Toward a Performative Ethnography

Situations such as the one described above, that deviate substantially from the conventional stereotype of the fieldwork interview suggested in monographs and described in textbooks on fieldwork method, led me to think about what exactly was going on. How was I to view encounters such as these which were not mere exercises in 'gathering data'?

In this connection Fabian speaks of performative as opposed to informative ethnography. Information is not there, in people's heads, ready to be called up and expressed in discursive statements which can then be collected by the ethnographer and taken home as 'data'. It has to be made present through enactment, performance.

> What has not been given sufficient consideration is that about large areas and important aspects of culture no one, not even the native, has information that can simply be called up and expressed in discursive statements. This sort of knowledge can be represented – made present – only through action, enactment, or performance. In fact, once one sees matters in this light, the answers we get to our ethnographic questions can be interpreted as so many cultural performances. Cultural knowledge is always mediated by 'acting'. Performances...although they can be asked for, are not really responses to questions. The ethnographer's role, then, is no longer that of questioner; he or she is but a provider of occasions, a catalyst in the weakest sense, and a producer in the strongest. (Fabian 1990a: 6–7)

In Fabian's sense the discussion between Lawrence, Pius and myself can be seen as a performance. It was an enactment, a making present, of cultural knowledge. But it was not merely enactment, it was also production. That knowledge was being produced rather than simply called up from some cognitive reservoir is clear from the text: when, for example, Lawrence made use of my lack of competence in the vernacular to take 'time out' to question Pius about gift markets before presenting me with his findings (150–9). Later this information, together with Pius's ideas about the role of certain types of food in the etiology of kwashiorkor, turned out to by highly idiosyncratic. In the meantime, however, Lawrence and I had added this information to our store of knowledge on the topic and discussed it with others, thus introducing it into the more general discourse.

Although the conversation was mainly between Lawrence and Pius, it is clear that I was the catalyst, the provider of the occasion. After all, they would not have been talking together like that, and in English, if I had not been present. But it can also be seen as a performance in the another sense. As Bauman has put it: 'Fundamentally, performance as a mode of spoken verbal communication consists in the assumption of responsibility to an audience for a display of communicative competence' (1977: 11).

Reading the transcript of that morning's discussion I cannot help having the impression that it is just that, a display put on for an audience: me. To what extent was this discussion just being staged for me? After all, they were speaking English, which was obviously for my benefit. And what are we to make of Lawrence's introduction (22–4) at a point when Pius must have known exactly who we were and what we were up to, as he and Lawrence had spent an evening together drinking corn beer. On the other hand, the fact that Lawrence also questioned Pius in Limbum surely shows that he was not only putting on a show; that at least some of it was serious enquiry. But then why switch to Limbum at exactly that moment, for those questions? Was it something I was not supposed to know, or was he just making some enquiries backstage before presenting me with his findings?

It was both an act, a performance in the conventional sense, and a serious enquiry. Now that I am in a position to interpret this conversation in the light of all that I learned subsequently, it is obvious that when Lawrence insisted on the nutritional cause of kwashiorkor he was just acting out what he thought I wanted to hear. In later discussions it became clear that he thought nutritional explanations of illness were pure nonsense. Pius tended to go along with him because Lawrence's position gave him the impression that this was what I wanted to hear. And when Lawrence asked whether the person who gave meat to the child was a family member (90) I am quite sure that he was making a display for my sake. This was something he must have known, and the way he asked about it supports my belief. Likewise, when he and Pius alternated and supported each other in the part about the cannibals and the witch market, and when Lawrence occasionally emphasised a point by asking a putative question, a performance really was being staged (see 104–14 and 131–46). I am not sure that all his questions about the cannibals in the market were only for my benefit, though. I suspect that he was familiar with part of what Pius was telling us, or perhaps he knew a different version, or versions, of the story and was asking questions for his own enlightenment as well (e.g. 162–9). His questions about the forest on the mountain, (149–59), were obviously genuine. As they were speaking Limbum this could not have been a display for me. For Lawrence the encounter was partly a serious enquiry and partly a show put on for my benefit.

The Production of Meaning

Presented below is an account that starts as an apparently simple translation of certain illness terms but ends up as an exploration of constellations of meaning, related in no fixed way to each other or to the terms which are used to talk about them; constellations of meaning which, at least as they are presented here, were partially produced or constituted during the process of fieldwork.

Some of these constellations constitute what would be called 'traditional etiology' or 'traditional cosmology' in a more conventional ethnography. But I do not attempt to describe 'the Wimbum medical system' or 'Wimbum cosmology' as though they existed separately from their realisations in concrete instances of interaction or enactment. Nor do I give an interpretation of my 'data' which attempts to reveal some underlying symbolic unity or coherence, thus making sense of apparently strange and incoherent phenomena and ideas by showing that they are really only transformations of universal themes,[2] or variations of what is already familiar to the reader.

I do not assume that there is a 'system of beliefs' in relation to which this ethnography is, or should be, a mirror-image representation. This does not mean that what are presented here as indigenous beliefs and understandings bear no relation to how Tabenken

2. Such as Godelier 1986.

people think about, and in particular talk about, these subjects. What is presented is a fiction, but it is a negotiated fiction, one which I negotiated with my informants and which they negotiated with each other during the course of my stay with them. I attempt to show the way in which knowledge about illness is produced and constituted and the essentially negative character of that knowledge: rather than being deviations from the norm fragmentation, inconsistency and indeterminacy are seen as the normal state of affairs (Fabian 1985, Friedrich 1986). This applies not only to indigenous knowledge, but also to anthropological knowledge of that knowledge. Not only were my informants' medical knowledge and interpretations normally fragmentary and indeterminate, my ethnographic presentation of this knowledge also reflects this. It is not a mirror-image reflection though: my presentation is fragmentary not because it is an accurate reflection of their fragmentary beliefs but because the praxis in which it is constituted is itself fragmentary (Fabian 1990b). In this sense my approach has been influenced by Tyler's conception of a post-modern ethnography:

> A post-modern ethnography is fragmentary because it cannot be otherwise. Life in the field is itself fragmentary, not at all organised around familiar ethnographic categories such as kinship, economy, and religion...nor do particular experiences present themselves, even to the most hardened sociologist, as conveniently labeled synecdoches, microcosms, or allegories of wholes, cultural or theoretical. At best we make do with a collection of indexical anecdotes or telling particulars with which to portend that larger unity beyond explicit textualisation. It is not just that we cannot see the forest for the trees, but that we have come to feel that there are no forests where the trees are too far apart, just as patches make quilts only if the spaces between them are small enough. (Tyler 1986: 131–2).

The negotiation began when I confronted people with my questions, biomedically derived concepts and anthropological categories, and attempted to elicit from them their translations and interpretations. It was not simply a matter of asking questions and obtaining answers that revealed 'medical beliefs' or 'culture'. I *confronted* people and obliged them, even *forced* them, to think about, and speak about, phenomena and connections about which they might not normally, perhaps ever, think. The direction which interviews and conversations took, the subjects discussed and the interpretations of terms, were influenced by confrontation, even provocation.

Relations of inequality and power played a role. I was the White 'doctor' carrying out research for the university, and if I wanted to weigh and measure children, or ask women awkward questions when they were hurriedly preparing breakfast before leaving for their farms, they may have felt obliged to comply because of this status (I say 'may have' because people did not seem to have scruples about making it clear when they had more important things to do). But obligations can be more subtle, and provocations less direct. I was also a visitor, the guest of very generous and hospitable people, and this status also carried with it obligations of cooperation for my hosts. Neither was it always necessary for me to ask questions in order to provoke answers: my very presence could provide the occasion, the motive, for spontaneous performance. Finally, it was not unusual for my hosts to spend a lot of time questioning me, which gave them a good impression of how I thought about various subjects, and this in turn influenced what they told me.

Informants did not always have ready 'information' in their heads that could be called up in response to my questions: there was no simple transfer of pre-existing information. Questions could be left unanswered, informants were able to go home think about them, discuss them and come back with tentative answers which they had negotiated with others. With these answers they confronted my own tentative answers, formed, in the meantime, in other discussions with other informants. On one occasion I discussed a point with Lawrence and he told me the opposite of what he had said on an earlier occasion.

'But now you're contradicting yourself,' I said.

'No I'm not,' he answered.

'Yes you are,' I said. 'I've got it all transcribed here.'

'Let me see that,' he said, snatching the transcription from my hand. After reading for a few minutes he said: 'Ah yes, I remember saying that then, but it's not what I really meant. What I'm saying now is what I really meant then.'

Interpretations were constantly changing for me as a result of my conversations with informants, but they were also changing for these informants as a result of their conversations with me, and with each other. And gradually we created between us a picture (unstable, indeterminate, contradictory) of how things were. This ethnography is the story of that experience.

Chapter 2

Background, Setting and Presentation

The Original Research Project

The western Grassfields of Cameroon, also known as the Bamenda Grassfields, were chosen as research location because, as was mentioned earlier, a national nutrition survey had shown that the region had the highest percentage of chronically malnourished children in the country and a relatively high degree of acute protein–energy malnutrition, even though it was a rich agricultural area. It seemed that under such conditions socio-cultural factors would be important in the genesis of malnutrition. Local health workers considered kwashiorkor to be a major health problem, and the Catholic Mission had established a health centre in Tabenken with the specific aim of treating kwashiorkor and providing health education (there was already a government health centre in the village).

The goal of my original research project was to discover the cultural factors related to infant nutrition and illness in Tabenken: to discover people's ideas or beliefs about food, nutrition and illness and the way in which they were related to incidence and therapy choice. These insights were to lead to recommendations for improving infant nutrition and health and providing acceptable health education.

Malnutrition and Kwashiorkor

Kwashiorkor occurs only in young children. There is no single definition of the disease on which all experts can agree, but oedema associated with hypoalbuminaemia (low serum protein) are generally accepted as the minimal criteria for diagnosis. Apathy and irritability are characteristic. Children with kwashiorkor have been described as 'the picture of misery. The child who can smile does not have kwashiorkor' (Hendrickse 1984: 430). Other symptoms include discolouration of the skin and hair, changes in hair texture and skin lesions which, in severe cases, may resemble second-degree burns (Hendrickse 1984: 430–1). In the biomedical literature kwashiorkor is usually described as a nutritional disorder, but its etiology is complex and has been subject to various interpretations.

The syndrome was discovered by Williams in Ghana in 1933, and she called it kwashiorkor, adopting a local term from the Ga language (Williams 1933, 1935). Since then there have been various theories about its cause and accompanying changes in terminology (see Cassidy 1982). Hendrickse (1985) lists twenty-five different terms. In an early paper on kwashiorkor Stannus (1935) referred to the syndrome as infantile pellagra and attributed it to niacin deficiency associated with a maize diet. In the early 1950s Brock and Autret (1952) and Trowell, Davis and Dean (1954) described it as a disease primarily affecting children who had just been weaned. They attributed it to a weaning diet which was high in carbohydrate but low in protein. A few years later Jelliffe (1959) included kwashiorkor and marasmus (characterised by wasting) in a single syndrome: protein-calorie malnutrition. In this interpretation kwashiorkor was thought to be caused by a high calorie/low protein diet, whereas marasmus is attributed to a diet deficient in both calories and protein.

In the 1960s these interpretations led to much concern about the so-called protein gap. In response Western countries sent large quantities of powdered milk to the developing countries to supplement children's diets, protein rich foods such as soya beans were promoted and there was a lot of effort to develop new protein-rich weaning foods.

Then in 1968 Gopalan showed that children on diets with the same protein/energy ratio could develop either marasmus or kwashiorkor, thus making the hypothesis that kwashiorkor was caused by protein deficiency in the presence of sufficient carbohydrate untenable. In an important article he suggested that kwashiorkor should be seen basically as a failure of adaptation to protein–calorie malnutrition and introduced the term 'dysadaptation' (Gopalan 1968). The earlier emphasis on protein was now widely criticised as 'the great protein fiasco' (McLaren 1974). Marasmus and kwashiorkor were no longer seen as separate nutritional disorders, but as different outcomes of the same protein–calorie deficiency. Nowadays the term 'kwashiorkor' is used less frequently and experts tend to speak more generally of protein–energy malnutrition (PEM). During the 1970s, research in West Africa showed the importance of infectious diseases, particularly measles (Morley 1973) and diarrhoea (Ebrahim 1983), in the etiology of PEM. There has been increasing interest in the hypothesis that kwashiorkor is not primarily a nutritional disorder but instead is related to the contamination of food by aflatoxins (Hendrickse 1984, 1985, 1986, Coulter, et al. 1986).

Finally, in some studies the attempt to identify a single causal factor has been abandoned altogether and PEM has been viewed as a result of a disfunction in the 'food system', a term used to include food production and availability, family income, household food distribution, individual food utilisation, living conditions, individual health and infectious diseases (Pacey and Payne 1985).

The Dilemma

It is against this background that I wrote my research proposal and planned my fieldwork. Personally I was not inclined to approach the topic from an explicitly applied perspective and I was opposed to the idea that the anthropologist studying health-related beliefs should adopt an evaluative attitude based on biomedical assumptions. Rather, I preferred to explore people's ideas about illness and food and place them in a wider cultural context. However, grant-giving agencies desired a more applied approach and obliged me to structure my proposal to suit these ends to a greater degree than that with which I felt comfortable. In particular I had great difficulty with the imposition of the explicitly 'practical' goal of distinguishing between 'beneficial' and 'harmful' beliefs and practices and making recommendations for the elimination of the latter. As a result there were tensions and contradictions inherent in the project right from the start: I was to attempt to understand local interpretations of illness and take them seriously while at the same time already knowing beforehand which ideas were to count as valid and acceptable and which were to be rejected as 'cultural blocks' that needed to be altered. These tensions emerged early in my fieldwork when it became apparent that informants did not have any developed 'food beliefs' and their ideas about the nature and etiology of kwashiorkor did not relate to biomedical ideas at all.

This led to a dilemma: should I focus on people's interpretations of kwashiorkor (such as Pius's talk of cannibalism), which practically inclined health providers would consider totally irrelevant to the immediate task of reducing the incidence of the disease, or should I direct my attention to the 'socio-cultural factors' which 'really' played a role in the genesis of kwashiorkor (e.g. ignorance of the role of nutrition in pathogenesis), but which were totally irrelevant to local people? I managed to free myself from the horns of the dilemma by dividing my research into two projects: a more 'conventional', applied project in which I studied the local diet, feeding habits, weaning practices, infant health, etc. as defined biomedically, and a more 'experimental' project in which I abandoned biomedical categories and conceptions of relevance and went along with my informants interpretations. What I present here is largely a report on this latter part of the project.

The reasons for maintaining this separation in the final ethnography are largely practical. On the one hand I have a large number of texts in which people discuss etiology, mainly in terms of intervention through witchcraft, and expound on the meanings, largely indeterminate, of key terms. On the other hand I have notes on local diet, anthropometric data (which was collected by Francis, the village health worker, and two Dutch nutrition-science students) and disease histories for all the under-fives in Kieku Quarter during my stay, as well as a number of detailed case studies of children with kwashiorkor.

These two bodies of data are, of course, related, even though local people did not relate kwashiorkor to malnutrition, but bringing them together between the covers of the same book would have resulted in a diffuse and unentertaining tome. Keeping the theme and the approach relatively limited has produced a more generally ethnographic and, I hope, readable text. It has also enabled me to deal with local etiology reasonably comprehensively (and with freedom from biomedical strictures), thus doing justice to its complex and indeterminate nature. Writing ethnography always involves choice and selection, and there are a number of important and relevant themes on which I have much more material than the merely superficial treatment here indicates (such as the influence of Christianity, the importance of twins, particularly so-called single twins, and bad death). Equally there are topics that are also relevant but which, for the sake of keeping the book concise, I have left out entirely (the notion of the devil, confession, transformation of people into animals and sacrifice).

I have also been reluctant to include the more practical material in this book because of its rather unexpected and problematic nature. As I have pointed out, the etiology of kwashiorkor is not clear-cut, even in biomedicine. But even the points on which there is general agreement (that it is a disease in children who have just been weaned, that protein–energy deficiency plays some role, whether exacerbated by diseases such as diarrhoea and measles or not) appear to be contradicted by some of my more practical findings. Most of the children in my case studies were well past weaning and were often six or seven years old. They also appeared to have adequate diets and there was not always a correlation with serious childhood illnesses such as measles and diarrhoea. In fact, my findings seemed to offer support the hypothesis that kwashiorkor is related to aflatoxines (Hendrickse 1984, 1985, 1986). However, the very limited number of blood and urine samples which I was able to collect during a subsequent fieldwork trip did not seem to bear this out.

Moreover, in the cases of kwashiorkor that I studied it did not make any difference to mortality or recovery whether the children in question were treated biomedically or traditionally (the traditional treatment being mainly ritual cleansing), and I even recorded a number of cases in which children actually developed kwashiorkor while they were in hospital for other illnesses and on protein-rich diets. There are, of course, various (possible) biomedical explanations for this, but local people tended to interpret it as supporting their non-nutritional explanations of the disease, especially in cases in which a child taken to a traditional healer recovered.

Therefore, despite the obvious overlap with the subject matter of the present book, the kwashiorkor case-studies, the illness histories and my discussions with parents, traditional healers and biomedical health workers on these topics justify a separate book in which all the relevant issues can be adequately discussed. Here I shall pass on to the interpretations of illness as they were discussed during my stay in Tabenken village.

Arrival in Wimbum Country

In 1934 F W Carpenter described the Wimbum landscape as 'a vast moorland covered with short grass, and here and there a clump of stunted trees. In the rains it is a bleak place of low temperature, high winds and scotch mists' (Carpenter 1934b: 2). In 1962, in a more enthusiastic vein, Jeffreys wrote of

> glorious mountains, moors and woodlands, falling from about 7,000 feet to the escarpment at about 4,000 feet. The high land consists of a lava flow, probably from the extinct volcano of Mount Mbinka... The rolling volcanic moors fall away to the north to be replaced at lower levels by the granites, with deep, narrow valleys. These moors have much of the European temperate-zone flora...I have picked wild violets, the buttercup, clover, both mauve and white and also four leafed clover. (Jeffreys 1962:83–4)

Carpenter must have visited the area in September or October, at the height of the rainy season, when early morning temperatures on the Ndu plateau can drop to freezing point and the mists may be so thick that you can hardly see your hand held out in front of you. Jeffreys probably strolled through the countryside on a sunny afternoon in May, just after the first rains when the temperature is mild, the valleys are lush and the hillsides covered in flowers.

I first arrived in Ndu in February 1985, at the height of the dry season. It was hot and dusty. I had taken a bush taxi from Bamenda, the provincial capital some 120 kilometres to the south east along the Ring Road, and after a four-hour journey squashed in the back of a twelve-seater Toyota Hiace, I was stiff and tired. My fellow-passengers and I had been transformed into a uniform red-brown by the fine dust which had billowed up around the vehicle and been sucked in through the open windows as soon as we left the tarred road out of Bamenda. When we arrived in Ndu my male companions all removed their shower caps, revealing black hair and ears contrasting with the red faces which had become familiar during the journey. At the start of our journey in Bamenda I had looked at them with some amusement when, with much ado, they had put on plastic shower caps. Now my neighbour turned to me triumphantly. 'You see', he said. 'We have kept our hair nice and black, while your own has become red.'

Ndu is the most important market town in Donga Mantung Division, in the north west of the Bamenda Grassfields (also known as the western Grassfields) in what is now the North West Province of Cameroon. The Wimbum occupy an area of about 1,500 square kilometres and are the most important ethnic group in the Division. Both Ndu and Nkambe, the divisional headquarters, are Wimbum towns.

The Wimbum are divided into three distinct clans, the Tang, the War and the Wiya, and although oral tradition has it that the clans arrived in the area from different origins and at different times, they none the less speak one language, Limbum.[1] There are three main Limbum dialects, but the differences between them are minimal and they do not coincide with the distribution of the clans, which occupy a number of smaller, non-contiguous areas. The dialects seem to correspond to the northern, central and southern parts of the Wimbum territory and may be the result of the influence of languages to the north and south.

A large number of languages and dialects are spoken in the western Grassfields,[2] many of which are limited to relatively small geographical areas, often only a few villages. If a language has more than 50,000 speakers then it is large.[3] Limbum, which, I estimate, is spoken by some 60,000–100,000 people, is one of the larger Grassfield languages. This meant that I could learn the vernacular and be able to use it over a relatively wide area. It was for this reason that Piet van Reenen, a Dutch linguist who had studied Limbum, had recommended the area. He had also recommended his erstwhile assistant, Lawrence, as a good language teacher. Lawrence was one of a handful of Limbum speakers who could write the language, he understood the tonal system, and, because he had collaborated with van Reenen, he also had some linguistic knowledge.

In Ndu I put up at the Baptist guest house and made some enquiries as to where Lawrence was to be found. I planned to go and see him the following afternoon, but I was forestalled. Early the next morning there was a knock at my door. I opened it to

---

1. There is little published material on the Wimbum. For historical data we must rely on early reports by colonial officials (Carpenter 1934a, 1934b, Hawksworth 1923, 1924), publications by Jeffreys (1962), a brief mention in some of the more general descriptions of the Grassfields (Chilver and Kaberry 1967, Nkwi and Warnier 1982) and P M Kaberry's fieldnotes compiled by Sally Chilver (Chilver 1981), to whom I am grateful for providing me with a copy. The only source of recent ethnographic data, apart from Probst and Bühler (1990) is a number of theses written by Wimbum students at the Roman Catholic Regional Major Seminary in Bambui (Tanto 1976, Njingti 1979, Mburu 1979, Bomnsa 1984) and a few locally distributed works (Mbunwe-Samba 1989).

2. See Stallcup 1980, Nkwi and Warnier 1982.

3. Van Reenen 1988: 102.

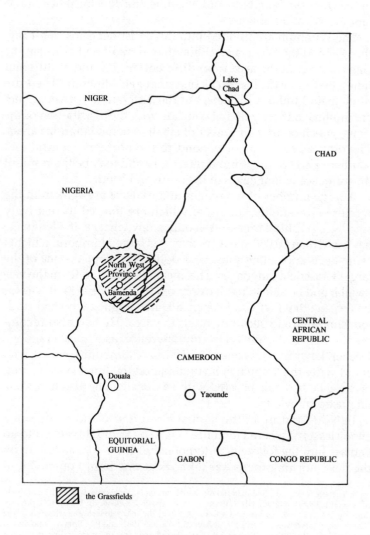

Map 1 Cameroon

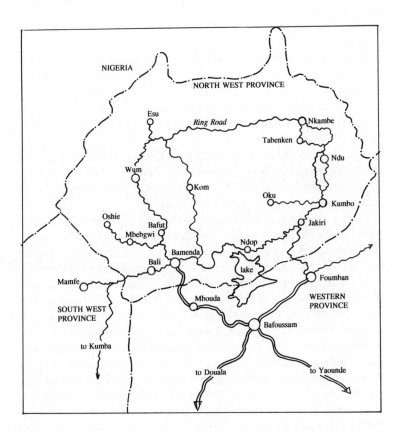

Map 2 The North West Province

find a short, very dark man with a small moustache standing on the doorstep. He reminded me of Charlie Chaplin. He was wearing a neat suit and a broad, floral tie with a large, 1960s-style knot. I estimated him to be in his early thirties, but he was, in fact, ten years older.

'I am Lawrence,' he said. 'I have come to assist you in your research.'

'Yes,' I said. 'I thought that you could teach me some basic Limbum during the first few months. I was planning to recruit a research assistant in Tabenken,' the village I had chosen as research location. I had always been advised not to accept self-styled research assistants who offered themselves to the field-worker as soon as he arrives.

'No, that won't be necessary,' he said. 'I will be accompanying you to Tabenken as research assistant. I am the only one who is fully qualified for the job.' He was adamant and, as time was to show, probably right. I agreed provisionally.

Lawrence, known in his native Ndu as 'The Green Revolution Man', had a vegetable and fruit stall where he sold 'European' vegetables such as carrots and lettuce. He had the only irrigated farm in the area and in the dry season, when the countryside was brown and desolate, it shone out on the hillside like an emerald. While everyone else cultivated the local staples, Lawrence experimented with new crops. Others looked down on fruit as not worth the trouble; he had orchards. They let their hens roost anywhere; he had a kerosene driven incubator. Sports, except football, were considered a waste of energy; Lawrence was an amateur marathon runner. When he took part in the gruelling international Mount Cameroon race (a marathon to the summit of Mount Cameroon, the highest peak in West Africa, and back) the following year, he finished just behind the leading group of international athletes.

Tabenken Village

The next day we left for Tabenken, the largest *Tang* clan village, situated in a deep basin about halfway between Ndu and Nkambe, right in the centre of the Wimbum area. Health workers at the nearby Catholic Mission hospital had recommended Tabenken as a research location because of the large number of

kwashiorkor cases and because they had established a health centre there specifically for treating kwashiorkor and providing
cooking lessons and nutrition education for mothers.

Tabenken has about 5,000–7,000 inhabitants and is spread over
a large area. It constitutes a single village to the extent that it is
divisional administrative unit. It has one chief, or *fon*, as they are
called in the Grassfields, one central market square, a government health centre (in addition to the mission health centre) and
an 'agric post', which is run by the Ministry of Agriculture and
provides fertiliser, seeds and advice to farmers. There is also a
government run coffee cooperative to which the farmers sell their
coffee, the only cash crop grown in the village. But Tabenken can
also be seen as a conglomerate of smaller villages. There are five
main wards, each under the leadership of a hereditary sub-chief,
or *kibai*. These are in turn divided up into numerous quarters
which are controlled by quarter-heads, or *fais*, again an hereditary position.

There is no published information on the history of Tabenken,
and it is not easy to reconstruct the history of the Grassfield societies generally, because the two main sources of historical data,
oral tradition and the distribution of languages, are often incom-
patible.[4] Not only is the available historical data fragmentary, but
so, it seems, is the very history itself.

> The present political-social units of the Bamenda Grassfields are for
> the most part composite units, sometimes grouped round intrusive
> dynasties or built by conquest, or by the slow adhesion of migrating
> groups in favoured areas, or, more recently, by the temporary
> agglomeration of smaller groups seeking protection from attack, The
> history of the Bamenda Grassfields, therefore, must do without sim-
> ple schematic maps showing broad directions of migration, though
> some of thè effects of invasions in the early 19th century or the expan-
> sion of particular states can be demonstrated. Further linguistic
> analysis faces an exceptionally difficult problem created by the nature
> of the settlement of the area – the scattering and combination of small
> speech groups, the isolation of some and the absorption of others, and
> the effects of local cultural predominance. Some of these factors might
> account for linguistic developments within the area, e.g. to differ-
> ences between neighbors, perhaps due to the overlay of different lin-
> guistic strata, rather than slow 'drift'. (Chilver and Kaberry 1967: 6–7)

4. Chilver and Kaberry 1967: 6, Nkwi and Warnier 1982: 149. See also Chilver 1961, 1966
and Chilver and Kaberry 1965.

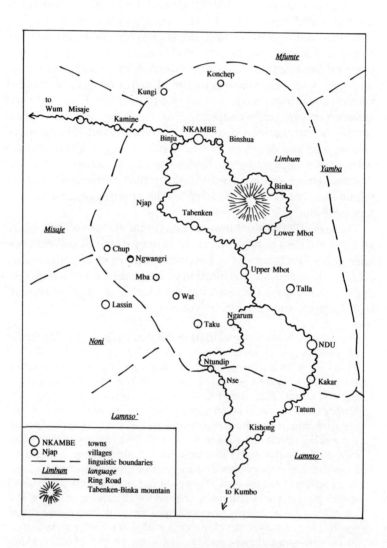

Map 3 The Wimbum Area

Oral tradition has it that the main wards in Tabenken used to be separate villages and the *kibais* chiefs in their own right. Now they fall under the authority of the *fon* of Tabenken. The old quarters in the centre of the village, near the *fon's* palace and the market square, form the nucleus of the village. Between these quarters and the palaces of the five kibais newer quarters have been established by immigrants from other Wimbum areas. The immigrants were often political refugees or were either fleeing from witchcraft or had themselves been ostracised because of witchcraft accusations. The house in which I lived during my stay in Tabenken was situated, somewhat symbolically, on the hillside opposite the health centre, and about halfway between the Mission and the palace, in a quarter called Kieku. Kieku is one of the newer quarters, though the leader of one of the resident lineages, who was a pretender to the throne, claimed that it had been the original centre of the village and site of the original palace. Later he took me to see the graves of the old chiefs which are situated in a small grove in the middle of the quarter.

When we arrived in Tabenken Lawrence and I went in search of Francis, the village health worker who ran the Mission health centre. He had been informed of my arrival and was to arrange for a place to stay. He was a lanky fellow, probably in his thirties, with a broad smile and a transistor radio permanently held to his ear. When Lawrence had gone off to look for a house for himself in the market square (he preferred to be in the middle of things) Francis took me up to the Mission to meet the parish priest. Although there are also Baptist and Presbyterian churches in Tabenken, the Catholic Church is probably the most important, and certainly the most conspicuous.

Tabenken parish was established in 1937 and the first Tabenkenian was baptised as a Catholic in 1914. Most of the people I knew claimed to be Catholic and attended mass every Sunday. The actual church building was an enormous structure, situated on a hill in the middle of the village. It was built in the 1930s under the supervision of the first parish priest, an Irishman, with sandstone blocks and tropical hardwood beams which, I was told, the parishioners had carried on their heads from the coast some 400 kilometers to the south. There is a large green neon cross on the top which, thanks to the Mission generator, can be seen for miles around at night.

I did not want to become too associated with the Mission or with the biomedical health-care sector, as I thought that this might interfere with my enquiries about beliefs relating to kwashiorkor, and particularly ideas relating to witchcraft and 'traditional' religion. I also thought that it might alienate non-Christian 'traditionalists' from my research. However, a visit to the parish priest was a necessary formality. I had been introduced into the village through the Mission and was to be involved, at least to some extent, in the activities of the Mission health centre. With some apprehension I asked Francis what he thought would be the best way to introduce my project to the villagers. 'There is no need to worry about that,' he said proudly. 'We made an announcement in church on Sunday before mass. The whole village knows you are here to study kwashiorkor.'

The following day, Lawrence and I had to fulfil another formality. Armed with a large bottle of whisky, we went to the palace to pay our respects to the *fon*. The palace is situated on the opposite side of the steep hill which separates Kieku, the quarter in which I lived, from the oldest part of the village. Kieku is, as I have mentioned, relatively new and the compounds are separated by orange, avocado and banana trees, and by several acres of coffee bushes. The compounds on top of the hill are closer together and when we descended into the oldest part of the village on the other side I found them to be so close together that there was no room for coffee bushes at all.

We entered a wide, open space only relieved by two enormous kola-nut trees. On the far side I saw a large building. The back and side walls were made of mud bricks, but the front was a lattice-work of raffia-bamboo. There were two thick wooden door supports, each carved in the form of a man standing on a woman's shoulders, illustrating the superiority of men over women according to Lawrence. It was the *Mfu'* lodge, where the warriors meet once every eight days to sing and drink palm wine and clash their cutlasses together in greeting. A row of carved wooden heads along the top of the entrance symbolised the skulls which hung there in the past as trophies of war, Lawrence said. Behind the *Mfu'* house and to the left was the meeting place of *Ngwerong*, the regulatory society to which the masked *jujus* belong.

Beyond the *Ngwerong* compound was the palace, a number of dilapidated mud brick buildings with collapsed thatch roofs and tumbling walls. In the middle was a small house with a corrugat-

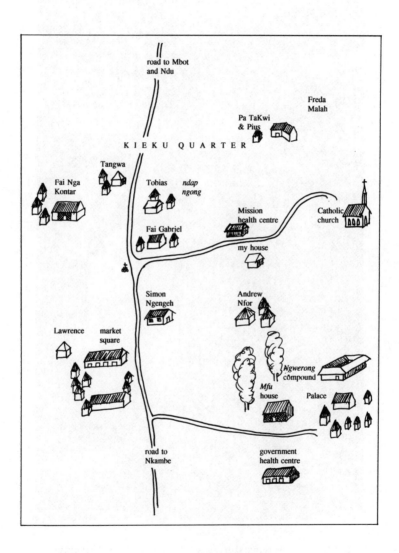

Map 4 Tabenken

5 Me and Lawrence during a *Mfu'* celebration. The carved
doorposts are visible on the left

ed iron roof and plastered walls: the *fon*'s residence. On either side of the palace were a number of thatched huts, the homes of the *fon*'s wives.

Lawrence sent a youth, probably one of the *fon*'s numerous sons (he was said to have more than 100 children), inside to say they we had come to greet the *fon*. We were led into a courtyard by another youth and told to sit down on raffia-bamboo stools. As we waited the courtyard filled with people who seemed to come from nowhere. As a sign of hospitality the *fon* would have to provide us, and anyone else who happened to accompany us, with palm wine. Such visits mean free drinking and word spreads quickly. After about ten minutes, when a courtier came out and gave us a sign that the *fon* was about to enter, the courtyard was full. Everyone stood up. The *fon* entered. He wore a blue robe and a peaked cap. He was a small, wizened man. He walked slowly to his own stool and sat down with some difficulty. Once he was seated we all sat down again. Two youths handed out glasses and filled them with palm wine from a large calabash.

Lawrence stood up, back slightly bent, hands cupped in front of his mouth. It was not permitted to speak directly to the *fon*. Lawrence explained who I was and the purpose of my proposed stay in Tabenken. The *fon* answered and Lawrence translated.

'The *fon* is very pleased with your arrival,' he said. 'He has been praying every morning for more than a year that God should send you, and now his prayer has been answered. He thanks God.'

'Oh,' I said, somewhat taken aback.

'Yes,' Lawrence continued. 'I told him that you have come to study kwashiorkor and he thinks you are a doctor. He is often sick and has always wanted the Mission to post a doctor in Tabenken to look after him. He is very happy that you will be staying here.'

The *fon* had been a devout Catholic since his youth. He was baptised in 1921 and had been a catechist until ascending the throne in 1946. Despite his ailing health he still attended mass every morning at six o' clock. The *fon* was also at the apex of an impressive traditional hierarchy, with which the church did not entirely agree, and this made his position somewhat ambivalent.

In contrast to the societies in the southern forests of Cameroon, Grassfield societies are extremely hierarchical. Each village has a *fon*, and under him there is an extensive hereditary nobility. The *fon* also controls the *juju* society *Ngwerong*, which is situated within the confines of the palace and which used, traditionally, to

be responsible for the execution of witches and those who committed adultery with the *fon*'s wives. In the past the Catholic
Church considered *Ngwɛrong* to be a devilish obstacle to
Christianity. The first parish priest constructed a high wall
around the Mission compound to protect it from attacks by *jujus*
belonging to *Ngwɛrong*. Both parties became more tolerant over
time. Many *Ngwɛrong* members, including the *fon* himself,
attended mass, but the church never really accepted the *jujus*.
Jujus no longer execute people, and although they still have a
social control function (people sometimes refer to them as 'the
traditional police') they are mainly active at mortuary celebrations and their main function is entertainment.

On the approach of a masked *juju* everyone, including the highest nobility, must crouch down to show respect. Anyone failing to
do so can be sure that the *juju* will humiliate him in public, and it
may even attack him physically. I once saw a *juju* drag a nobleman
from the crowd by his hair, throw him into the mud and stand on
him. On another occasion a passing *juju* caught sight of me taking
a disrespectable photo of it. It ran over and, as I crouched down, it
stood on me, much to the amusement of the crowd. This is all
intended playfully, however, and there is an element of reversing
the local hierarchy. When else are young men (who are 'in' the
jujus) allowed to trample title-holders and visiting anthropologists? The Catholic Church tends to interpret the crouching as
'bowing down to graven images' or 'worship', however.

There is an uneasy relation between Christianity and what, for
want of a better term, I will call tradition, and this is epitomised
in the position of the *fon*: ex-catechist and devout Christian but
formally responsible for the activities of the *jujus* belonging to
Ngwɛrong. The two are opposed, yet inseparable because they are
combined in one person. This uneasy and ambiguous relationship between Christianity and tradition is one of the underlying
themes in the following pages.

Language and Translation

Everybody in Tabenken, except the few teachers and other government workers who had been transferred from other areas,
spoke Limbum as their first language. Most people also spoke
Pidgin English, though in different forms and with varying

6 On lookers crouch for Mabu during a celebration in Ndu.
The *Ngwɛrong* compound is visible in the background

degrees of fluency. The Pidgin of old traditionalists is not the same as that of young urbanites, because Pidgin in the anglophone cities is moving closer to standard English and developing a more elaborate vocabulary. Some old people in Tabenken only had a very limited knowledge of Pidgin, and men generally spoke better Pidgin than women. All those with some basic education, as well as many without any formal education, spoke English (also with varying degrees of fluency). Those who had reached secondary school, and those who had worked in the francophone part of the country spoke at least some French. There were also still a few old men who spoke German, which they had learned when Cameroon was a German colony before the First World War.

Since unification in 1960 Cameroon has been officially bilingual, the national languages being French and English. The western Grassfields are situated in that part of the country which was formerly part of British Cameroon. French is taught as a second language in anglophone schools and is becoming increasingly popular as a sign of education and status. Pidgin English continues to function as the *lingua franca* throughout the South West and North West Provinces and is widely used in some of the major francophone cities.

Cameroon Pidgin is not simply a mixed language arising in a contact situation in which people meet for limited purposes, which is how Hall (1966) defines a pidgin. It is highly developed and could function as a first language.

> It is for most speakers an auxiliary language though it is frequently acquired by children at the same time as they learn their vernacular mother tongues. Cameroon Pidgin would certainly be capable of serving as a community's first language. In the Bamenda Grassfields and in coastal communities Pidgin is used in church, in the market, on public transport, in intertribal gatherings, among educated and uneducated, for proverbs, for work-chants, for story-telling and for creating an atmosphere of intimacy. Many people who use it have a good command of standard English but Pidgin is felt to have some advantages over English...it is not an elitist language and in many of its structures it reflects vernacular usage and so, in a very real sense, can be considered a Cameroon language. (Todd 1979: 6)

The condescending remarks which ethnographers are apt to make when they hear that a colleague has worked through the local pidgin are not justified in the case of Cameroon Pidgin.

During my fieldwork about 60 per cent of the interviews and conversations were in Limbum, mainly through an interpreter. The remaining 40 per cent were in English or Pidgin. This is a very general stetement, however. In practice conversations were, at least to some extent, a mixture of all three. English interviews were full of Pidgin and Limbum terms and Limbum interviews were full of English and Pidgin terms,[5] with different people often using the same term to refer to different things, and even the same person using the same term to refer to different things, depending on the context in which the term was being used. The fluctuation and even outright contradiction on the level of the meaning of terms was often paralleled by the sometimes seemingly chaotic mixing of linguistic codes.

People often used English words in ways which deviated significantly from their meaning in standard English. Sometimes this was part of standardised Pidgin usage, such as when people say 'sometimes' in Pidgin meaning 'maybe' in standard English, or 'I hope so' to mean 'I think so'. It will be obvious that this can lead to confusion, as on one occasion when I asked a villager whether he thought that a sick relative was going to die. He answered 'Yes, I hope so.' But deviation may also be idiosyncratic. Tobias, one of my assistants, called those ordinary people who cannot see the invisible activities of witches, but only the material world, 'short sighted materialists', and Pius often referred to witches as 'domestic politicians'. The meanings of key terms also tended to vary, as they were translated back and forth across linguistic boundaries. The word "diarrhoea" did not have the same meaning for a health worker at the local hospital that it did for a villager, and if the health worker switched to "purging", the Pidgin translation of "diarrhoea", in order to facilitate communication with the villager, he usually did not realise that they may still be talking about completely different phenomena because the villager might be using "purging" as a translation for a Limbum term which has no semantic overlap with "diarrhoea".

Neither was the relation between English and Limbum static for me. Initially I did not understand a word of Limbum and my understanding of Pidgin was not much better. By the time I left I had no difficulty with Pidgin, and, though I still could not confi-

5. For example, on one occasion when Pius was telling Lawrence about twins he said: '*O ka tɛ* treat *wowi* from the childhood *ka' o ka ku'o la baa.*' (If they are not treated from childhood then when they grow up they will be mad).

dently conduct more than relatively simple conversations in Limbum, I could understand a great deal of what people were saying in Limbum and, perhaps more importantly, I could read the Limbum texts which I had collected. This means that in the first interviews I was entirely dependent on an interpreter, whereas later I could understand what people were saying in Limbum interviews before it was translated and could therefore make use of both the original Limbum statements and the translations. As my Limbum vocabulary increased and informants became used to my pronunciation, they could also increasingly understand my mixture of English and Limbum. Also, the more we discussed, the more they could anticipate what I meant, and vice versa. In addition, I still have the Limbum transcriptions of most of the interviews and conversations.

Interpreters

Lawrence and Tobias, my main interpreters, played an important and creative role in the process of translation. Lawrence did most of the translating, particularly during the first year, and he also transcribed most of the Limbum discussions from the tapes. At first I had intended to learn the basics of the language and dispense with an interpreter as soon as possible, as, we are led to believe, most anthropologists do in the field. Limbum is not an easy language to learn, however. It is a tonal language, and for the untrained ear it is difficult enough to distinguish between the high, low and middle tones, let alone to be able to recognise and cope with such phenomena as tonal downsteps, in which a middle or low tone drops a little lower. Two words, which sounded perfectly alike to me, could refer to two completely different things because of the different tones with which they were spoken. For example *nkvúu* is chief and *nkvùu* is farm. I still have recordings of discussions with Tobias which go like this:
    'Say *nkvúu*.'
    '*Nkvùu*.'
    'No, *nkvúu*.'
    'That's what I said.'
    'No you didn't. You must say *nkvúu*, you said *nkvùu*.'
    '*Nkvùu*.'
    'No, no, no. Can't you hear what I'm saying? I'm saying *nkvúu*,

nkvúu, nkvúu!'

The more Limbum I learned the more I realised that I would not acquire sufficient competence during eighteen months to be able to conduct more than relatively simple conversations without the help of an interpreter, let alone discuss such matters as the existence of the ancestors or the nature of god. How other anthropologists succeed in discussing such complex matters with informants in the vernacular during first field trips is a mystery to me. I am reminded of Robert Lowie's remark about nobody trusting a translation of Proust based on a similar competence in French.

I also realised that Lawrence and Tobias played an important *constitutive* role in what I was doing. They were not merely neutral channels, necessary but distorting filters or invisible 'thirds' (Crapanzano 1980), but active co-producers. Even if an informant and I could understand each other quite well, the exchanges between Lawrence or Tobias and the informant during the interview, my discussions with them during and after the interview and, later on, the talks we had about the translations and transcriptions, always shed new light on a problem or called my attention to some aspect or connection which I had not previously noticed. They developed an interest in the topic, or rather, they already had an interest, which is why the project developed in the direction it did and also why we could work together so well.

In the conversations which I present below I attempt to make visible the contribution of all parties to the dialogue. I disagree with the way many ethnographers make use of interpreters or assistants in the field only to render them invisible later on in the process. It reminds me of the way colonials used the locals, whose presence they found so disturbing, to mediate in their most intimate spheres of life, as houseboys, nannies, cooks, while at the same time rendering them invisible, acting as though those whom they would like to keep out of sight were not right there, in the intimacy of their homes.

Recording and Transcription

Before leaving for the field I had been advised to tape-record my interviews but to transcribe only what was 'relevant'. Somehow, though, this did not seem adequate. How is one to decide what is relevant? Something which does not seem relevant at the time of transcription may become crucial at a later stage, as I discovered with early remarks about the relationship between kwashiorkor and ostensibly unrelated phenomena such as witchcraft, twins and abominations. These later proved to be crucial to an understanding of how people talked about and interpreted the illness that is called kwashiorkor.

So, not wanting to risk losing anything I (perhaps somewhat compulsively) recorded and completely transcribed most conversations and interviews. In the case of the Limbum interviews conducted through an interpreter this usually included my English questions, the Limbum translation of my questions, the Limbum answers given by the informant and the English translation of those answers. It also included any discussion in English between the interpreter and myself and any discussion in Limbum between the interpreter and the informant, as well as any remarks by, and discussion between, anyone else who happened to be present. Here I was fortunate that Lawrence was one of a handful of people who could write Limbum, and if it were not for him the transcription of many of the Limbum texts from which I now work would have been impossible.

After the Limbum text had been transcribed I asked Lawrence to make a more or less literal inter-linear translation. This enabled me to compare his on-the-spot translation with his later literal translation. With my own increasing knowledge of Limbum I could read the Limbum texts and discuss them with him. I also recorded and transcribed our conversations about the texts and translations.

In studying these texts, various changes of meaning came to light. Sometimes neat and coherent interviews turned out to be chaotic and incoherent when everything had been transcribed and translated, and incoherent and contradictory stories sometimes became clear and understandable in the light of a more thorough study of the full transcription. In this way the production of meaning continued into the texts, and was influenced not only by translation but also by the mode of recording and transcription. The replacement of the notebook by the cassette recorder as the basic tool of ethnographic research must have had a significant influence on the form and the content of the ethnographic material which ethnographers take home and use as the basis for their publications. How different would *Argonauts of the Western Pacific* or *Witchcraft, Oracles and Magic among the Azande* be if Malinowski and Evans-Pritchard had worked with a tape recorder and been able to make use of verbatim transcriptions, not only of their interviews, but also of casual conversations?

Yet neither are the transcribed interviews definitive: transcription does not fix the meaning of what was said. While I was in the field it occurred to me that although anthropologists are very touchy about colleagues quoting from their first drafts, they themselves often construct whole cosmologies based entirely on what may well be called natives' 'first drafts' (and verbal first drafts at that). I wondered why informants should not be allowed to reread and edit the interviews in which they had participated. After all, if anthropologists can spend years writing up their results, why should their informants not have a second chance to correct their spontaneous statements?

This led me to experiment with letting informants edit the texts of the conversations in which they had participated. The results were disappointing, however. The fiery enthusiasm for debate soon waned into poorly concealed boredom when I presented them with piles of transcripts. Interviews were fine, discussions about the transcriptions okay, but hours of reading was going just a bit too far. So, the conversations presented below are all first drafts.

The 'final' ethnographic text is not definitive either. The content and composition of this text is the realisation of one possibility out of many. As Fabian has stressed, ethnographic writing is not a neutral means of presentation. It is not merely a matter of form but also part of the content. Writing does not *record* external reality, it is part of the process that *constitutes* that reality. Ethnographic texts do not mirror other cultures but are products of intercultural communication (see Fabian 1990b). It is with this in mind that the present book should be read.

Texts and Autobiography

In presenting my ethnography in the form of a series of conversations or dialogues I more or less follow the chronological development of my fieldwork, so that the way my narrative is built up resembles the way in which my own knowledge and understanding of the subject developed. I say 'more or less' because my understanding did not exactly parallel the way this knowledge develops in the conversations. This is because the meaning of texts is not stable or fixed: the significance of remarks or answers to questions often only became clear to me much later, long after they had been uttered, recorded and transcribed, when I was in a better position to interpret or reinterpret them in the light of what had been said later, and of my own growing knowledge of both the subject and the vernacular. I can never attain *the* final interpretation of what my informants 'really' meant because there is no final interpretation. Meaning in texts (and in the events which generate them) is recursive: it depends on the meaning of what has preceded it and it may lead to a revision of earlier interpretations (Dwyer 1982: 274–5). The texts continue to reveal new meanings, depending on how I read them, what I know and what it is I am looking for. Though, of course, the number of different readings which are acceptable at any given moment is not infinite. There are criteria for distinguishing adequate from inadequate interpretations, but these are culturally and historically contingent rather than absolute (Fish 1980).

As they run to more than a thousand pages, neither, obviously, do I present here all the conversations that I recorded and transcribed, but only a selection of fragments, which for me, as I re-read them now, evoke the memory of discovery and frustration, revelation and puzzlement, understanding and chaos, which gave me partial access to my hosts' interpretations of illness and misfortune. In this sense my presentation is autobiographical. I do not claim to speak for others, and if they were to write their own reports of our encounters they would undoubtedly be different. Putting their names on the title page and pretending multiple authorship, suggesting that they had an equal say in the form and content of the final product, would be dishonest. Of course, I could never have written this ethnography without them, but should I hide my responsibility as the final author and autocratic editor of their statements behind the pretense of equality and multiple authorship?

Basing my presentation on conversations or dialogues is not a question of 'giving the natives a say', rather, it follows from the assumption that there is no clear distinction between 'data gathering' and 'interpretation', and from the belief that anthropologists should give an account of the whole process of interpretation (Fabian 1985). I shall come back to this in the final chapter.

Chapter 3

Malnutrition, *Ngang* and Twins

From Kwashiorkor to *Ngang*

The first two encounters described in Chapter 1 provided me with an introduction to indigenous conceptions of kwashiorkor. Within a few days of moving into Tabenken I had established that there were children with kwashiorkor, that local people did recognise the illness as a problem and that there were traditional healers who specialised in its treatment. In addition I had two Limbum terms which seemed to be the vernacular equivalents of kwashiorkor: "bfaa" and "ngang". I did not assume that "bfaa" and "ngang" were exact translations of "kwashiorkor": this was hardly possible, given that "kwashiorkor" is a disease term in the technical vocabulary of Western biomedicine, and as such has denotations which *could not* be part of the meaning of terms from a non-biomedical system. For example, hypoalbumenemia (low serum protein level), which usually forms part of the biomedical definition of kwashiorkor, could not be part of the meaning of "ngang" because, for one thing, the technical means of establishing hypoalbumenemia are not available to Wimbum medicine men.

I did assume, however, that the terms had more or less the same meaning, that is I assumed that "ngang" and "bfaa" referred to the more visible and easily recognised symptoms of kwashiorkor: the spectacular swelling, discolouration, apathy and lesions. I did not exclude the possibility that the vernacular terms might also have meanings which were not covered by "kwashiorkor", but I assumed that their meanings overlapped to a large extent and that the terms could be used as synonyms in discussions without producing serious misunderstanding. After all, biomedical health workers had been translating the terms in this way and using them in practical situations for years.

What began to emerge from discussions, however, was that the Limbum words "ngang" and "bfaa" could not be treated as approximate equivalents of the biomedical term "kwashiorkor". They had multiple meanings which were not covered by "kwashiorkor".

During my first conversation with Pius he described the initial symptoms of *ngang* as rashes, skin lesions resembling fire burns and changes in hair colour and texture. He said that after about two years the feet and face start to swell. What he described as *ngang* closely resembles kwashiorkor. He mentioned various causal factors, such as eating garden eggs and elephant stalk, and prostitution and cannibalism. He said that *ngang* was the more recent name for the sickness and that it had previously been called *bfaa*.

Confidence (described in Chapter 1) was the first case of kwashiorkor I encountered in Tabenken. A week later Henry, one of the village health workers, informed me of another case, the three-year-old son of Fai Nga Kontar. I decided to go and visit him and have a look at the child.

As Lawrence and I approached the compound we were met by a tall, stately man in his sixties. He was wearing a simple, light-blue robe and wore a curious cap, which I can only describe as resembling an udder with hundreds of teats. He carried a spear. Lawrence exchanged a few words with him in Limbum (which I did not understand) and told me that this was the man we were looking for. In Pidgin Fai Nga Kontar said he would take us inside, show us the child and explain what he knew about the illness. We followed him for a few hundred metres until we came to a mud-brick compound in a clearing. There were two main buildings standing next to each other, about four metres apart. The space between them had been made into an enclosure by a raffia bamboo lattice-work. As we entered the clearing Lawrence stopped. Fai Nga Kontar opened a sliding door in the lattice-work and disappeared inside, pulling the door closed behind him. I looked questioningly at Lawrence. 'We must enter by the door on the other side,' he said. 'Only the *Fai* himself may enter through this one.'

Fai is a traditional title, which people translate into English as 'quarter-head'. Fai Nga Kontar was head of one of the quarters of Kieku, the part of the village in which I stayed. He had not been born with the name 'Nga Kontar' either. He was a member of the traditional nobility and one of the hereditary title holders in the regulatory society *Ngwerong*. The name Nga Kontar was inherit-

7 Fai Nga Kontar wearing his 'udder' cap. In the background
   the bamboo lattice-work of his compound

ed from his father when he died, and the *Fai* would pass it on to his eldest son when he himself died. Only those with such high titles were permitted to decorate their houses with raffia bamboo lattice-work, and they had separate entrances which no one else was allowed to use.

By the time we had walked around the building and entered the enclosure through another sliding door on the opposite side the *Fai* was seated on a traditional carved wooden stool, awaiting us with a handful of kola nuts. We sat down opposite him on similar stools and he offered us the kola nuts. He then had the child, Marcel, brought in for us to see.

It was another textbook case of kwashiorkor. He was miserable and apathetic, with a big, round, puffy face. His hands, feet and legs were so swollen that the skin was taut and shiny and there were skin lesions on his legs. His hair was a pale ginger colour and soft to the touch. The *Fai* told us that Marcel had *ngang*. He said that the disease was now referred to as *ngang* but that it had previously been known as *bfaa*. *Bfaa* meant 'mistake from the mother's compound', he said. Though he was a medicine man himself, he claimed to have no idea what the cause of his child's illness was. He said that Marcel was the son of his second wife who had left him. The *Fai* had recently obtained custody over the child through the courts, and he had become sick since coming to stay in his father's compound.

Some weeks later, during a visit to Taku, a nearby village, a young woman called Mungvu came to see me with her child because she had heard that I was interested in children's diseases. The child looked miserable, with a big, round, puffy face, pale skin and very light-coloured hair. She said that the child was suffering from *bfaa*. I asked her why she thought it was *bfaa*. She said that the child had been hot and had had diarrhoea and that whenever she ate she vomited. Her skin and eyes had become red and there had been red spots on her head. Mungvu had taken her to a medicine man in her village and he had said that the child had *bfaa*. When I asked her why she called the sickness *bfaa* and not *ngang* she replied that *ngang* was different, that it was wet (*shong*).

The next person to mention *ngang* to me was Fai Gabriel. Fai Gabriel was one of my neighbours and his compound was just down the hill from my house. He was in his late forties. Like Fai Nga Kontar, he was a member of the traditional nobility, but he had come into conflict with the chief and renounced his title, which was really Fai Nga Mcε. Now he was known simply as Fai Gabriel. He was a devout Catholic and went to mass every Sunday. But he also referred to himself as a 'neo-pagan' because he had married two wives, which was forbidden by the church. He worked for the Catholic Church as a builder. He spoke fluent English. One day I visited him to ask him about the illnesses which were common in his compound.

He was pruning the coffee trees behind his compound. I asked him whether he could spare some time for a talk. He said that he would be finished later in the afternoon and I could call in then. As I turned to leave he said 'What topic are we going to talk about. If you tell me beforehand then I can think about it and prepare.'

'I want to know about the most common illnesses in your compound,' I said.

'Good, I will think about it.'

When I returned, Fai Gabriel received me in his sitting room, where we sat on lounge chairs without cushions (just as many people build houses with windows but cannot afford the panes, so many people have lounge suites made but cannot afford to buy the foam-rubber cushions). In his slow, systematic way he summed up all the illnesses he could remember. He also mentioned *ngang*.

[3.1] 'Then you have *ngang*,' he said. 'We call it *ngang*, when the child peels. It has been around for quite a long time, but since this Mission health centre arrived here most of the mothers take their children there and they know the cause, so now they give their children much food and vegetables, and *ngang* is not coming up so much in this village anymore. Most of the people have been taught to feed their children to protect them from *ngang*.'

'Have there ever been cases of *ngang* in your compound?' I asked.

'A long time ago, some thirty years, but since then nothing. My wife delivered twins for the first time, but they died in hospital. Then she delivered twins again, but they also died because of *ngang*. Only one is still alive, a son who is fifteen. Since then there has been none in the house.'

'So they died because of *ngang*?'

'Yes. I remember that the first teeth were already coming out.

After the sickness attacked he only stayed for a few weeks before dying.'

'How did you know it was *ngang*?'

'Well, there is a woman from Ngwangri [a nearby village] who treats this disease. When people go there with children like that she tells them: that is *ngang*.'

'What are the symptoms?'

'The child becomes very thin and the legs may be just like this,' he said, holding up his little finger. 'The arms also. He will be very thin. Then the hair changes. It will be very smooth, like your own, but yellow in colour. It will not coil but be straight.'

'And that's *ngang*?'

'Yes, these are the signs of *ngang*.'

Lawrence and I also visited a number of traditional healers, both in Tabenken and neighbouring villages, who were said to treat *ngang*. Manasas Yangsi was one of them. He lived in the neighbouring village of Taku. An unsmiling man in his fifties, he only spoke Limbum. At the time we visited him he was treating his grandson, Linus, whom he said was suffering from *ngang*. During our visit the child sat on a chair in the corner of the room staring miserably at the floor. He clearly had kwashiorkor. His arms and legs were so swollen that the skin was taut and shiny, his hair was soft and yellow, his skin was discoloured and there were skin lesions on his legs and arms. Linus's parents, Manasas's son and daughter-in-law, lived in Limbe on the south coast, and they had left the child with Manasas for treatment.

[3.2] 'I'll tell you about *ngang*,' he said, in response to a question from Lawrence. 'Sometimes when a child is sleeping at night and he makes a noise with his teeth, that is a sign that makes the *ngang* come out. When you hear a noise like that the child has to be treated. When a child is delivered we know whether it is a twin or not. This child,' he said, pointing to his grandchild, 'was born in Limbe, so we don't know whether he is a twin or not. He was delivered in hospital so there was no [traditional] midwife to tell me whether the navel was crossed to show he was a twin. So I'm just giving him different kinds of medicine, for twins and *ngang*. When I take a child who has been attacked by *ngang* I raise his head like this, I will see *ngang* in his eyes. The corners of the eyes are yellow. The nose and the area around the mouth become red. Those are the first symptoms, before it really comes out in the

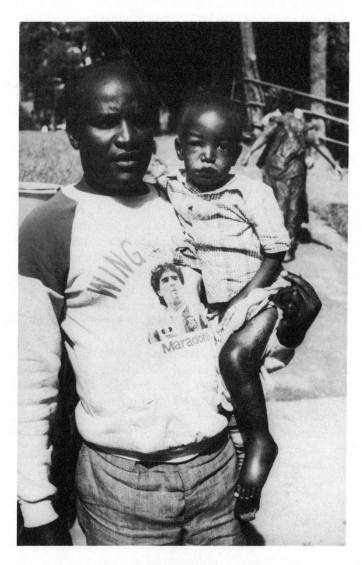

8 Child with kwashiorkor/*ngang*

form of swelling. After delivery you can see the nose
becoming red. These are the first signs and then you know
that the child is attacked. *Ngang* is when the child has just
been delivered and is very young. If it continues then it
becomes *bfaa*. *Bfaa* is when it comes out seriously, when the
jaws and feet swell and there are bruises or sores on the
body. That is *bfaa* and the people who treat it are quite different.'

What emerged from these early conversations was that most
of the people I spoke to in Tabenken referred to the syndrome
which I described or pointed out to them (i.e. kwashiorkor) as
ngang rather than *bfaa*. In fact many of them had never even
heard of the word "bfaa" in this connection. One or two, mainly
medicine men or more knowledgeable elders, repeated what
Pius and Fai Nga Kontar had told me earlier, that the disease
used to be called *bfaa* in the past, but that it was now referred to
as *ngang*. Only one of the informants mentioned above, Mungvu,
used the term "bfaa" instead of "ngang", and Manasas Yangsi
said that *ngang* develops into *bfaa*. So I initially assumed that the
two terms were equivalent but that, for reasons yet unknown to
me, one had replaced the other, just as in the discourse of some
of those who considered themselves modern "ngang" was being
replaced by "kwashiorkor". This is why I concentrated on *ngang*
and did not talk about *bfaa* in early discussions.
    But at the same time, I also began to realise that kwashiorkor
and *ngang* were not as similar as I had originally assumed, and
that I could not use the word "ngang" as a simple translation of
"kwashiorkor". People distinguished between wet and dry forms
of *ngang*, and they described early and late stages, conceptions
which were not covered by the term "kwashiorkor".

Wet and Dry *Ngang*

The third case of kwashiorkor that I encountered was also at the
Mission health centre. Winifred lived in a neighbouring village
and had brought her six-year-old son, Francis Ngweh, to
Tabenken for treatment because she thought he was suffering
from *ngang*. The village health workers diagnosed kwashiorkor.
    On the day following their arrival I went to see them. The child

did not seem to have kwashiorkor at all. He did have rather full cheeks and his hair was slightly discoloured at the temples, but there was no sign of oedema and I saw him laugh quite frequently (children with kwashiorkor do not laugh). Henry, the village health worker, told me that the symptoms had greatly reduced. Winifred also said that her son's condition had been fluctuating for the past few months. She said that he had had diarrhoea, had no appetite and had been sleeping a lot.

When I asked her what she thought was wrong with the child she said that he had *ngang*. It was the dry variety, she added. She said that there was a dry form, which she called *ngang yur* in Limbum, and a wet form, *ngang mshong*. Henry, who was present during the conversation, confirmed this, and he went on to talk of dry and wet kwashiorkor. He said that wet kwashiorkor was characterised by swelling of the feet and legs, whereas in dry kwashiorkor there was no swelling. He thought that this child had dry kwashiorkor.

The next day I spoke to Winifred's husband, Isaac. He was not the father of the child, he said, but had 'inherited' Winifred as a second wife when her husband (Isaac's brother) had died. He said that the child had been sick for two months. He had been apathetic and spots had appeared on his stomach. Then his face and later his feet had become swollen. Isaac said that it was a 'family disease' because some of his own children had also had it. He said that when the symptoms of *ngang* first appeared Francis was already being treated because he was 'followed by twins'.

One morning Lawrence came to tell me that he had arranged for us to interview a girl of about twenty years of age about *ngang*. This was an unlikely story, as young people generally had little knowledge of such matters. I suspected that Lawrence had an eye on her and wanted to impress her. In order to humour him I said it was a good idea and we set out on the long walk to the compound in which she stayed with her mother. When we arrived we went into the dark, smokey kitchen and sat down. The girl was busy cooking breakfast before leaving for her farm. On the opposite side of the cooking fire her mother lay sick in bed.

In Tabenken, as is most Grassfield societies, each married woman has her own kitchen, which is usually a separate hut in her husband's compound. They are usually square buildings consisting of a raffia bamboo framework which has been filled in with mud and a thatched roof. More recently the walls have been made from sun-dried mud bricks. There are no windows and smoke from the fire has to seep out through the thatch. When meals are being prepared the kitchens are like smokehouses. The women usually sleep in their kitchens, which are more like multi-purpose living quarters than their Western equivalents.

Lawrence did not find much chance to show off to the girl because her mother, Freda Malah, started to tell us about her illness. She spoke Limbum, which Lawrence translated for me. After she had finished describing her illness I casually enquired about other illnesses which were common in their compound. At the end of a long list of illnesses she mentioned *ngang*. She said that there were two kinds: wet *ngang* and dry *ngang*. Wet *ngang* was caused by weaning the child too early and not feeding it properly. It could also be caused by eating bananas which have split open and in which flies have excreted, she said. She did not know what caused dry *ngang*.

Some people distinguished between wet and dry forms of the disease (*ngang mshong* or *ngang yinto'* and *ngang yur* respectively). Opinions diverged considerably on the matter, however. Whereas some informants, including Henry, were convinced that wet and dry forms of the disease could be distinguished, others only knew of one form which they simply referred to as *ngang*, though sometimes their descriptions of it resembled either the dry or wet *ngang* in other people's descriptions. Among those who distinguished two forms, swelling was usually mentioned in descriptions of the wet form. Lawrence claimed on one occasion that the wet form was kwashiorkor while the dry form was marasmus. Here he was equating the Limbum terms with the biomedical terms for two acute forms of protein–energy malnutrition, and was perhaps influenced by his biomedical knowledge. Actual cases of marasmus were infrequent and were not referred to as dry *ngang*.

Yet the situation remained confused. Swelling seemed to be the defining characteristic of wet *ngang* for those who made a distinction and was sometimes the defining characteristic for general *ngang* for those who did not. What exactly dry *ngang* was never became clear. The symptoms that people described usually included wasting and some form of skin disorder, but no two versions were the same, and the descriptions usually fitted some other disease as well. For example, when I asked someone to describe dry *ngang* they might describe the symptoms of what is usually referred to as scabies. When I pointed this out he might say that it did indeed resemble scabies, but that it was different, though he could not explain in what way. The people who did distinguish between dry and wet *ngang* usually described the dry form primarily in terms of symptoms manifested on the skin, though they refused to classify it as a skin disease.

Early and Late *Ngang*

Most people seemed to agree that *ngang* could be diagnosed immediately after delivery, the signs being scabies-like spots on the child's skin (see Pius's description in [1.1]). They said that these spots were on the child's skin when it was delivered or appeared shortly afterwards. If the disease was recognised and treated at this early stage then it would not develop any further. If it was not treated, however, then the spots would disappear, but after a few years the disease would reappear in its second and more serious phase. This second phase is then the wet or dry *ngang* characterised by swelling and discolouration or wasting and skin disorder respectively. Some thought that once the second phase had been reached the disease was inevitably fatal.

It is worth noting here that the distinction between wet and dry *ngang* sometimes coincided with that between early and late *ngang*. For example, Pius described the difference between early and late *ngang* in terms of skin rashes and swelling respectively, which is exactly the same way in which other informants described the difference between wet and dry *ngang*.

Kwashiorkor and *Ngang*: The Indeterminacy of Meaning

So, if I may sum up for the moment, it is possible to distinguish three ways in which the terms "kwashiorkor" and "ngang" are related to each other in discourse on disease:

1   "Ngang" is a synonym for "kwashiorkor". People assume that they have the same meaning, though what that meaning is may be unclear. This is how most people who have both terms in their vocabulary use them most of the time, including biomedical professionals who use "ngang" to speak to

villagers about kwashiorkor, and villagers who use "kwashiorkor" to speak to me about *ngang*.
2   The meanings of "kwashiorkor" and "ngang" overlap. The
extent of this overlap varies from one situation to another.
3   Finally, there may be no overlap whatever, as in the case of
some descriptions of dry *ngang* in which oedema and apathy,
the defining characteristics of kwashiorkor, are absent.

These three ways in which "kwashiorkor" and "ngang" are related do not necessarily appear in the discrete forms I have
described above. I have introduced this three-fold distinction to
facilitate my description, and in doing so I have created more
order and coherence than there actually was. In practice, in ordinary conversation, all three may be present together, and an individual may hold different views during different encounters, or
at different moments in the same encounter.

Take, for example, the conversation with Henry and Winifred
which I mentioned earlier. Together with Francis Henry ran a
health centre which was specifically set up to treat kwashiorkor
and teach mothers to cook healthy food and feed their children
properly. He was trained at a Catholic Mission Hospital and was
therefore familiar with the biomedical definition of, and theories
about, kwashiorkor. When he spoke to me he used the terms
"ngang" and "kwashiorkor" as synonyms. He defined "kwashiorkor" biomedically, thus implying that "ngang" means the
same as biomedically defined "kwashiorkor". When treating his
patients he acted in accordance with these statements. If a
woman came to him with a child who had *ngang* he assumed that
she had not been feeding the child properly. He admitted them,
gave the mother cooking lessons and made sure that the child
received a high-protein diet. But in the situation described above
he said that the child had kwashiorkor, even though it obviously
lacked the two defining symptoms of kwashiorkor, oedema and
apathy. Then, following the mother's distinction between wet
and dry ngang, he went on to speak of 'dry' and 'wet' kwashiorkor, saying that the child had 'dry kwashiorkor,' which is not a
biomedical concept at all but Henry's biomedicalisation of *ngang
yur*, dry *ngang*. In other words, he had come to use "kwashiorkor" and "ngang" as synonyms, but defined "ngang" traditionally, thus implying that "kwashiorkor" has the same
meaning as the traditionally defined "ngang".

These shifts in meaning were influenced by the setting in which the conversations took place. In conversation with me he kept to biomedical assumptions and categories, in the presence of local people who had ideas which deviated from those of biomedicine he compromised and moved more into their universe of meaning. In this way he was able to bridge biomedical and traditional discourses. What he really believed remains an open question and, probably, an unanswerable one. What he believed depended on who he was talking to and in what context.

A discussion I had with Simon Ngengeh provides a further illustration of the way in which the meanings of "kwashiorkor" and "ngang" fluctuated in the same conversation. Simon Ngengeh was a large, stern-looking man of about fifty. He was the 'discipline master' at the Nkambe Government High School. One day I had visited him at the school and in the passage outside his office I encountered a queue of trembling, white-lipped pupils, awaiting his judgement on their misdemeanours. He lived opposite the market square in Tabenken. A great drinker of palm wine, any conversation with him was always lubricated with many litres of the sour, white liquid.

[3.3] 'In Limbum people call kwashiorkor *ngang*, but sometimes they also refer to it as *bfaa*. How do you see that?' I asked.

'Firstly, I don't know the symptoms of kwashiorkor, except as I have seen it in pictures of the Biafran war. Until the war I never heard the word "kwashiorkor", but the disease *ngang* existed in this community, and the symptoms as we know them are small blisters appearing on the body of the baby, just like pimples, but when they are broken they produce liquid, colourless liquid. This is what we know as *ngang*. The picture of kwashiorkor which was given us was one of a child with emaciated body and a protruding belly. This was the picture we got from the war front. Compared to what we call *ngang* we see that where you have children who are undernourished the tendency is to have falling hair, this skinniness, in fact in some cases the legs are even swollen.' He paused to empty his glass.

'Then it appears that *ngang* is also a disease which can be inherited, because certain couples produce children who from birth have to be treated for *ngang* or it will eventually show, no matter how much good feeding. So I still have a feeling that there is a difference between *ngang* and kwashiorkor... The question now is: what of *ngang* appearing in homes where children are fed with both breast milk and this *biberon*? Some people have children and they are taking care of them properly, but they still have to go to native doctors for the treatment of *ngang*. It would appear, therefore, that *ngang* is something right inside the body and they have to destroy the root with this traditional treatment so that it does not develop as the body grows. It is an organism, a negative organism, in the body trying to develop and overtake the normal growth of the hormones and make them less effective, and then create the disease kwashiorkor.'

He leaned forward in his chair. 'I would like to ask you this question: Will any person placed under conditions of starvation become a victim of kwashiorkor?'

'Not necessarily,' I said.

'Therefore, if it is only some of them, then those with the rudimentary gene of *ngang* in them are likely to be victims of kwashiorkor.'

Simon initially distinguished between *ngang*, which he described as a type of skin disorder, and kwashiorkor, which he related to malnutrition. He saw *ngang* as a possibly hereditary sickness, and one able to develop no matter how well-fed the child. He emphasised that *ngang* and kwashiorkor are different illnesses. But then, and this appears to be contradictory, he wondered how it was possible that *ngang* (sic) can occur in children who are well fed (that is to say he appeared at that point to be using "ngang" as a synonym for "kwashiorkor"). Some children, it appears, are well fed but they still have to be treated traditionally to prevent the illness. He then switched to a biological idiom which lead back to the term "kwashiorkor": '*ngang* is something right inside the body...and create the disease kwashiorkor.' Because not all malnourished children develop kwashiorkor he finally described it as being connected to a 'rudimentary gene of *ngang*'. Simon started off by distinguishing between *ngang* and kwashiorkor as two different illnesses, went on to use the term "ngang" to refer to kwashiorkor and finally separated them again into kwashiorkor as sickness, not necessarily related to malnutrition, and *ngang* as 'negative organism' and 'rudimentary gene'.

Fixing Twins

In my conversation [3.1] with him, Fai Gabriel said that his wife delivered twins but that they died of *ngang*, Isaac mentioned that when his child first developed *ngang*, he was already being treated because he followed twins, and Pa Manasas Yangsi [3.2] said that because he did not know whether his grandchild was a twin or not he was treating him with medicine for both *ngang* and twins.

In early discussions about *ngang* twins were, in fact, mentioned quite frequently together. When I asked medicine men which illnesses they treated a typical answer would be 'I treat headache, stomach ache, side pains, *ngang* and twins.'

When, the first time Lawrence and I went to see Pa TaKwi and he was not home, Pius told us that if we wanted to be absolutely certain of meeting his father we should come on a 'Country Sunday'. The Wimbum calendar has an eight-day week and all major activities, except going to church, are fitted into this cycle. Every village has its market day once every eight days, and once every eight days there is a traditional rest day on which the women do not work on their farms and traditional healers see their patients. These rest days are called Country Sunday in Pidgin. (The word "country" refers to anything considered traditional. There are country doctors (traditional healers), country chop (local cuisine), country fashion (rituals), etc.)

So, two weeks later, early one 'Country Sunday' morning, Lawrence and I set out for his compound once more. To my horror Lawrence brought along a large transistor radio with a shoulder strap, which he had recently purchased at the market in Ndu.

'What's that for?' I asked.

'I've brought it along for some entertainment,' he said with a broad smile. I wondered how much of my recordings it would be possible to understand against the background of blaring African pop music. But then I consoled myself with the thought that he would not be able to play it anyway in the solemn context of Pa Takwi's treatment session.

When we arrived at the compound the door of Pa TaKwi's room was open and smoke seeped from the dark interior and dissolved in the crisp morning air. Pius, who was in the yard washing his jeans in a bucket, called to his father that we had arrived and then led us into the dark interior of his den. Lawrence and

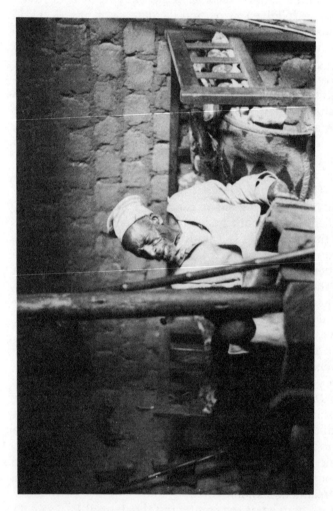

9 I could make out the form of a very slight old man wearing a tattered raincoat and a tall cap with a feather in it ... Pa TaKwi at work

Pius disappeared into the gloom and I stumbled after them feeling my way to a stool which Pius said was in the corner behind the door. The room was full of smoke from a small fire which was burning in the middle and my eyes soon began to water profusely.

I sat down and looked around. I could make out the form of a very slight old man wearing a tattered raincoat and a tall cap with a feather in it crouched in the middle of the room near the fire. He was grinding some herbs in a stone mortar and paused in his labours to lean forward and shake my hand. He repeated Pius's greetings in Pidgin and gave me a kola nut, a sign of hospitality. The room was traditionally furnished with a low wooden bed covered with ragged blankets along one wall, a central three-stone fireplace, a few bamboo stools and various boxes and trunks. In one corner, behind where I sat, there was a bamboo pole cutting diagonally across the corner from wall to wall. On it hung a few tattered garments, the old man's wardrobe. There were none of the 'cushion chairs' (Western-style chairs with foam-rubber cushions), tea tables and cupboards which are the usual furnishings in the houses of the younger or more affluent villagers.

The low bamboo ceiling was black and shiny from years of exposure to wood smoke. The surfaces of the mud bricks from which the walls were made had the same glazed appearance and resembled black bathroom tiles. The rear wall and ceiling were clustered with bags, packages and bundles of all shapes and sizes: small raffia bags, large bags made of snake skin or the pelt of some animal, with bunches of feathers protruding from them, bundles of bones bound with leopardskin thongs, packages made from old fertiliser sacks with porcupine quills threaded through the twine keeping them together, calabashes and clay pots, all of them covered in a shiny black glaze, the result of years of smoke and soot and the countless sacrificial sprinklings of fowl's blood and palm wine.

While I inspected the interior of the room, Pa TaKwi continued to grind his herbs and Pius went out to fetch a calabash of palm wine with which to entertain us. Lawrence turned his radio on and fidgeted with the dials, while Pa TaKwi removed a large bundle of leaves from where they had been roasting in the fire. He contemplated them before solemnly crossing himself and placing them in a bowl on the ground in front of him. Next to the

bowl were other instruments of his trade: calabashes with bunches of leaves protruding from their stems, small bottles, two large
snail shells embellished with cowries, rattles, bunches of green
leaves and small yellow flowers.

Three small boys entered the room and sat on one of the beds,
chatting among themselves and giggling. Pius returned with the
palm wine and some glasses, and while we drank he explained
the uses of the different 'medicines' hanging on the walls. Most of
them were protective medicines, he said. There was a large bag
with a bundle of feathers attached to it which protected the compound against evil spirits and a calabash containing medicine
which protected against fire (this included protecting the people
in the house from fire burns as well as preventing fire from
destroying the house). Pius recounted that the house had, indeed,
once caught fire, but that the fire had quickly died out because of
the working of these medicines. While Pius talked Pa TaKwi continued to grind his herbs, working with concentration and delib-
eration, like a chemist.

When he had finished grinding the herbs Pa TaKwi asked Pius
to fetch some palm oil from the kitchen, which he then mixed
with the herbs he had just ground. He then took a piece of bamboo from the fire and, laying it on the floor in front of him,
rubbed a lump of eucalyptus resin on the red-hot tip. This produced a thin column of aromatic smoke which soon filled the
room. It reminded me of the incense used in church during the
mass. The Catholic imagery increased when, a few seconds later,
Pa TaKwi stood up, removed his cap, folded his hands in front of
him, one enclosing the other, closed his eyes and prayed solemnly. After praying he crossed himself, genuflected, first in the
direction of the medicines on the wall at the back of the room and
then toward those on the ground in front of him, crossed himself
again and, after replacing his cap on his head, sat down. He was
now ready to commence with his treatment.

The two boys who had been waiting on the bed came forward
and stood in front of the medicines, calabashes, rattles, herbs and
shells behind which TaKwi was crouching on his small bamboo
stool. He took the bunches of yellow flowers and rubbed them on
the boys' foreheads, after which he went outside and threw the
flowers into the air. Next he took a calabash containing palm wine
and sprinkled some of it over the two boys and the medicines, took
a swig of it himself and let the boys drink some of it from his hand.

At this point I began to wonder why the third child was being excluded and asked Pius, who told me that the boy was a neighbour's son and 'not involved' in the treatment. The other two boys were his own sons, the older one was 'a twin' and the other 'his follower'. This was apparently the reason for their being treated.

In the meantime Pa TaKwi had filled the two large snail shells with palm wine and, taking a shell and a bunch of leaves in each hand he let the boys drink from each of the shells in turn. He then dipped the bunches of leaves in the wine which still remained in the shells and sprinkled it over the boys' heads. After replacing the shells he removed a small bottle from one of his medicine bags and from it poured a small amount of black powder onto the palm of his hand. He mixed this with castor oil and let the boys lick some of it from his finger tip before using the remaining paste to draw a black stripe on the stomach of one of the boys while he sat on the bed and distractedly scratched the bed post with a stone.

Lawrence's radio now produced a continuous background of static, occasionally interrupted by a man's voice saying something in an unknown language. I had always thought that treatment rituals were solemn affairs. The radio crackled, Pius and Lawrence chattered on like fishwives about some local scandal, the children alternated between boredom and noisily romping and giggling, hens strutted in and out, clucking as they scratched around for titbits. Perhaps I had been too strongly influenced by Western medical settings.

Pa TaKwi went back to his mortar and continued to grind the herb and red oil paste for a few more minutes. When he seemed satisfied with the consistency he took some of it on the tip of each index finger and let each of the boys take a lick, after which he crossed his hands in front of him and licked some of the paste from each finger himself. He then wiped his hands on the younger boy's legs and drank some more palm wine from the shells. After this he put down the shells and took up two of the rattles. He shook these above each boy's head, mumbling something which was inaudible to both Lawrence and myself. Then, taking a hollow bamboo, he blew into each child's ears, shook the bamboo next to his own ears and tapped himself on the forehead with it before returning it to its place on the ground. Finally he took another rattle, shook it next to both boys' ears and replaced it on the ground. He then returned to his stool and the boys went outside to resume whatever it was they had been doing when they were called. The 'treatment' had been completed.

I had gone to see Pa TaKwi in the hope that I would see him treating kwashiorkor, but as it turned out no children with kwashiorkor were brought to him for treatment on that occasion and all I witnessed was him 'fixing' his two grandsons. Pius had said that his two sons were being 'fixed' because 'the older is a twin and the younger is his follower'. This was not the first time that I had heard of twins being 'fixed'. During my first meeting with Pius he had mentioned that his father treated twins ([1.1] 20), and I later heard that Pa TaKwi was in fact a specialist in fixing twins.

Are Twins Prone to *Ngang,* or do they Just Become Fools?

The connection between twins and *ngang* became clear during a second visit to Pa TaKwi two months later. As on the previous occasion, Lawrence and I arrived at his compound early in the morning of a 'Country Sunday'. There we found a woman of about twenty with her three-month-old baby waiting outside, while Pa TaKwi was preparing his medicines inside. We went inside, where Pius offered us the usual hospitality of palm wine and kola nuts, while his father busied himself with his preparations. After a while the woman with the baby came inside and sat on one of the beds. She had brought her child for preventive treatment for *ngang*. This was what I had been waiting to see.

Pa TaKwi proceeded with the treatment, and to my surprise it closely resembled the treatment of the twins we had seen on the previous occasion. He followed the same steps, including all the praying and genuflecting, and he used the same medicines, also giving the child palm wine to drink from the large snail shells. Indeed, Pius's two sons, who had been treated as twins on the previous occasion, were called inside and treated together with the baby. After the woman had left, taking with her a bundle of leaves for continuing the treatment herself at home, TaKwi explained to me, partly in Limbum, which was translated by Lawrence, and partly in Pidgin, that the medicines which were spread out in front of him (the snail shells, calabashes, rattles, etc.) were for treating twins and *ngang*.

**10 Pa Andrew giving a child palm wine as part of the
treatment for twins and ngang**

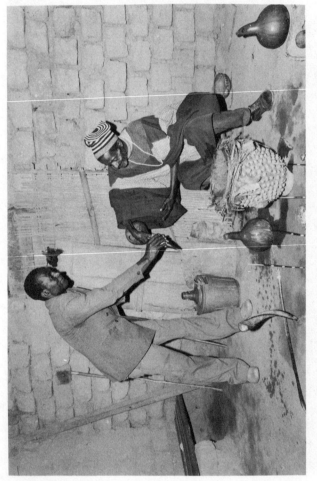

11 Pa Andrew fills Tobias's cup with palm wine. It is not only the children who are being treated who drink the palm wine. A treatment session is also an occasion for social drinking in which all who are present participate

In the days that followed I found out that other medicine men who specialised in the treatment of *ngang* were also specialists in fixing twins. The two forms of treatment appeared to go together, and, what is more, the medicines which were used also seemed to be the same. The treatment of twins appeared to be the same as the preventive treatment of *ngang* in babies. I wondered whether twins were thought to be more susceptible to *ngang*.

A month later I met Pius on the main road. He had his medicine bag over his shoulder and he said that he was on his way to Njap, a nearby village, to treat a child preventively for kwashiorkor. He was helping his father out because the old man had gone to treat patients in a different village and would not be back in time. He asked me to accompany him. I was not very keen on the long walk, but I thought that it might be worth while to see what the treatment involved.

We walked along the dusty main road and then branched off along a narrow path which meandered down through the valley separating Tabenken from Njap. Pius chattered on about his father's skill and his own ambitions as successor. Then he started to tell me about his 'handicrafted' daughter. The girl, who was about thirteen, did, in fact, have deformed hands. Instead of four fingers she had one large finger on each hand. Apart from that she was perfectly normal and could do anything with her single-fingered hands that other children could do with five fingers. She attended the local Catholic school, where she was in fact doing very well. Pius, however, claimed that she was an invalid and that she needed special schooling which he was too poor to provide. He used all the rhetorical skills at his command in an attempt to persuade me to pay him a large sum of money to finance this. I started to suspect that this was why he had invited me along and became irritated. By the time we reached the bottom of the valley, the halfway line between the two villages, he had fallen silent and we each retreated into that inner world of daydreaming and reflection which makes long journeys seem short.

When we arrived at the compound we were welcomed by the compound head. I was ushered into the sitting room and given a glass of palm wine while Pius was hurried off into an adjoining room to commence treatment. The family was obviously not wasting any time.

From where I sat I only caught occasional glimpses of what Pius was doing through the half-open door. His treatment seemed to be the same as that which I had seen his father administer on previous occasions. After he had finished he came back into the sitting room and the women of the household brought in bowls of fufu corn and a dish of chicken fried in palm oil, which they had been preparing while Pius was administering his treatment. We ate in silence, and when the meal was over we left after saying a brief farewell.

[3.4]   'What's the reason for treating that child?' I asked, once we were on the path back to Tabenken.

'It was not well matured,' Pius said, looking over his shoulder. I was surprised. 'Not well matured?'

'Yes,' he answered. 'In the stomach. It was born too early.'

'And what does the medicine do?'

'Pa treats the whole house, not only one child.'

I thought that perhaps he had not heard me. 'But what's the purpose of the treatment?'

'To make the child healthy, and also for kwashiorkor. The first child in the compound was also treated for that. There were six or seven.'

'Treated to prevent kwashiorkor?' I asked.

'Yes,' he said. We walked on in silence, passing through fields where women with bent backs were weeding with short hoes.

'That child was almost a twin,' Pius said suddenly, as though there had been no pause.

'Almost?'

'Yes,' he said. 'Just the same as a twin, that's why I've named it Tumi. That's a twin's name.'

'You mean it's a single twin?' I said, thinking that the child's sibling must have died.

'The herbs are used for treating both twins and kwashiorkor. That's what we are treating there,' Pius said, ignoring my question.

'When you say it's a single twin do you mean...?'

'Yes,' Pius interrupted, 'like mine. They came in plural and divided themselves.'

'If they're twins what happened to the other one?'

'There isn't another one, only this one.'

I was puzzled. 'But then how can it be a twin if there isn't a second one?'

'When the child was delivered there was a sign.'

'What kind of sign?'

'You have a line like this,' he said, tracing a diagonal line over his shoulder and under the opposite armpit. 'Just like a chief. It came out of the mother's womb with the sign.'

'You mean marks on the skin?'

'Yes.'

'And those marks mean it is a single twin?'

'Yes, it's almost a chief.'

'But why do twins have to be treated like that?'

'You know, there's no kwashiorkor without twins and no twins without kwashiorkor. They are both in one. But the twin medicine is quite different.'

'What does the illness which twins get if they're not treated look like?' I asked.

'They become dry,' he said, using the Pidgin term for "thin". 'They become very dry and small and pale. The child gives a lot of trouble, demanding all the time. Then it may just go and sleep and die. It just goes back. But in the case of kwashiorkor you see the eyes and the legs and the body swelling, and if you don't care for the twin it will go back.'

'Go back where?' I asked.

'To another person...'

After this discussion I was quite sure that there was some connection between *ngang* and twins and determined to find out more. I thought that the medicine men who specialised in the disease would be able to provide me with the relevant information. Manasas Yangsi gave the following explanation.

[3.5] 'Sometimes twins have *ngang*, but not because they are twins. It is not that all twins will get *ngang*. But if they are not fixed [*kubci*] as twins they will not have *ngang*. They will have a different illness. They will become fools [*lvur*].'

And on a visit to Fred Ngiri, another medicine man, I asked:

[3.6] 'Is the treatment that you give to twins the same as that for *ngang*?'

'There is some difference,' he answered.

'But the treatment for twins and *ngang* is similar. Does that mean that there is some relationship between twins and *ngang*?'

'They are not related, though some twins may be attacked by *ngang*.'

'Some people say that if you don't treat twins then they are more likely to get *ngang*.'

'Any child can be attacked by *ngang*, but when they are treating twins they also give the wine for *ngang* because the twins may
likely be attacked by *ngang*.'

So is there a connection between *ngang* and twins, and if so
what is it? In my conversation with Pius [3.4], he said he was
going to Njap to treat a child because it was 'almost a twin' and to
prevent kwashiorkor. He said that the herbs he used were for
both twins and kwashiorkor and that 'there's no kwashiorkor
without twins and no twins without kwashiorkor. They are both
in one.' But he then apparently contradicted this by saying that
the medicine for twins is different.

Manasas Yangsi said that the treatments of *ngang* and of twins
are different [3.5], and that although twins may get *ngang* they do
not necessarily get it because they are twins. The treatment of
twins seems to prevent not *ngang* but to stop the children from
becoming fools.

Fred Ngiri [3.6] agreed that the treatments for *ngang* and that
for twins are similar. Yet he denied that *ngang* is related to twins.
He then went on to suggest that the two treatments are combined, because, he says, 'twins may likely be attacked by *ngang*'.

What is one to make of this last remark? Part of the confusion
may be a result of translation. We spoke English, which Fred
speaks fluently, but he used English words which have probably
been influenced by meanings from related Limbum terms and
which do not have exactly the same meaning for him that they do
for me. The problem lies in the term "relationship". Fred agreed
that the treatments for twins and *ngang* are similar. I asked
whether this meant that there is a *relationship* between twins and
ngang. What I meant was a causal relationship: the fact of being a
twin as a cause of *ngang*. Later, when I was able to read the
Limbum transcriptions of other interviews, I discovered that in
the translations of my questions about relationships between
phenomena the word "relationship" was usually translated as *e
mo'sir*. Literally this means 'it is one'. This could mean 'they are
different but connected' as well as 'they are one and the same
thing'. These two meanings are clearly different. In these conversations I found that, in the context of the questions above, informants usually gave *e mo'sir* the latter meaning. This usually led to
them denying that twins were 'the same as' *ngang*. This was then
explained to me as 'there is no connection between them.' Now,
although Fred spoke English fluently I suspect that the meaning

he ascribed to "relationship" overlaps at least slightly that of 'one
and the same thing'. This would explain why he admitted that
the treatment is similar, denied the relationship when I asked
explicitly, and then concluded that twins are treated for *ngang*
because they are likely to get it.

Clearly twins and *ngang* are not the same thing. But are they
related? Do people perceive a causal connection? Are twins more
prone to *ngang* than ordinary children? And does fixing them
prevent them from developing *ngang*? It did seem that people
were suggesting this, though I could not be sure. Perhaps they
saw a connection, perhaps they were responding to my suggestion that there was one (if I did not think there was a connection
then why was I asking everybody about it in the first place?). The
treatment of twins resembled the treatment of *ngang*, even
though some informants (Manasas Yangsi [3.5]) said that the two
were different, but it is not clear whether these informants saw
treating twins as automatically preventing *ngang* as well. What
everyone did agree on was that fixing twins prevented them from
becoming fools.

Chapter 4

Abominations, Bad Death and *Bfaa*

An Accidental Death

One day a man went missing. He had been drinking in one of palm wine bars in the village square and by the time he left late in the evening he was quite drunk. He was last seen stumbling along the path in the direction of his compound. His relatives organised a search party the following morning but they found no trace of him.

Early one morning, four days after his disappearance, I drove down to the village square to pick up Lawrence for a trip to the market in Nkambe. There was much more activity than usual. A crowd had formed on the main road and people were moving about excitedly and pointing in the direction of Nkambe. As I watched from the car, a group of women emerged from a side street and ran off, in single file, in the direction in which everyone was pointing. Then the car door opened and Lawrence got in.

'What's going on?' I asked.

'I'm not sure,' he replied, as we drove off. 'But I suspect that they have found him.'

Nkambe is on a high plateau, and after leaving Tabenken the road climbs steeply. We approached the top of a hill and rounded a bend and there we encountered another crowd of people standing on the hillside and staring down into the wooded valley. People were moving busily up and down the path leading to the stream below.

'He must have hanged himself down there,' Lawrence declared.

We drove on, and after doing our business in Nkambe returned to Tabenken about an hour and a half later. When we reached the same spot there were a lot more people and some of the women were wailing. A large crowd had gathered on the slope of the hill on the opposite side of the valley. I stopped the car and we went to find out what had happened. A woman told us that the missing man had indeed been found. He had apparently fallen into the stream and drowned. The woman said his relatives had started to dig a grave on the hillside, opposite the spot where they had found the body. I looked across the valley and could see two young men, stripped to the waist, digging.

'I thought that people were always buried in their own compound,' I said.

'Burial in the bush without a death celebration is the normal thing in the case of such accidental deaths,' Lawrence replied. 'Yes,' he added after a while. 'Now they will have to *kvu bfaa.*'

'*Kvu bfaa?*'

'They will have to fix the *bfaa* before they can bury him.'

Before I could ask what he meant there was a sudden outburst of wailing and two women burst out of the undergrowth. Four or five other women were trying to restrain them. The two seemed to be hysterical and surged forward, dragging their restrainers with them across the road and down the hill into the valley.

'The dead man's wife and sister,' someone explained.

More women at the roadside took up the wailing. They cried that the man should not be buried on the hillside but in his compound as tradition demanded. The wife and sister reached the spot where the two youths were digging the grave. There was some commotion and then the whole group broke up and started to move back toward the stream. They emerged from the trees a few moments later and ascended to the road. In the middle of the crowd four men carried a bamboo stretcher on which the corpse lay wrapped in a purple blanket.

After a brief discussion with those waiting at the roadside the stretcher bearers moved off in the direction of the dead man's compound, followed by the crowd.

What had happened, I found out later, was that one group of relatives had decided that because it was a bad death the man should be buried where he had died without any celebration. They had brought spades and started to dig a grave. The man's wife and sister, supported by another group of relatives, had disputed this interpretation and insisted that he be buried at home. The latter group had won the day.

Lawrence and I spent the whole day at the dead man's compound where, by afternoon, hundreds of people had gathered. There was a lot of discussion and speculation as to what would happen next. Most people seemed to agree that the man could not be buried properly until the *kvu bfaa* ritual had been performed. But in the afternoon his oldest son arrived from Bamenda, where he worked as a school teacher. He swept away all indecision and ordered a grave to be dug in the compound. He would not hear any talk of bad death and that was the end of it. A few hours later the man was buried normally.

From *Ngang* to *Bfaa*

The first person to mention *bfaa* to me had been Confidence's mother, during the very first interview I conducted in Tabenken, when she called her child's illness *bfaa in* Limbum. Shortly after this Pius and Fai Nga Kontar both used the word "bfaa" as a synonym for "ngang". They said that the illness which people now called *ngang* had previously been referred to as *bfaa*, but that the latter term was no longer fashionable. Fai Nga Kontar said that "bfaa" meant 'mistake from the mother's compound'. Then in Taku Mungvu used "bfaa" in the same way as Confidence's mother, to refer to her child's illness, which I diagnosed as kwashiorkor. Finally, also in Taku, the traditional healer, Manasas Yangsi, said that *ngang* was the early stage of the disease, which then develops into *bfaa* when swelling appears.

In order to clarify some of these distinctions Lawrence and I paid another visit to the medicine man Manasas Yangsi. Shortly after our arrival Manasas's wife came in carrying their grandson Linus. His condition had deteriorated since our last visit. He was extremely miserable and he legs and feet were even more swollen. I wondered whether or not I should advise them to take him to a hospital or the health centre in Tabenken. While I was speculating on the best course of action, Lawrence asked Manasas to explain the relation between *ngang* and *bfaa*.

[4.1]   'If you don't treat *ngang* right at the start then it will become a sickness which people used to call *bfaa*,' Manasas said. 'It will enter into the body and be like *bfaa*. *Ngang* and *bfaa* are different. The people who treat *bfaa* are different. It is not we *ngang* people [*ngaa ngang*], we fix *ngang* so that it can not turn into [*beengir*] *bfaa*. When it is in a child like this,' he said, pointing to his grandchild, 'then it is *ngang*. But if he is not given medicines early it will enter

into the body and become *bfaa*, and the body will become red.'
The next day we went to see Pa TaKwi, who was also an *ngang*
specialist. His ideas on the matter were somewhat different to
those of Manasas Yangsi. In response to a question about the relation between *ngang* and *bfaa* he said:

[4.2]   '*Ngang* and *bfaa* are different. *Ngang* attacks young children. It
attacks the face and the head. It gathers in the stomach. It comes
from the stomach, it all starts there. Then it has to be fixed. It
appears like scabies, sometimes it is red. And as it has colour on
the outside, it is the same in the stomach. *Bfaa* is when a person
has killed himself. It only attacks adults who have been there, not
children.'

Then we went back to Freda Malah, the mother of the girl
Lawrence fancied. This time we arrived later and the daughter
had already left for her farm. Lawrence was disappointed, but at
least we could get straight down to business. I asked Lawrence to
ask Freda about the difference between *ngang* and *bfaa*.

[4.3]   'I have heard of the sickness called *ngang*,' she replied, 'but never
of a sickness called *bfaa*. I have heard of *kvu bfaa*. They do that
when someone has committed suicide. If a person in the family
has committed suicide then they come and fix the compound
[*kubci la'*]. They fix the compound by *kvu bfaa*. This kind of *bfaa* is
not on the body [i.e. is not a sickness]. There are also other kinds
of *bfaa*. When someone is murdered or gets killed during war, or
when someone has died a strong death, like being killed by a
spear. If the death occurred on someone's farmland then medicine men will be called and they will come and *kvu bfaa*, because
if corn is being farmed there then it will not be good. That is the
one I've heard of, I've never heard of it as a sickness. *Bfaa* and
ngang are not one thing.'

In my conversation [4.1] with him, Manasas Yangsi said that
ngang, if not treated, will become *bfaa*. He seemed to agree with
Pius and Fai Nga Kontar that "bfaa" is an older term which is
being replaced by "ngang". He also agreed that *ngang* and *bfaa*
are different, and this was supported when he said that they are
treated by different specialists. But he saw them as related: they
may be different, but *ngang* does develop into *bfaa*.

Pa TaKwi agreed with Manasas Yangsi, that *ngang* and *bfaa* are
different, but he did not describe the difference as one between

different stages in one illness process, but as different phenomena. For him *ngang* is an illness which starts in the stomach and appears on the skin like scabies, whereas *bfaa* is related to suicide; *ngang* attacks young children whereas *bfaa* only affects adults. This confirmed what Pius had said in our first conversation ([1.1] 66–73), but it is puzzling when placed next to an earlier exchange between Lawrence and Pa TaKwi, in which Lawrence asked him whether *bfaa* (sic) is related to twins, and Pa TaKwi answered that *ngang* (sic) and twins are separate, that is to say he treated the two terms as synonyms.

Freda Malah, like Pa TaKwi, used the term "bfaa" in connection with suicide, but whereas Pa TaKwi spoke of *bfaa* attacking people, as an illness, Freda Malah initially referred only to *kvu bfaa* as an activity through which a compound is 'fixed' when someone commits suicide. She had never heard of *bfaa* as an illness. Then she said that there are other kinds of *bfaa*, that they are related to violent death, and have to be fixed through *kvu bfaa*. She suggested that this kind of death can affect farming on the ground on which it occurs. She again explicitly denied that *bfaa* is a sickness and also denied any connection between *ngang* and *bfaa*.

As we walked back from Freda's compound, single-file along the narrow path, I questioned Lawrence about what we had just heard.

[4.4]   'Well,' I demanded, 'what's that kind of *bfaa* she was talking about?'

'That's the action from committing suicide. When you commit suicide it's called *bfaa*, it's not a sickness.'

'So does "bfaa" refer to suicide then?' I had my cassette recorder in my hand and aimed the built-in microphone at Lawrence's back to catch as much as possible of what he was saying.

'Errr...' Lawrence hesitated. 'It's not really suicide, it's...' He fell silent. We walked on and after some time he resumed. 'If I commit suicide then they will have to fix that otherwise it will affect other people in the compound, and they will do the same without knowing. So they have to disturb that traditionally. It's not really sickness, the sickness which is called *bfaa* is different.'

'How would you talk about that in Limbum?'

'You might say: "Someone has committed suicide so they are

fixing *bfaa* over there." Or maybe: "Someone has fallen in the stream and drowned."' He fell silent again. 'It's mostly related to accidental death.'

'So if I'm crossing the road and a car runs over me and kills me then they will have to fix the *bfaa*?'

'Yes.'

'What happens if you don't fix it?'

'Then someone else in the compound will also have an accidental death.'

'It's a kind of prevention?'

'Yes.'

'So Freda Malah was talking about this kind of *bfaa*?'

'Yes, I think that when someone speaks of fixing *bfaa* he means that kind of *bfaa*, but there is also the *bfaa* which is related to *ngang*, only I don't think she has any idea about that.'

'Do you think that the one word refers to these two different things?'

'I think that there is some relationship between them...' He paused. 'It's something I will have to think about.' There was a long silence as we plodded on down the hill and back into the village. 'You know,' he said, when we had reached the path leading to my compound, 'sometimes when a child gets such a sickness they say that the mother has made something like *bfaa*...that she has made a mistake before the sickness attacks the child. So then they call that *bfaa*.'

I was puzzled. 'What kind of mistake?' I asked.

'Like,' he hesitated, 'either the mother went and slept with her brother or...the mother made...' His voice trailed off. 'Well, it's just something relating to very dangerous things,' he resumed, 'like trying to...to kill somebody. If you try to kill somebody and hide it then the thing appears on your child and they call it *bfaa*.'

'Do you think that's how they relate?'

'Yes...well, we'll have to get some elders to explain the difference. We'll ask Pa Manasas Yangsi, he should be able to explain the difference. He was saying that *ngang* comes out like scabies on the child's skin, and that this later becomes *bfaa*. So we will ask him what the difference is between that *bfaa* and the *bfaa* they fix because someone has had an accident.'

Lawrence seemed to be familiar with the use of the term "bfaa" in connection with violent death though, in contrast to

Freda Malah, he did use it to refer to sickness, and he saw a connection between *ngang* and *bfaa*. At one point he translated "bfaa"
as "mistake", as Fai Nga Kontar had done previously, and related
it to incest. He claimed that a 'mistake' by the parent can affect
the child. Judging from the way he and Freda Malah used the
term, there is some semantic overlap with the English "abomination". Though the term "bfaa" was not new to Lawrence it is also
clear that he was not aware of all its meanings and not sure of
how the various meanings related to each other. I suspect that he
(and others) previously knew of *bfaa* as a kind of mistake or
abomination, and *bfaa* as an illness related to *ngang*, but that he
probably used the terms as homonyms. He did not pretend to
know all the answers, though, and suggested that we ask Pa
Manasas Yangsi.

Later the same evening, while I was relaxing with a cup of coffee, Francis Kongor, one of the village health workers, called in to
see me. He lowered his lanky body into a chair and poured himself a mug of coffee from the thermos. He added a generous helping of powdered milk and three dessert spoons of sugar. While
he stirred the syrupy mixture I decided find out what he thought
about the subject of the day's investigations.

[4.5] 'What's *bfaa*,' I asked?

He looked up and frowned. '*Bfaa? Bfaa* means mistake.'

'How do you use that word in Limbum?' I asked.

'If somebody makes a mistake then we call it *bfaa*.'

'You mean even a simple mistake, like putting something in
the wrong place?'

'Yes,' he said, and held out his cup of coffee. 'Suppose I should
put this cup here, but I put it there instead, then I would say *mɛ
bfaa se*, I have made a mistake.'

'Do people use the word "bfaa" when they are talking about
kwashiorkor?'

'Err...no,' he said, somewhat taken aback.

'Some people say that *bfaa* is the same as *ngang*,' I said.

'For me *bfaa* is something which you have done...' He leaned
back in his chair and reflected for a moment. 'Let's say I do something wrong in that compound down there. Then after some time
my child falls ill. When that happens people will call it *bfaa*. The
mistake I made down there has come back to my child and that is
bfaa.'

'Is the sickness of your child called *bfaa* or is it that the sickness of your child has been caused by *bfaa*?'

'The sickness is caused by the *bfaa*, by the mistake that I have done. And the thing doesn't affect me but only my child.'

'How would you say that in Limbum?' I asked.

'We would say *bfaa be koo muu*, the mistake will attack the child.'

'Have you ever heard people calling kwashiorkor *bfaa*?'

'No,' he said. 'Kwashiorkor is always ngang. *Ngang e koo muu* [*ngang* has attacked the child].'

'Someone told me that *bfaa* was the same kind of sickness as *ngang* and that it was caused by a mistake which the mother had made.'

'No,' he said, shaking his head.

'So if someone gets sick because of *bfaa*, can that be for any kind of mistake or only certain kinds of mistake?' I asked.

'There are certain kinds of mistake which are very bad. For example, if I have sex with my sister and she delivers a child. Then in the long run she gets married and her husband gives me *mimbu* [palm wine or beer] to drink and I take it then the mistake will prove itself. Either her child or my own will die. Maybe she will just be getting thinner and thinner, and she eats and doesn't grow and I eat and don't grow, then they will say *bfaa e koo mɛ*, the mistake has attacked me.'

'If someone kills himself is that also *bfaa*?'

'Yes, if you hang yourself then it is *bfaa*. If I hang myself here then I have made a mistake in this compound and the owner has to fix it.'

'Fix it?'

'Yes, he will come and my parents will come with a goat and fix it.'

Francis, like Lawrence and Fai Nga Kontar, translated "bfaa" as "mistake". For him it referred to both simple mistakes such as misplacing an object and more serious abominations, such as incest or suicide. These abominations have to be 'fixed' and if they are not they may affect the perpetrator's child. He denied that "bfaa" can be used as a translation of "kwashiorkor", saying that kwashiorkor is always called *ngang* in Limbum (here he agreed with Pius). And he also denied that *bfaa* is a sickness which is related to *ngang* and which is caused by abominations (here he was in agreement with Freda Malah, but not with Lawrence, Pa TaKwi, Manasas Yangsi and many others).

By the time we returned to Manasas Yangsi a month had elapsed since our previous visit. After we had settled down with the usual palm wine and kola nuts I enquired about his grandson, Linus. Manasas said that the child had greatly improved and was outside playing. He sent an older child to find him. In the meantime I asked what treatment the child had been receiving. Manasas said that he had been treating him himself with *ngang* medicines four times a week. He had started the treatment shortly after our last visit.

While Manasas was talking Linus was brought in. He had indeed greatly improved. The oedema had disappeared and his hair had been restored to its natural black. He still looked rather miserable, but this was because he had had diarrhoea for the last few days, Manasas said. He had a lot of sores on his toes, mainly round the edges of the nails and along the edges of the sole, which were probably the ravages of jiggers, small sand fleas which burrow into the feet and lay their eggs there. The soft feet of children may contain hundreds of jiggers if they are not removed regularly, and irritation and infection can cause gaping wounds.

Lawrence broached the subject of *ngang* and *bfaa*.

[4.6] 'Do you think there is any difference between *ngang* and *bfaa*?' he asked.

'There is no difference,' Manasas said. 'It is one thing. *Ngang* is *bfaa*. [*Yu yu e mo'sir. Ngang ege ba bfaa*]. If you leave it and it stays in the body for a long time then it turns into *bfaa*.'

'Do you think that the *bfaa* which attacks children is the same *bfaa* that they talk about when somebody commits suicide. Or is it a different sickness?' Lawrence asked.

'The medicine used to fix *bfaa* is the same as the one used when somebody commits suicide,' Manasas explained. '*Bfaa* is sickness. The sickness is *ngang* when it enters the body for long and starts to look red. The jaws and the feet become swollen. The child doesn't have its natural colour, it is red.'

'Do you think that if a person commits suicide and I go there and they don't treat [*kvu*] me, and I then give a woman a child that the child will have *bfaa*?' Lawrence asked.

'The child will have *bfaa*. Even if somebody commits suicide

on a woman's farm and the farm is not treated [*kvu*] then the food
will be attacked [*koo*] by *bfaa*.'
    '*Bfaa* will attack the food?'
    'The food which they grow there will not be good.'
    'So they have to fix [*kubci*] the farm?'
    'Yes, and if a person is killed there then they have to fix it,'
Manasas confirmed.

In our previous interview [4.2] Manasas had said that *ngang*
turned into *bfaa*, or something which resembled *bfaa*, but he had
insisted that they were different and were treated by different
specialists. This time, while still claiming that *ngang* turns into
bfaa, he clearly stated that they are one and the same thing. He
then went on to say that the same medicines are used to fix both
the sickness called *bfaa* and the consequences of suicide. He clearly linked the *bfaa* which is related to abominations such as suicide
to the *bfaa* which affects children and which resembles kwashiorkor. He seemed to view this latter kind of *bfaa* as the developed
stage of *ngang*. If a man visits the place where someone has committed suicide and he is not treated, and he then has sex with a
woman who becomes pregnant, her child may be attacked by the
sickness *bfaa* as a result. So *bfaa* is contagious, but it passes over
those directly involved and affects their children, which is also
what Francis said about *bfaa*, even though he denied that it had
anything to do with *ngang* or kwashiorkor.

The description which Manasas gave of *bfaa* is a more or less
complete list of the symptoms of kwashiorkor, and these were the
very symptoms his grandchild had manifested on our previous
visits. However, he continued to refer to this child's illness as
ngang and not as *bfaa*.

He also repeated what Freda Malah had told us about *bfaa*
affecting the ground on which the abomination had been committed. She had said that if someone was killed on a farm then the
corn harvested there would not be good.

It now seems possible to distinguish a number of different
ways in which *ngang* and *bfaa* are related:

1 *Ngang* and *bfaa* are one and the same thing (Manasas Yangsi
   [4.6]).
2 *Ngang* develops or turns into *bfaa* (Manasas Yangsi [4.1],
   though he is ambiguous).

3 *Bfaa* is related to both *ngang* and to abominations (Lawrence and Manasas Yangsi [4.6]).

4 There are two kinds of *bfaa*, one is an illness resembling kwashiorkor and the other is related to abominations (Lawrence, though he is ambiguous).

5 There is only one kind of *bfaa*, it is related to abominations and has nothing to do with *ngang*: *ngang* and *bfaa* are two different things (Pa TaKwi, Freda Malah, Francis).

Abominations and Bad Death

Some people used the term "bfaa" to refer to an illness which resembles kwashiorkor and which may or may not be seen as the developed stage of *ngang*. The term "bfaa" literally means mistakes. It can refer to simple mistakes, like misplacing an object, or to more serious mistakes, such as failing to pay the bride price. Informants also often used it in connection with violent death, incest and suicide. These topics were first seriously discussed in an interview with Pa Andrew Nfor, a medicine man, president of the Tabenken Traditional Healers' Association and, like Pa TaKwi, a devout Catholic. He was a slight man in his late seventies. He had a narrow face, sunken cheeks and protruding eyes. His voice was high-pitched and, in his wide, traditional robe, he reminded me of a small bird. He lived together with his wife and an unmarried daughter near the palace, about ten minutes' walk from my house. I went to visit him one morning and he received me in his sober treatment room. There were none of the bags of medicines, bundles of feathers and snakeskins which characterised the rooms of most medicine men in Tabenken.

After some preliminary social chat and the usual palm wine and kola nuts, I asked him about the role of witchcraft in the etiology of *ngang*.

[4.7] 1.'Can *ngang* also be caused by witchcraft?'
   2. 'There is a sickness like that which can be caused by a person,' he said. 'And you can die of it.'
   3. 'You mean *ngang*?' I asked
   4. 'Yes, because normally when someone dies of *ngang* he is swollen and we consider that kind of death a bad death [*rkwi rbibip*]. When someone swells up it is a bad death. Passing blood

is a bad death.'

5. 'And that is caused by somebody?'
6. 'Sometimes it is being caused by the person himself and some-times somebody else is causing it.'
7. I was surprised. 'Caused by the person himself? How does he do that?'
8. 'The person can cause it himself if he is trying to use his witch-craft [*tʋu'*] on somebody else who is also a witch but is stronger than him. Then he will be caught and get that illness.'
9. 'When children are affected with *ngang* does that mean that they may also have caused it themselves?'
10. 'The one in children is just an illness that comes. It isn't caused by anybody.'
11. 'So it's only when adults get it that it is caused by somebody?'
12. 'Yes.'
13. What about *bfaa*, is it the same as *ngang* or is it different?'
14. '*Bfaa* is a sickness that your colour changes and you become red. When you die like that it is called *bfaa*.'
15. 'Does it look like *ngang*?'
16. 'It's just like *ngang*.'
17. 'Is that *bfaa* different from the *bfaa* that people talk about when somebody commits suicide [*kɛrni*]?'
18. 'The *bfaa* of suicide is more serious than the *bfaa* of *ngang*.'
19. 'Are they related?'
20. 'What actually causes [*gee*] *bfaa* is suicide, then the sickness *bfaa*, the one which is like *ngang*, is less serious.'
21. 'Do you think that if someone commits suicide and a pregnant woman sees that and doesn't get treated, that her child will get *ngang* or *bfaa*?'
22. 'If a pregnant woman happens to see a man who has committed suicide she has to say so, she cannot be quiet, and then they will give her certain medicines to fix her. But if she doesn't say it or they don't fix her properly then she will die and the child will also die. But if she says it and all the ceremonies are carried out then she will be healed together with the child.'
23. 'Can it lead to *ngang*?'
24. 'Not if it has been fixed.'
25. 'And if it hasn't been fixed? Does the child get *ngang*?'
26. 'If they don't fix it the child will get *ngang*, and it is *bfaa*.'

Andrew said that people who die of *ngang* are swollen. Dying swollen is a 'bad death' and bad deaths are caused by somebody, though that somebody could be the victim himself. A witch may find that a person whom he is trying to bewitch is, in fact, himself a witch, and a stronger one at that. The potential victim is not affected and the first witch himself becomes the victim of his own nefarious use of his powers. He gets *ngang*, swells up and dies a bad death. This does not apply to children. If an adult dies of *ngang* people may suspect that he was a witch, but *ngang* in children is 'just a sickness' and not caused by anybody. At this point Andrew said that the death of an adult from *ngang* is a form of bad death. Although he initially appeared to be referring to a separate illness which only resembles *ngang* (2), in his next statement he explicitly referred to *ngang* as bad death (4).

I then introduced *bfaa* into the discussion (13), and Andrew distinguished between the *bfaa* that is 'just like *ngang*' (16), and a more serious form of *bfaa* which is related to suicide (18–20). But when I tried to relate *ngang* to suicide (21, 23) he seemed to agree that if a pregnant woman witnesses a suicide and is not fixed, her child will get *ngang* (23–26). The way in which he used both terms and interchanged them suggests that they had almost the same meaning for him here.

A couple of days later I was drinking palm wine with Simon Ngengeh in his house. I thought that he might be able to shed some more light on the meanings of the terms I have been discussing.

[4.8] 1. 'Some people say that *bfaa* is a sickness related to *ngang*, whereas others say that it has nothing to do with *ngang* but is related to things like suicide,' I told him. 'What do you think?'
   2. 'It is believed here, in our tradition, that if anybody commits an abomination, and suicide is such an abomination, another being incest, then it will run through the family for generations unless there is a cleansing rite which is performed to remove that abomination from the family. It is an abomination to commit suicide, or to raise your cutlass to someone, even if you don't actually strike him. If the knife draws blood, even symbolically, then the error, and *bfaa* means error, must be cleansed by a ritual. This usually involves paying some fines.'
   3. 'What do you call that cleansing rite?'
   4. 'When a person commits suicide it is an abomination to carry him from the scene of the suicide back to his compound and have him

buried like someone who has died normally. Traditionally we have been told that people had to go there, dig the grave under the tree and cut the person down so that he falls in. But today people do not like to have the body of their relatives treated like that and would rather pay a fine and have him buried normally. They call that cleansing rite *kvu bfaa*. Where there has been an abomination, or a conspiracy against a member of the family, and they have to be reunited then you have the ritual called *ncvu la'*.'

5. 'Is that different to *kvu bfaa*?'

6. 'Yes. *Kvu bfaa* is associated with suicide, dying what is called a bad death, *rkwi rbibip* in Limbum. If a person dies and gets swollen, or dies from a wound, or a woman dies during child-birth, then that is regarded as an abomination and is associated with *kvu bfaa*. So *kvu bfaa* is associated with someone who is dead through an accident which is not considered normal, and through suicide. But where you have a reconciliation which is also resulting from an error, the error being either incest or conspiracy, then you will have *ncvu la'*.'

7. 'You mentioned bad death. What's the Limbum term?'

8. '*Rkwi rbibip*, when a person dies swollen.'

9. 'Have you ever heard of people referring to a sickness which looks like kwashiorkor as *bfaa*?'

10. 'That is it!' he exclaimed. 'That is the adult who dies swollen. It is believed that he did some serious wrong and concealed it. He was expected, while living, to confess publicly and perform the cleansing rite. But if he is a patient for a long time and is carried to the hospital but he remains in that state and he is finally sent home and he dies in that swollen state then he has died a bad death, that is, he has died swollen.'

11. 'Is that kind of death ever associated with witchcraft?'

12. 'Of course. It is, it is.' He got up and went through the back door and into the kitchen where his mother, who was in her eighties, was cooking. After a few minutes he returned. 'She says that there are many aspects to it,' he said. 'When a person knows of his death, he knows the cause of his death, but refuses to confess then he is responsible. But where others, through envy, use witchcraft to spoil his death so that there will be no ceremony, then the cause is from outside, as opposed to the cause being from within.'

13. 'So he can cause it himself?'

14. 'He can cause it himself and others can cause it. And where they cause it, the element of envy is there.'

In this discussion Simon Ngengeh immediately linked *bfaa* to abominations such as suicide and incest. If a person commits suicide and the body is removed from the site where the suicide took place without a cleansing ritual (*kvu bfaa*) being performed then this is also an abomination. He said that the *kvu bfaa* ritual is associated with bad death. Dying swollen, from a wound or in childbirth (accidental deaths, deaths which are not considered to be normal) are all abominations which require *kvu bfaa*.

He had already said that the term "bfaa" means error (2). When I asked him whether there is also an illness called *bfaa* which resembles kwashiorkor (9) he agreed that there is, and linked the illness *bfaa*, bad death and kwashiorkor together on the basis of one common symptom: swelling (10). He agreed that such a death can be caused by witchcraft. Like Pa Andrew he said that the victim himself may be responsible for his own bad death. He did not explicitly state that such a death could be result of the victim's own witchcraft, and defined responsibility in terms of committing an 'error' and not publicly confessing to it. There is also the possibility that the victim is innocent and that a witch is causing him to die swollen in order to 'spoil his death' and prevent him from having a proper death celebration, out of envy or spite (10–12).

Everyone I spoke to agreed that when someone dies a bad death there will be no death celebration and the deceased will be buried unceremoniously in the bush away from the compound. As the event documented at the beginning of this chapter illustrated, however, it is possible to make exceptions in practice. Simon did say that in the case of a bad death it is possible to pay a fine in order to be able to bury the victim properly, though I do not know whether this happened in the case at the beginning of the chapter.

A few days after my discussion with Simon Ngengeh, Lawrence and I paid another visit to Fai Nga Kontar, the traditional quarter-head and father of one of the first kwashiorkor cases I saw in Tabenken, to ask him to explain how he saw the difference between *ngang* and *bfaa*. He told us, as he had done on our first visit, that the illness which I had been calling kwashiorkor used to be called *bfaa* in Limbum, but that nowadays it is called *ngang*. He emphasised that *ngang* and *bfaa* are synonymous. I then asked him whether this *bfaa* is the same as the *bfaa* which is usually mentioned in connection with suicide.

[4.9] 1. 'When a person commits suicide it is different,' the *Fai* said. The *bfaa* of suicide is different. In Limbum that one is called *njong*. *Bfaa* medicines and *ngang* medicines are not different. They are one thing.

2. 'Why do you call it *bfaa* when a person commits suicide?' I asked.

3. 'Because he has made a mistake [*bfaa*] by committing suicide. There is a reason for this *bfaa*. It has to do with wars between the *WiYa* and the *WiTang*.[1] You make/cause *bfaa* [*a gee bfaa*] when you cut a person. If you marry someone from *Ya* [Ndu] without fixing it then later your children have *bfaa*. If a person gets burnt by fire then it is *bfaa*. Then they have to go and fix it, they have to fix with different medicines and they will say the person has made/caused [*gee*] *bfaa*. They call that *kvu bfaa*. It is the same as in Limbum. At first when we referred to *ngwɛɛ mcɛp* we just said *ngwɛɛ mcɛp* [literally medicine man]. Now people call him a native doctor. "Native doctor" is not a Limbum word, it is English, but in Limbum people have started to say native doctor.'

4. 'If someone dies a bad death, swollen up, what people call *rkwi rbibip* in Limbum, do you also use the word "bfaa"?'

5. 'If somebody dies a bad death they don't call it *bfaa*. If a person dies an accidental death then they *kvu bfaa*, and carry the basket called *nko' blung*.'

6. 'Can a person die swollen because he has made a mistake [*e muu gee bfaa*]?'

7. 'If a person dies swollen they will not consider it to be *bfaa*, they will say he has made witchcraft [*e muu gee tvu'*].'

Fai Nga Kontar initially said that the *bfaa* which is related to suicide is different to the children's illness. He then went on to claim that the medicines for *ngang* and *bfaa* are the same. There seem to be two "bfaas", one which is synonymous with "ngang" and a homonym related to suicide. Thus Lawrence, during the same discussion, explained that *ngang* and *bfaa* are the same because their medicines are the same, but that different medicines are used for *bfaa*.

I tried to find out whether these two "bfaas" were related, but the *Fai*'s answer was confusing. He said that suicide is a mistake (*bfaa*). The reason for this mistake is wars between Tabenken and

---

1. Two of the three Wimbum clans, inhabiting the Ndu and Tabenken areas respectively.

Ndu in the past. If someone is wounded or killed by a cutlass during such a war it is an abomination (*bfaa*), which has to be fixed before an inter-clan marriage can take place. So far this was consistent with what he had already said, but then he went on to say that if there was an inter-clan marriage without the abomination having been fixed then the children resulting from that marriage 'will have *bfaa*', which is to say that he was then referring to the illness *bfaa* and relating it directly to *bfaa* as abomination. Suicide, accidents with fire and children getting the illness *bfaa* all seem to be linked to the same ultimate cause: failure to fix a mistake or abomination which has occurred in the past in the context of inter-clan wars (3).

He then went on to say that this is 'the same' as the adoption of new English words in Limbum, which eventually replace the Limbum originals. I can only speculate on the relevance of this comparison. Perhaps he was referring back to what he had said previously about "bfaa" being the original Limbum term for the children's illness and "ngang" being a foreign word which was introduced from a neighbouring area and soon became fashionable. It seems reasonable to assume that he meant that the illness *bfaa* and abominations form one conceptual complex, but that the newly introduced term "ngang" subsequently came to be applied to the illness. This speculation does not, however, explain why the *Fai* was initially so adamant in denying this connection. Perhaps the suggestion of a direct link between the illness and suicide was unacceptable to him, and he could only agree with a connection between them through their relation to a common ultimate cause.

The *Fai* did not think that *bfaa* was related to bad death, as Simon Ngengeh had suggested. He used the term "bfaa" in connection with accidental death, not bad death (i.e. dying swollen), and did not seem to regard suicide or deliberate killing during war as forms of bad death, as did other informants (4–7). My next question (6) was motivated by Simon Ngengeh's remarks ([4.8] 10) that a person may die a bad death because he has made mistakes to which he refuses to confess; that he 'knows of his death' ([4.8] 12).

The *Fai* did not think that bad death can occur because a person has made mistakes to which he refuses to confess and that he 'knows of his death,' as Simon Ngengeh said. He said that if someone dies a bad death then people will say that 'he has made witchcraft' (4.9:7). In this he repeated what Pa Andrew and Simon Ngengeh had already told me.

A discussion which I had with Fred Ngiri and Mathias Tomla three months later shed some more light on the relation between *bfaa* and bad death. Fred and Mathias were brothers in their late thirties. They lived in Upper Mbot, a village just outside Tabenken and on the road to Ndu. Their father had been a renowned medicine man. Since his death a few years earlier his practice had been taken over by Fred. Mathias was a teacher at a nearby Roman Catholic primary school. Mathias's wife, Susan, also worked for me as an assistant. All three of them spoke fluent English, and all our discussions were in English. I had gone to Mbot on a 'country Sunday' so that Fred could explain their *ngang* medicines to me. We sat in his treatment room and Fred systematically explained the uses of the various medicines.

[4.10] 1. 'What do you think causes *ngang*?' I asked at one point.
2. 'We can't really know the cause of *ngang*,' Fred said. 'Sometimes it is said that it is caused by the sins of our great grandfathers, or by the parents, and that is the reason for it attacking the child. When it attacks the child in a different way, that is, when the child changes colour, then it is called *bfaa*.'
3. 'Is *bfaa* the same as *ngang*?'
4. '*Bfaa* is *ngang* which has become swollen.'
5. 'So if a child has *ngang* then later it turns into *bfaa*?'
6. 'If it is not treated then it turns into *bfaa*.'
7. 'What is the difference between the two?'
8. '*Ngang* usually appears on the body like scabies. Then when it turns to *bfaa* the colour of the child changes. The child becomes fat, sometimes instead of it becoming fat the eyes become swollen and the body changes. With that we now use different medicine. It has now become *bfaa*.'
   Fred went on to describe the kinds of medicines he used in treating *ngang* and *bfaa*. During this exposition Mathias, his brother, entered the room and sat down opposite us. When Fred had finished his exposition, Mathias spoke.
9. 'I wish to give some light on the issue of *bfaa*,' he said. 'It is generally believed that if you are attacked by *bfaa* then there is a cause behind it. The cause may rest with the parents, for example, if somebody hangs himself in the forest and nobody is allowed to fetch wood there, but you go there to fetch wood then you will

eventually be attacked by *bfaa*. If you are lucky it may not attack you, but then it will attack your children because they are weak. It could be that as a man you are armed with medicines. It will just appear like *ngang*). But nowadays it is believed that nearly all children who are delivered, for one small reason or another, will be attacked by *ngang*. Nobody is believed to be all right, and this will eventually lead to the child getting *ngang*. So the difference between *bfaa* and *ngang* is in the cause.'

10. 'So *bfaa* can be caused by something like somebody committing suicide, but not *ngang*?' I asked.

11. 'Yes,' Mathias agreed. 'And in the case of *bfaa*, very serious types can attack grown-ups like ourselves. You may be healthy and then the disease of *ngang* that appears in children could just attack. And sure enough, if you investigate you will find that you have gone against some custom, especially like the one I have mentioned.'

12. 'Does that mean that if someone commits suicide and you go there then your child will get *bfaa* without first having *ngang*?'

13. 'Yes,' Mathias said. 'If somebody commits suicide and everybody rushes there then you can't go back to your house until a doctor has given everybody medicines. If you go without the medicine then you will be attacked by *ngang*.'

14. I was still puzzled. 'But what will the sickness that affects you look like? Will you immediately swell up or will you first get the kind of scabies which you described as a symptom of *ngang*?' I asked.

15. 'It's of many kinds. You may begin to grow very lean and your body will eventually turn yellow. Others may have swelling like little children.'

16. 'What else can cause that apart from someone committing suicide?'

17. 'If you go to certain forbidden places.'

18. 'What kind of places?'

19. 'Like *ndap ngong*. Not everybody is supposed to go there. But going to any forbidden place when you're not supposed to can cause it.'

20. 'I've heard that you can also get *bfaa* by falling into a latrine and not getting treated,' I said.

21. 'Yes, that's also a cause. Because a latrine is where all bad things are dumped.'

22. 'Is there some similarity between a latrine and the *ndap ngong*?'

I asked.

23. 'The *ndap ngong* is a forbidden place, the latrine is a place where bad things are dumped. People say that just the fact of falling into the latrine means that there must have been something. It could be that even if you did not fall in you would still have been trapped in another way.'

24. 'You say: "there must have been something." What kind of things are you thinking of?

25. 'There are always mistakes which you have committed, either knowingly or unknowingly, and they are against you. Either the gods or the customs.'

26. 'People say that children can get *ngang* if the mother continues breast feeding when she is pregnant again. What do you think?'

27. 'Yes, we see that this *ngang* can be caused by the woman weaning before time and continuing to breast feed when she is pregnant, without giving the child proper care.'

28. 'Why do you think people give such different explanations as suicide and falling into latrines for the same sickness?'

29. 'For us Africans there is always a reason for sickness. Especially this *ngang*. If you get it there must be a fault somewhere.'

30. 'Can it also be caused by witchcraft?'

31. '*Ngang* is not caused by witchcraft,' Fred interjected.

32. 'If an adult gets *bfaa* and becomes swollen can you also call that *rkwi rbibip*?' I asked.

33. '*Rkwi rbibip* is when a person is already dead,' Fred explained.

34. 'So if I get *bfaa* and swell up and die then you'd call it *rkwi rbibip*?'

35. 'Yes, Fred replied.

36. 'Do you speak of *rkwi rbibip* when a child dies of *bfaa*?'

37. 'With a child they don't say *rkwi rbibip*...' Mathias began, but Susan interrupted him.

38. 'Then what do they call it?' she demanded.

39. 'It's the same, it's the same,' Fred insisted.

40. 'But people tell me that if someone dies swollen like that there must be some witchcraft involved,' I said.

41. 'Yes,' Fred said. 'That is the one in which the stomach swells, not the whole body. That one is caused by witchcraft.'

42. 'So that's different to *bfaa*?'

43. 'Yes,' Fred affirmed.

We then drifted off into a discussion about witchcraft, which is the subject of Chapter 6. This led on to a discussion of the differences between diviners and medicine men, which prompted met to ask whether medicine men specialise, so that some only treat witchcraft related disorders and others only use herbal remedies. Fred said that most medicine men carried out both kinds of treatment.

44. 'For example,' he continued, 'if we treat a child for *ngang* and we see that it is not working then we go and find out whether it's being caused by witchcraft. Because here in our practice we can't treat a child having serious *ngang*. If we treat three times and don't see any change, though there usually is some change, then we have to find out whether witchcraft is involved.'

45. 'How do you find that out?'

46. 'In some cases the medicine tells us. For example, if there is a child with *bfaa* and I rub the child with the medicines and they do not stick but come loose as soon as I apply them, then I know that it is caused by witchcraft.'

47. 'If you get a child like that do you then send it to someone else in order to find out who is behind the illness?'

48. 'You tell the person to go and find out more about the sickness before coming back. Then they go to a diviner before coming back to tell us.'

Fred said that *ngang* and *bfaa* are two phases in the same illness: '*bfaa* is *ngang* which has become swollen'. He said that he did not really know the cause, but that people say it is a result of 'sins' committed by parents and grandparents. Mathias, who had not heard Fred's remarks on 'sins' as a cause of *ngang*, said much the same thing about *bfaa*: if someone has the illness called *bfaa* then there must be a reason, and that reason may rest with the parents. In his example he linked *bfaa* directly to suicide. He said that there are only slight differences in appearance between *ngang* and *bfaa*.

He then went on to say that nowadays it is believed that almost all children will be attacked by *ngang*, 'for one small reason or another,' because 'nobody is all right', and he concluded that the difference between *ngang* and *bfaa* is in the cause. At first he suggested that *ngang* has the same ultimate cause as *bfaa*, and in this he agreed with Fred that they are phases of the same illness and can be attributed to some wrong committed in the past. But when he stated that the difference lies in the cause he may have been suggesting that they are different phenomena, or perhaps he meant that most children are likely to get *ngang* because of wrongs committed by parents, but that this will only develop into the more serious *bfaa* if more serious wrongs have been committed (he mentioned the connection with suicide). This is only speculation, however. Further on he agreed with me that *ngang* and *bfaa* are different, but proceeded to use the terms interchangeably anyway. My attempts to elicit what I would consider a systematic statement on the precise relationship between *ngang* and *bfaa* were in vain (10–15).

I resigned myself to the fact that he was using the terms interchangeably, and attempted to set off in another direction: what are the other causes, apart from those connected with suicide, which lead to *ngang* or *bfaa*? (16). He mentioned going to forbidden places such as the *ndap ngong* and falling into a latrine, where 'bad things' are dumped.[2] Here 'bad things' may refer, I think, to the polluted nature of the primary product which is usually dumped in latrines, or to bad medicines which, I occasionally heard, were also disposed of in latrines (17–22).

Then there was some disagreement about whether a child who dies of *bfaa* (i.e. swollen) has died a bad death. Mathias said it would not be a bad death, Fred said it would (36–9). Fred distinguished between *bfaa* and bad death by saying that *bfaa* is when the whole body swells, whereas in the case of bad death it is only the stomach which swells. He only thought the latter to be caused by witchcraft (40–3). When I asked him explicitly, Fred quite emphatically stated that witchcraft was not a cause of *ngang* (30–1). But later, in the context of a discussion about different kinds of healers he spontaneously described how he finds out whether *ngang* is being caused by witchcraft (44–8). This shows quite clearly how people would say different things depending on whether they were talking spontaneously or answering my explicit questions.

People use the word "bfaa" in relation to abominations such as suicide, incest, accidental death, death from a wound, from bleeding or in childbirth. All kinds of violent and unexpected death are generally referred to as bad death (*rkwi rbibip*). Dying swollen is bad death *par excellence*. Through the symptom of

---

2. Translated literally, *ndap ngong* means 'house of the land'. It is where sacrifices are made to ensure good harvests. Informants sometimes described it as 'a sort of traditional church'. I will come back to this Chapter 7.

swelling people tend to relate the illness *bfaa* to abominations (also called *bfaa*) and to bad death. Fai Nga Kontar disagreed with this, however, and distinguished between bad death (dying swollen), on the one hand, and other forms of (violent) death related to the term "bfaa", on the other. For him bad death only occured when someone dies swollen, and for such cases he did not use the word "bfaa".

What people told me about bad death varied. They disagreed with one another and adjusted their interpretations in the discussions. But there *is* a notion of bad death, which everyone who spoke to me shared, at least minimally. And it is a notion that has been widely reported in the ethnographic literature, and not only that of Africa. Lack of control and unpredictability are often seen as the most important aspects of bad death (see Bloch and Parry 1982: 15). Writing about Hinduism, Parry describes bad death as unexpected death for which the deceased has not been able to prepare himself, the paradigmatic case being death by violence or as a result of a sudden accident. It is an untimely or uncontrolled death (Parry 1982: 83). For the Lugbara, according to Middleton, bad deaths have in common that they occur 'outside' and unexpectedly. This may include death outside the home, while in the bush hunting, death in warfare or through homicide away from one's compound and before the proper time, death as a result of witchcraft or sorcery and dying outside Lugbaraland as a migrant (1982: 143).

Bad death is often opposed to good or natural death in which, after a full life, a person comes to a peaceful (and predictable) end surrounded by family and friends. According to Parkin, bad death mars or detracts from the completeness of such good deaths: the living are left with an incomplete picture of the deceased (Parkin 1985: 7–8, see also Parry 1982). In the Western literature on death the notion of good death tends to over-shadow that of bad death (see, for example, Kellehear 1990).

There Must Have Been Something...

When a person dies a bad death there is no death celebration and he is buried outside the village in the bush. Such a death can be caused by someone (a witch) who, out of envy or spite, causes the person to swell up in order to 'spoil his death'. But it may also be caused by the person himself. If a person does something wrong, commits an abomination (*bfaa*) such as homicide or incest and does not confess then he may also die a bad death. In that case he 'knows of his death'. And, similarly, if you are attacked by the illness *bfaa*, then this is because you must have done something wrong and not confessed.

If abominations are not fixed then they will be passed on from one generation to the next. 'The mistakes walk, they move from blood to blood,' Tobias said on one occasion. As a result, new abominations will continually be caused through the failure to fix previous abominations. In his discussion of bad death in Hinduism, Parry (1982: 83–4) notes that bad death in a family is cumulative, with one bad death leading to another: 'the sins of the father may be visited on the son, and...the attenuation of this life may be a consequence of the wickedness of those with whom the individual is most closely associated'. And with regard to bad death among the Giriama in Kenya, Parkin writes:

> The metaphysical ideas relating to 'bad death' centre on the notion that men and women who kill – in battle as warriors, in village quarrels or by accident – have the blood of their victims in them, and are now subject to the negative state of what is known as *kilatso* (derived from *mulatso*, blood). Bad death (or *viha* death [i.e. violent death]) refers to the subsequent murders, suicide, acts of violence or accidents, which these individuals carry out and which are attributed to this condition. Actual motivations for these acts may certainly be identified... But *kilatso* is held to subsume them, translating them, so to speak, into action. (Parkin 1986: 213)

The act of committing suicide or killing someone can be referred to as *bfaa* (abomination), but the effect of the uncleansed act, the defilement itself, which is passed on through the generations, is also called *bfaa*, and this latter *bfaa* in turn leads to new abominations, also referred to as *bfaa*.

This is clear in the conversation with Fred and Mathias above [4.10]. Mathias said (23, 25): 'just the fact of falling into the latrine means that *there must have been something*. It could be that even if you did not fall in you would still have been trapped in another way... There are always mistakes which you have committed, knowingly or unknowingly, and they are against you.' Earlier Fred had said that ngang may be caused by the 'sins' of the parents (2), and Mathias had claimed that if you are attacked by *bfaa* there must be an ultimate cause (9). What becomes apparent here is that an occurrence like falling into a latrine can be seen both as a mistake or abomination (*bfaa*) in itself which, if not ritually fixed, can be a cause of illness (*bfaa*), and it can also be seen as the consequence of a previous and as yet unfixed abomination. This is what Mathias meant when he said that if you did not fall in the latrine then you would have been trapped in another way. The *bfaa* (abomination) is always there in the background as a potential cause of all sorts of calamities, and it will remain there, passing on from one generation to the next until a diviner points to it and it is ritually fixed.

One question which arises here is how this is thought to work. Are people punished for mistakes through some impersonal moral cosmic mechanism like karma, or is a personalistic agent responsible, as Mathias suggested when he mentioned 'gods' and 'customs'. I will return to this question in chapters 7 and 8.

Bad Breast Milk and 'Children's Illness'

When I asked people what causes *ngang* and *bfaa* they generally said that they did not know. But in the course of many discussions the meanings of these terms became richer and more complex and I gradually built up a picture of what people meant when they used them. When I thought that my knowledge of *ngang* and *bfaa* was more or less complete – when it did not seem as though I would acquire any new meanings or uncover any new contexts in which the terms were used – I moved on to enquire about etiology more generally.

At the same time I also continued to work on the more practical, biomedically oriented, branch of my project. I recorded case histories of a number of children with kwashiorkor and collected details on all the factors which were thought, from a biomedical perspective, to play a role in the genesis of infant malnutrition: socio-economic status, diet, feeding habits, ideas about infant feeding, etc. When I arrived at the topic of breast feeding and weaning I once again encountered, much to my surprise, *ngang* and *bfaa*, this time as part of a 'bad breast milk syndrome'.

Lawrence and I had been interviewing a group of about forty women who lived in Kieku Quarter about diet, infant feeding, weaning, and so on. At one point I was trying to find out the reasons for neglecting or terminating breast feeding. I asked them about all kinds of situations which women in other cultures sometimes consider a valid reason for terminating breast feeding, such as when the child has diarrhoea or fever. The women claimed that they did not stop breast feeding for any of these reasons. The only reason which they gave for the early termination of breast feeding was a new pregnancy.

At one point in an interview with a young woman called Hilda I asked: 'Would you stop breast feeding if you became pregnant again?'

'Yes,' she said.

'Why is that?'

'I've heard that it isn't good,' she replied.

'What will happen if you do?'

'The child will have kwashiorkor,' she said, using the biomedical term.

'Is that caused by the breast milk?'

'Yes,' she said, 'it shows that the milk is not good.'

In another interview with an older woman, Ita, I asked what would happen if a woman continued to breast feed during pregnancy.

'If you are pregnant and you give the child the breast then it can die,' Ita said.

'Why is that?' I asked.

'Because the breast is bad [*bibip*].'

'What kind of sickness would the child get if you continued breast feeding when you were pregnant?'

'*Yang bobkɛ*,' she told me.

'What's that?' I asked. I had never heard the term before.

'That's children's illness,' Lawrence explained casually.

'Yes, it's the same as *ngang*,' Ita added.

'Is it like kwashiorkor?' Lawrence asked.

'Yes,' she replied, 'just like kwashiorkor'.

Another young woman, Rose, used the term "bfaa" in the same context.

'It's not good for a pregnant woman to breast feed,' she told me.

'Why not?' I asked.

'If you do that the child will not become strong. It will be sick and purge [have diarrhoea]. After that it will have the sickness called *bfaa*. It will not look good.'

'What does it look like when it has *bfaa*?'

'It will have swollen jaws and feet and the colour will change.'

'Is that the same as *ngang*?' I asked.

'Yes,' she said.

'Is it also the same as *yang bobkɛ'*?'

'The same.'

'Sometimes *bfaa* or *yang bobkɛ'* just comes and sometimes it comes from breast feeding when you are pregnant,' Røse's mother added.

'Why do you think that breast feeding during pregnancy can cause a sickness like that?' I asked.

'Because the breast is bad,' Rose said. 'There is another child in the belly and that makes the breast bad.'

This sudden re-appearance of *ngang* and *bfaa* surprised me. In the previous discussions about *ngang* and *bfaa* nobody had used the term "*yang bobkɛ'*" or mentioned bad breast milk. Now suddenly, in the context of interviews with women about pregnancy and breast feeding, a new term comes to light. The term "*yang bobkɛ'*" means literally 'children's illness'; it is also sometimes referred to as *yang gharbee*, which means the same thing. The women also related it to the term "kwashiorkor", which they used more frequently than the (male) traditional healers, probably because women are more exposed to biomedical health education.

The appearance of *yang bobkɛ'* in these circumstances should not suggest that it is part of a submerged female conceptual domain: when I went back to the men with whom I had discussed *ngang* and *bfaa* I found that they knew all about *yang bobkɛ'* and bad breast milk. Then why had they not told me about it? Well, they said, I had not asked, and it had not occurred to them. Indeed, as far as I know, the interview I had with Ita was the first time *yang bobkɛ'* was mentioned during my research. When I asked 'What's that?' in an excited voice, Lawrence casually replied 'That's children's illness', as though it was the most common thing in the world. He was obviously familiar with the term. Why had he not mentioned it to me previously? Somewhat paradoxically, if I had limited my enquiries to *ngang* and *bfaa* and not continued with my parallel research on kwashiorkor I might never have heard of *yang bobkɛ'*.

Later it became clear that people also related *yang bobkɛ'* to *bfaa* and abominations. Women are supposed to abstain from sexual relations during pregnancy and lactation (which is the reason that men give for having many wives and mistresses on the side), and the early termination of breast feeding is a sure sign that this restriction has been broken. People said that for a woman to have sexual relations while pregnant or breast feeding is an abomination similar to those already discussed above, and is the cause of the illness *ngang, bfaa* or *yang bobkɛ'* in children.

So it is that the children's disease which we call kwashiorkor is related, through its most spectacular symptom, swelling, to both abominations and bad death. As such it can be attributed to the activities of jealous witches, the unconfessed sins of the parents, abominations committed by past generations, a pregnant woman inadvertently stumbling on a person who has committed suicide and not telling anyone, or a mother breast feeding her infant when she has resumed sexual relations with her husband. Where the responsibility for a specific case of the illness lies is a matter for the diviner to decide.

Chapter 5

Illness, Medicine and Etiology

Naturalistic and Personalistic Etiologies

Between the mid-1970s and mid-1980s a number of publications appeared in which earlier ethnographies of illness and misfortune in Africa were criticised for placing too much emphasis on supernatural causation and neglecting natural causation and practical medical behaviour. Indeed, since Warren's (1974) first criticism of Field (1937, 1960), there has been what almost amounts to a crusade to prove that Africans traditionally recognise a separate medical domain in which they interpret illness primarily in empirical and practical rather than in social and moral terms.[1] These discussions are based on a distinction which is usually made between naturalistic and personalistic etiologies.

> A personalistic medical system is one in which disease is explained as due to the *active and purposeful intervention* of an *agent*, who may be human (a witch or sorcerer), nonhuman (a ghost, an ancestor, an evil spirit) or supernatural (a deity or other very powerful being). The sick person is literally a victim, the object of aggression or punishment directed specifically against him, for reasons that concern him alone. Personalistic causality allows little room for accident or chance...naturalistic systems explain illness in impersonal, systemic terms. Disease is thought to stem, not from the machinations of an angry being, but rather from such *natural forces or conditions* as cold, heat, winds, dampness, and, above all, by an upset in the balance of the basic body elements. (Foster 1976: 775, emphasis in the original)

Foster sees etiology as the key to cross-cultural comparison of non-Western medical systems; the independent variable which

---

1. See for example Fortes 1976, Loudon 1976, Gillies 1976, Prins 1981, Warren 1974, 1979a, Yoder 1981, 1982a, 1982b. Here I am, obviously talking about a tendency, albeit a very dominant one, in recent medical anthropology and not about all medical anthropologists. There have, of course, been studies which have continued to stress the supernatural nature of traditional etiologies. See, for example, Jacobson-Widding and Westerlund 1989, Nordstrom 1989 and Feinberg 1990.

determines other elements of the medical system (p. 776). He also distinguishes between comprehensive and restricted etiologies. Personalistic etiologies are usually part of more comprehensive explanatory models and illness is seen as being just one form of misfortune. Naturalistic etiologies, on the other hand, are limited to explaining illness (pp. 776–7). So, for example, in India the hot–cold theory is only used to explain illness, whereas in Africa witchcraft explains not only illness but all kinds of misfortune.

It is an emphasis on comprehensive personalistic etiologies in medical ethnography that some authors see as a problem. Fortes (1976) and Yoder (1982b) trace the problem back to W H R Rivers, who was one of the first medically trained anthropologists to make a systematic study of what was then referred to as primitive medicine. In his *Medicine, Magic and Religion*, Rivers (1924) claimed that etiology is the central element of medical systems, and that the study of etiology naturally leads on to the study of diagnosis and treatment. This explains his focus on indigenous theories of disease causation. He distinguished between three main kinds of cause: human, supernatural and natural. He stated that all three are also recognised in Western societies, but here natural causes are by far the most important, and it is on the notion of its natural causation that people base their attitude to disease. Among 'savage or barbarous people', on the other hand, beliefs about disease causation fall mainly into the first two categories, and natural causes are hardly recognised at all (Rivers 1924: 7–8). Human and supernatural causes correspond to the domains of magic and religion respectively, and as a result the distinction between 'primitive medicine', magic and religion becomes blurred. Because of its mainly magical and supernatural nature, Rivers concluded that primitive medicine was fundamentally different from Western medicine (Rivers 1924).

This focus on etiology as a basis for indigenous illness classification and the emphasis on comprehensive personalistic etiologies was common in many other early studies (Clements 1932, Field 1937). It is also found in more recent ethnographic studies (see Beidelman 1963, Price-Williams 1979, Ngubane 1976), as well as in attempts at a more general synthesis: G P Murdock's world survey of theories of disease is based on a two-fold distinction between natural and supernatural theories of causation. Referring to Africa, Murdock states that 'a disproportionate number of societies emphasising witchcraft theories were found' (Murdock 1980: 42).

The question now is: what is wrong with this emphasis on personalistic etiologies? Why so much trouble to prove that Africans
traditionally explain most illness in naturalistic terms? In his
foreword to the collection of papers presented at the 1972 confer-
ence of the Association of Social Anthropologists on social
anthropology and medicine, Fortes claimes that the gap which
has been described between Western and non-Western medicine
is a result of the influence of early twentieth-century medical science on such early medically qualified anthropologists as Rivers
and Seligman (Fortes 1976: xii–xiii). They were 'obsessed with
native theories of magical causality' (p. xiii) and as a result they
'*reduce* the study of health and disease to studies of witchcraft,
sorcery, magic and in general curative or socially re-adjustive ritual practices, with herbalist and empirically rational diagnoses,
treatment and prophylaxis as residual categories' (pp. xiv–xv, my
emphasis).

Yoder, in his introduction to another collection of papers, this
time on 'African health and healing systems' (Yoder 1982b)
agrees with Fortes, though he is more critical with regard to the
influence of biomedicine. Yoder points very explicitly to some of
the more important problems in ethnomedical studies in Africa:
anthropologists 'have tended to accept uncritically biomedical
definitions of what is relevant in the study of health care and
medicine'; they have accepted a dichotomy between biomedicine
and other medical systems and there have been variations in the
way the limits of medical systems are established (pp. 1–2).

But in spite of this perceptive criticism, Yoder agrees with
Fortes on the negative influence of Rivers' conclusions about
'primitive medicine' on later generations of anthropologists. As a
result of this, he says, referring to Evans-Pritchard and Turner,

> the study of medical beliefs and practices became *subsumed* under the
> rubric of magic, witchcraft and religion...

in particular

> ...Their emphasis upon belief and etiology has led them to neglect
> other crucial aspects of medical systems, in particular nosology, pro-
> phylaxis, and the patients' choice of medical practitioners. *Indeed,
> there has been little interest in the study of medical systems per se.* (Yoder
> 1982b: 4, my emphasis).

The issues raised by Fortes and Yoder can be summed up as follows: the focus on etiology, and in particular on comprehensive personalistic etiologies in the medical ethnography of Africa has led to the blurring of the distinction between the domains of medicine, magic and religion. Anthropologists have been too eager to relegate indigenous disease theory to the realms of religion and magic by describing witches or supernatural beings as the most important, or only, etiological agents recognised by Africans, who are seen as interpreting disease primarily in social and moral terms. This has led anthropologists to accept (implicitly or explicitly) that there is a fundamental dichotomy between Western biomedicine on the one hand and all other medical systems on the other. The focus on etiology accentuates the contrast between biomedicine and other medical systems. This has in turn led to the neglect of the practical, behavioural aspects of non-Western medical systems, and therefore to a neglect of medical systems as such.

But Yoder notes with apparent satisfaction that 'Recent research, with a *broader* focus on *medical* ideas and practices in Africa, presents a rather different picture of both disease etiology and medical knowledge in general' (Yoder 1982b: 13, my emphasis).

His reference is to the work of a number of anthropologists who have made the medical system their object of study and who 'conclude that people regard most illnesses as having natural causes'.[2] Because of their 'wider' research interests, which include 'all aspects of medical systems in Africa', they provide a 'more reliable data base from which to generalise' (Yoder 1982b: 13).

Bibeau, for example, claims that 'many studies of African traditional medicine are fragmented...breaking up reality' which is in fact continuous (Bibeau 1982: 45). Indigenous pharmacopoeias, psychopathology, anatomo-physiological knowledge, and so forth, should be viewed holistically as aspects of a medical system (Bibeau 1982: 45). He found it necessary to analyse Ngbandi medicine by establishing the boundaries of the medical domain: defining the 'semantic domain covered by Ngbandi medical terms, such as care, heal, drug, disease', identifying medical behavioural settings in which these terms are used and observing the behaviour of 'the actors of the medical scene' (Bibeau 1981: 297, 1982: 49).

2. Gillies 1976, Bibeau 1979, 1981, 1982, Janzen 1978, Warren 1974, 1979a, 1979b, 1982, Young 1975, 1976, 1977.

Both the preparations for my fieldwork and the research itself were influenced by these discussions. At the start of my fieldwork I considered myself to be working largely within medical anthropology: I took the 'medical domain' as my object of study. I started from the visible symptoms of a biomedically defined syndrome (kwashiorkor) and from there tried to find out how people interpreted this syndrome and how they related it to disease classification and etiology more generally: I tried to delineate the medical domain.

Illness and *Yang*

It should be clear from my presentation of people's statements about *ngang* and *bfaa* that any simple classificatory scheme that is supposed to represent indigenous disease categories would be inadequate. Indeed, it is not clear whether the concept of disease is even relevant here. Disease is, after all, usually defined biomedically, and this definition automatically excludes many indigenous conceptions of physical disorder, not to mention various forms of non-physical disorder.

The Limbum term that is generally translated into English as "sickness" or "disease" is "yang". The meaning of "yang" is less specific than that of "disease" and it can refer to a disease (*yang binji* = gonorrhea), to pain (*yang rbvuu* = pain in the stomach) or to certain kinds of physical discomfort (a person feeling the intense need to defaecate might say *tung e yang mɛ* = stools are causing me discomfort). Therefore "dis-ease" seems to be a better gloss for "yang". In what follows I will translate "yang" as "illness", adopting the distinction often made in the medical anthropological literature between *illness* and *disease*. Biomedical doctors diagnose and treat diseases, which are abnormalities in the structure and function of bodily organs and systems. Patients suffer illnesses, which are experiences of dis-ease not necessarily correlated with disease biomedically defined (see Eisenberg 1977).

At the time of my first discussions about *ngang* and *bfaa* I also started to compile a list of Limbum illness terms. I asked various people to give me the Limbum names of all the illnesses (*byang*) they knew. These enquiries resulted in lists that varied from three or four terms to more than forty. These lists were mainly in Limbum (I had specifically asked for Limbum terms otherwise people would have only given English or Pidgin names), though there were also English terms ("malaria", "cough", and sometimes even "cancer" and "AIDS") and Pidgin terms ("gonococcus", "purging", "catarrh") which had been adopted into the Limbum illness vocabulary. My final list contained more than a hundred terms, and I am sure that it is still far from complete.

There was a common core of about sixteen terms representing the most common illnesses which were mentioned by most people. There was relative agreement about the physical symptoms that these terms denoted. The degree of consensus gradually faded, however, once discussion shifted to the periphery of general knowledge. When I read them my list most people recognised many more terms than they had originally told me, but there was no one who had heard of all the terms in my complete list.

Some Common Illness Terms:

"tu lu" (headache: *tu* = head, *lu* = bite)
"rbvuu lu" (stomach ache: *rbvuu* = stomach, *lu* = bite)
"kosi" (cough)
"facifaci" (catarrh)
"mbimnyor" (side pains: *mbi* = side, *nyor* = body)
"njee" (backache: *njee* = back)
"coro" (measles)
"mbɛp" (fever)
"mkar" (scabies)
"bumnongsi" (rheumatism)
"yur" (filaria, itching: *yur* = dry)
"wakinta" (fainting, convulsions)
"ngang"
"bfaa"
"malaria"
"purging"

The English terms in parentheses are not meant to be the biomedical equivalents of the Limbum terms. They are the English terms often used by the people themselves, either to translate the Limbum terms for me, or to refer to the illnesses in question in their own multilingual discourse. When these English terms are used by local people they may be given meanings which are very different to those which they have for biomedical health workers. For example the term "scabies" can refer to a large variety of skin ailments, most of which would not be called scabies by a biomedical practitioner. Similarly, "catarrh" can refer to the biomedically distinct colds and hay fever. "Headache" and "malaria" are often used to refer to fever.

There are also a number of terms which, if literally translated, refer simply to parts of the body, but when used in conversation about illness refer to pain or dis-ease in that part of the body. So when I asked someone to give me the names of illnesses in Limbum he or she might say *tu* (head), *rbvuu* (stomach), *njee* (back), *mbimnyor* (side of the body), etc. and mean sore head, stomach pains, backache or side pains respectively. If there is any doubt they may add the term "yang" and say *yang rbvuu, yang njee*, etc. This way of naming illness has been reported from other parts of Africa (see Harley 1941: 199, Bibeau 1982: 52).

There were terms in my extended list which some informants described as synonyms. But as the meanings of most terms are indeterminate to a greater or lesser degree it is usually only possible to see them as synonyms in the context of a conversation with a specific informant. The Pidgin term "purging", for example, is usually translated into English as "diarrhoea" and in English and Pidgin conversation in hospitals and health centres "diarrhoea" is seen as an accurate translation of "purging". I initially accepted this translation but began to doubt its accuracy when I noticed that some women said that their child was purging if they thought it defaecated too often, even though the stools were hard.

Indeed, the situation proved to be even more complicated. "Purging" is used in English, Pidgin and Limbum discourse about illness with varying shades of meaning. There are also at least five Limbum terms which are translated into Pidgin as "purging" and into English as "diarrhoea".

Pidgin terms related to "diarrhoea":

"purging"
"mixing"
"belly bite"

Limbum terms related to "diarrhoea":

"rbvuurto'" (*rbvuu* = stomach, *to'* = to boil)
"gorbvuu" (*go* = illness, *rbvuu* = stomach)

"rbvuubir" (*rbvuu* = stomach, *bir* = red)
"rbvuufingci" (*rbvuu* = stomach, *fingci* = to mix)
"gobar" (*go* = illness, *bar* = excreta)[3]

These terms have in common that they refer to dis-ease related to
bowel function. "Rbvuubir" and "rbvuufingci" refer to stools
that are mixed with blood. When talking about bloody stools
people may also simply say that someone is "mixing". Together
with "gorbvuu" and "gobar" these terms need not necessarily
refer to watery stools. Indeed they may also refer to constipation.
This leads to situations in which people use the terms "purging"
or even "diarrhoea" to speak about being constipated. In one
interview with a mother I asked her whether she fed her child
beans. The answer, translated by Lawrence was: 'No, not beans.
They are not good for children, they cause diarrhoea.' In Limbum
she used the term "rbvuurto'" and she may simply have been
referring to flatulence and accompanying discomfort caused by
eating beans (*rbvuu* = stomach, *to'* = to boil). Most of the people I
spoke to were not familiar with all these terms, and there was not
much consensus about the exact meanings of those they were
familiar with. A conversation I had with Tobias Ngwang is characteristic.

Tobias also lived in Kieku Quarter, about fifteen minutes' walk
from my house along the main road. He was a compound head in
his forties. I am not sure how much formal schooling he had, but
he spoke fluent English and could read and write well. An auto-
didact, he learnt French from his son's school textbooks and also
studied some of the mystical texts, such as *The Great Napoleon
Book of Faith* and the *Sixth and Seventh Book of Moses,* which circu-
lated in literate circles in Ndu and other towns. He was also a
devout Catholic. About half-way through my stay in Tabenken I
hired him as a second assistant. We became friends and often
drank coffee together. Although most people in Tabenken cultivated coffee as a cash crop, they did not actually drink it, and
some people did not even know what it was used for. If they did
drink coffee it was the Nescafé which was sold in the market, to
which they added large amounts of powdered milk and sugar.
My habit of drinking large amounts of black coffee without sugar

---

3. "Go" refers to illness or dis-ease and has the same meaning as "yang", though in conversations I only heard the word used in reference to these stomach illnesses.

soon caught on, and I taught Tobias how to roast and grind some
of the coffee beans he cultivated behind his compound (some villagers had no idea that this was the raw material from which the
Nescafé was made). By the end of my stay Tobias could proudly
say, in true Dutch fashion, that if he did not have his black coffee
in the morning he could not function properly for the rest of the
day.

[5.1] 'Do people recognise different kinds of diarrhoea, or do they just
see all diarrhoea as the same thing?' I asked.
'They just call it *gorbvuu*, that is diarrhoea', Tobias said.
'Is that the term for all kinds of diarrhoea or only for the one
mixed with blood?'
'No, for all kinds.'
'What about *rbvuurto*'?'
'*Rbvuurto*' means purge, belly bite when it is purging.'
'Does purging mean the same as diarrhoea or is it different?'
'Purging is different.'
'How is it different?'
'You can take purge to wash your bowels, that is not diar-
rhoea. You can take purge and when you purge you call it *rbvuu
le to' mɛ, rbvuurto*', that is rbvuurto' is not diarrhoea. That's the
difference.'
'If someone says that his child is sick because it is purging then
what does he mean? How is that different to when he says that
the child has diarrhoea?'
'Well, if someone complains that his child is not well because it is
purging then that is always attributed to diarrhoea. Because if you
are sick and purging and you die then they say that you have died
of diarrhoea, that is *gorbvuu, e rkwi rbvuurto*'. That means when you
were sick you were purging, and when you die it did not stop.'
'So if somebody has *gorbvuu* what would you say in English:
He was purging or he had diarrhoea?'
'In English they say: He is purging. In Limbum we say he has
gorbvuu, e tvur yang gorbvuu, gorbvuu e ce to' e, he is purging, *rbvuu
e ce to' e*.'
'So there's really no difference between diarrhoea and purging?'
'There is really no difference. No difference.'
'Do people distinguish between diarrhoea and diarrhoea
mixed with blood?'

'When you are purging, when you are sick, the people will try to witness it. If you just do local purging then they will just say that you are purging. But if there is blood then they will call it diarrhoea, which is *gorbvuu*. But if they identify that you are purging, you may be purging as frequently as that, but if there's no blood then they will say that you are only purging.'

'What would they say in Limbum?'

'They would say: *e to' rbvuu, e ce to' le rbvuu.'*

'So *gorbvuu* is always with blood?'

'With blood. Even if you are not purging, if you go to stool and the stool is hard but it is mixed with blood then it is attributed to *gorbvuu.'*

'So *gorbvuu* is always with blood?'

'With blood.'

'And if the stool is hard and there is blood would they call it *gorbvuu*?'

'Yes, then it's *gorbvuu.'*

'And if they speak of *rbvuurto'* can it also be hard, or is *rbvuurto'* always soft?'

'Well, *rbvuurto'* can never be hard because if you are purging and when it becomes hard and you are trying to force the faeces to go out then normally blood must come out. But with normal purging, *rbvuurto'*, there is no mixing. The bowels are washed. It comes down very clear, just faeces alone. But that which is attributed to *gorbvuu*, or diarrhoea, as known, it is mixed. Sometimes you purge, you go to stool but you can't even excrete. When you try to excrete it becomes hard. But then after a few minutes it may even try to come out in your clothes, with some mixture of blood. That is what is called *gorbvuu.'*

'If you have *rbvuurto'* does it make any difference whether you excrete only once a day or twenty times?'

'Whether you go once or twenty times, they will still call it the same *rbvuurto'.'*

'Are there other names for diarrhoea in Limbum?'

'Only *gorbvuu*, the illness of the stomach.'

'And *rbvuurto'*?'

'And *rbvuurto'.'*

After a number of interviews such as this what are we to conclude about the exact meaning of illness terms, or the way in which they relate to each other, or the physical reality they are supposed to denote? In the case of biomedical terms we can consult textbooks, whereas here the relevant knowledge can only be produced and reproduced in encounters of this nature. Is it useful in such cases to speak of a 'system of illness classification'? And, if so, on whose authority should it be based: on that of the traditional healer, the educated intellectual, the average villager?

Can we simply collect lists of vernacular terms from a few representative key informants and arrange them in tree-diagrams and tables of contrast sets which then represent, unproblematically, the indigenous disease classification system, with each term referring to a more or less distinct syndrome? According to Warren:

> once the domain for diseases had been defined by a single indigenous healer – whose classification was to be regarded as the traditional model for the domain – this model was compared with the classifications as articulated by other indigenous healers as a test for the cultural validity and reliability of the traditional model...

this then reveals

> ...the core competences which allow the various members of the Techiman-Bono society to interact adequately and appropriately when dealing with this particular domain. (Warren 1979a: 38–9)

This is, of course, the classic ethnoscience approach which, although it seems to have become extinct in mainstream anthropology, is still very much in vogue as a research method in certain sections of medical anthropology, as well as in applied development oriented anthropology more generally.[4]

Given my experiences as presented above, I tend to conclude that there is no ideal level of cultural competence which can be revealed by eliciting the categories and classifications of 'knowledgeable' informants. Rather, there are a number of clusters of more or less indeterminate terms, which together and across many instances of communication, refer to a loose constellation of symptoms. It is not simply a question of polysemy: one term

4. See for example Warren 1974, 1979a, 1982, Boutin and Boutin 1987 and Kleinman 1980 for medical anthropology and Brokensha, Warren and Werner 1980 for development studies. I would not wish to be mistaken as claiming here that these authors have got it all wrong and that there are no systematic illness classifications in Africa. I am simply maintaining that classification systems are more indeterminate and subject to variation from one situation and one individual to another than they suggest. As a consequence I am opposed to the way models are constructed, based on research in one (limited) cultural context and then assumed to apply to other situations and cultures.

having different but more or less fixed meanings (in the sense of a reasonable degree of consensus), the meanings are fluid and vary as the term is used in different contexts and by different people, and the variations are not necessarily systematic.

The situation is further complicated by translation. People not only speak of *ngang* and *bfaa*, they also translate these as kwashiorkor, and even malnutrition. And when they talk about diarrhoea they may be referring to what we would call constipation.

It would be more accurate to talk of complexes of loosely defined but interrelated terms (such as diarrhoea/*purging*/*gorbvuu*/*rbvuurto*// etc.) rather than specific well-defined diseases. There are, in fact, a number of such complexes which I will not describe here (see Bibeau 1982: 59 for similar examples).

Limbum speakers would generally consider the phenomena I have been discussing to be forms of *yang* and these phenomena could, without much stretch of the imagination, be called illness by an English speaker, even though a biomedical expert may not grant them the status of disease. But it has often been claimed that Africans classify illness together with all sorts of misfortune which we would never call illness, even though the two may be distinguished lexically.

In an early interview, when I asked Pa TaKwi to tell me what he treated, he answered (and here I condense a very extended account):

> I fix *ngang*, twins, rib pains, headache, burns. When a person commits suicide I fix the place where it happened. I treat heart pains. If a person can't sleep I give medicines [*mcɛp*]. If a woman doesn't menstruate for a long time I give medicine. If you build a new house and can't sleep in it I give you medicine. If you want to marry a girl but she doesn't love you I can make her love you. If you have a child at school who doesn't do well because of witchcraft then I will give you medicine.

When I asked medicine men what kind of conditions they treated or fixed (*kubci*) without referring explicitly to illness (*yang*) they would mention, in addition to the illnesses listed above (and those in my extended list), all sorts of misfortune, from failure in love to motor accidents and poor performance at school, which we would not classify together with illness. *Yang* only refers to what we would call illness, in the broad sense of (physical) disease. Other misfortunes would not be called *yang*.

When I asked people to tell me about ngang they would sometimes ask: 'Do you mean *yang ngang* or the *ngang* which dances?'[5]
The fact that both *ngang* and (some kinds of) *bfaa* could be
referred to as *yang*, and were in fact mentioned in many people's
lists of illness terms, seems to justify (at least provisionally) my
classifying them as illnesses.

Medicine and Mcεp

The Limbum term "yang" is used in a similar way to the English
"illness", and the meanings of the two terms overlap to a large
degree. This is not the case with that other term which is so central in the ethnographic description of medical systems: "medicine". The illnesses mentioned above are generally treated with
medicines, but so are various other kinds of misfortune, as the
quotation from Pa TaKwi above shows.

"Medicine" is the term which people use, in both English and
Pidgin, to translate the Limbum "mcεp" (singular "ncεp"). But
"mcεp" has a much broader meaning than we assign to "medicine", so when local people speak English or Pidgin they use the
term "medicine" in a much wider sense than Westerners would.
In what follows I will briefly mention some of these meanings.

Firstly, people in Tabenken use the term "mcεp" to refer to
more or less the same things as Westerners would call medicines:
both Western pharmaceuticals and local herbal remedies for illness. They extend this meaning by also using it to refer to herbs
and other substances or combinations of substances used to 'fix'
or prevent various non-illness misfortunes, and to enhance the
chances of success of various undertakings.

Secondly, they call certain objects "mcεp". A *ncεp* may be a
bundle of leaves, feathers, porcupine quills, a mixture of pow-
ders, contained in a small leather pouch or other package or container, or some other object, black and shiny because of layers of
sacrificial blood and soot and encrusted with beads or cowrie
shells. The house in which I stayed in Tabenken had been abandoned by the owner because witches had continually tried to
harm him there. Throughout my stay I kept discovering the anti-
witchcraft medicines which he had hidden in almost every nook

5. There is a *juju* (masked figure) called *ngang* which dances and which is used to find
harmful 'medicines' that have been hidden in the ground by ill-doers.

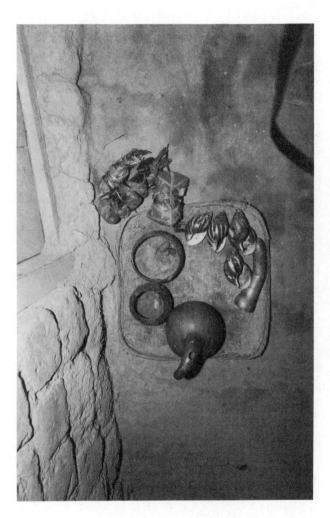

12 Medicines for treating *ngang* and twins

13 Medicine in a bottle, buried in the drive to someone's compound

and cranny: bundles of porcupine quills and feathers stuck in holes in the wall, a small leather package in the crevice above the door, bottles containing leaves, buried near the entrance, with only the opening visible. These *mcɛp* are what used to be called 'fetishes' in the older literature.

Thirdly, in some compounds an oval stone or other object that symbolises the unity of the compound or the lineage is kept in a separate room or corner. This object is also called a *ncɛp*. The compound head makes regular sacrifices to the *ncɛp*, performing a ritual which is referred to as *kubci ncɛp* (fixing the *ncɛp*). This *ncɛp* unites the whole family or lineage around it and binds them to their 'old compound', giving the compound head who looks after the *ncɛp* power over those who leave the village to work in the city or the plantations in the south. These migrants are supposed to maintain contact with their village and their home compound, coming home regularly to *kubci ncɛp*: perform the ritual and sacrifice a fowl on the compound *ncɛp*. Failure to do this can lead to all kinds of misfortune from illness and accidents to failure at school and lack of promotion at work or low profits in business. The urban *evolué* who consults a diviner because he has been meeting with one misfortune after another is likely to be told that he has been neglecting his contacts with the village, that the *ncɛp* is vexed and he should return as soon as possible with fowls or a goat and calabashes of palm wine in order to *kubci ncɛp*. Diviners often trace illness, not only of migrants but also of those who remain behind in the villagers, back to the sufferer's neglect of the family *ncɛp*.

In relation to this there are hints of a connection between *kubci ncɛp* and *bfaa*. Lawrence described neglecting the family *ncɛp* as a 'mistake', an abomination, which causes sickness and misfortune to those involved until it is 'fixed' by the appropriate ritual.

Twins, particularly so-called 'single twins' (*rfar mo'sir*), are referred to as *boo ncɛp* (*boo* = children, singular *muu*). Single twins are children who are born with the umbilical cord around their shoulder and under the opposite arm (as Pius described in conversation [3.4]) or wrapped around their neck, or who are born feet first or already have teeth when they are delivered. They are very active children whom it takes a lot to satisfy. They are said to become great leaders (see Pius [3.4]), good musicians and renowned medicine men if they are treated properly. If they are not they go mad or, according to some, become witches. They are

14 A *juju* belonging to *Ngwɛrong*

15 *Nko'*, a particularly violent *juju*, also belonging to
Ngwɛrong

called *boo ncɛp* because they have a special relation to a *ncɛp*, and neglect of rituals which are part of this relationship will affect the child adversely. This is related to the issue of *ngang* and twins to which I referred in Chapter 3, but I will not go into the matter here as it is complex enough to warrant a separate study.

Jujus (masked figures belonging to *Ngwerong* and other lodges) are also referred to as *mcɛp* in Limbum. It is worth noting that although people use the English "medicine" to refer to all the kinds of *mcɛp* mentioned above, they would never refer to a *juju* as medicine.

Finally, there are various objects which come from outside local society and which are also considered to have mystical power. Some old men still had knives or bugles which they had been given as gifts when they worked for the Germans in pre-First World War days, and many of the chiefs and sub-chiefs had collections of Toby Jugs which they cherished even more than their masks, elephant tusks and carved wooden stools. Like the masks and other important *mcɛp*, these objects were only brought out on special occasions. When old chiefs persuaded me to take an official photo of them in full regalia, their courtiers had to employ all the rhetorical skills at their disposal in order to persuade them to display their bugles and Toby Jugs. More recently have come the new forms of medicine described by Probst and Bühler (1990), which are related to improved communication and increasing literacy: *The Great Napoleon Book of Faith, The Sixth and Seventh Book of Moses* and the 'powerful Hindu talismans, rings and preparations capable to solve all your life problems' that are imported from Nigeria (Probst and Bühler 1990: 453, see also Probst 1989).

What these kinds of *ncɛp* have in common is that they possess the power to influence people, events, outcomes, and this power and these effects cannot be readily explained in terms of observable connections. Geschiere calls the Maka equivalent of *mcɛp* 'charged objects' (Geschiere 1983), which is to say objects that are charged with some kind of (supernatural) power, and this does indeed seem to be their essence.

Lawrence distinguished between two singular forms of the word "*mcɛp*": "*ncɛp*" and "*rcɛp*", though no one else seemed to agree with him on this. He claimed that the singular term "*ncɛp*" could refer a bundle of leaves and feathers, a round stone or a juju, as described above, but that it could not be used to refer to medicine in the conventional English sense of pharmaceuticals and herbs. For these the correct singular term was "rcεp". Both "ncεp" and "rcεp" were rendered in plural as "mcεp". He said that "ncεp" referred to a composite object, a bundle of leaves and feathers for instance. Here each individual herb would be rcεp, but the bundle as a whole would be ncεp. Two bundles would then be mcεp.

My other informants in Tabenken said this was all nonsense, that there was no such term as "rcεp" in Limbum and that "ncεp" was the only singular form, referring to both composite charged objects and individual herbs. Lawrence continued to insist that he was right and that everyone else was wrong. I suspected that perhaps differences in dialect were responsible (Lawrence came from Ndu where a different Limbum dialect is spoken) and Lawrence agreed that this was possible. But some weeks later, while we were drinking in a bar in Ndu and chatting to a few local acquaintances, I decided to put the question to them. They did not seem to be familiar with "rcεp" either. Lawrence became involved in a heated discussion during which even the beer was forgotten, but he was unable to convince them. A moody silence descended and we left shortly after.

'Well,' I said, somewhat provocatively as we walked back to the car, 'so much for your theory.'

'Tut!' he snapped. 'These people are not linguists, they don't know the function of the concord marker.' It is quite possible that Lawrence was right on this issue. In spoken Limbum all three terms tend to sound like *cεp*, the *r, n* and *m* only being audible on very close listening, if at all.

In a paper on medicine, politics and social change in Ndu, Probst and Bühler (1990) stated that the plural "mshεp" refers to 'good' medicines and the singular "nshεp"[6] refers to 'bad' medicines (though they added that such verbal distinctions are hardly made in everyday life and that the social context determines the meaning of the term). Good medicines are public and harmless whereas bad medicines belong to the secret and dangerous realm of magic (pp. 447–8). Good medicines include modern drugs and herbal remedies, whereas bad medicines include all kinds of 'charged objects for the achievement of personal aims as well as special remedies against ailments whose cause is suspected in the

6. In the dialect spoken in Ndu the /c/ in words like "mcεp" is replaced by /sh/.

realm of the supernatural' (Probst and Bühler 1990: 449–50). This is a distinction which people in Tabenken also seem to make in conversation. When they talk about pharmaceuticals and medicinal herbs they always use the plural "mcɛp", as they also seem to do for the packages and bundles of feathers and leaves. When discussing compound stones, single twins and *jujus*, however, they seem to use the singular "ncɛp". It could be that the two terms have different meanings, but I tend to think that the difference in usage is related to the quantities in which people encounter the objects in question: people are not likely to purchase single tablets or single leaves for an illness, but *jujus* and compound stones are usually encountered (and discussed) singly.

Thus when people use the term "medicine" it refers to a much wider spectrum of meaning than we would associate with the same term. This has consequences for the attempt to identify and delineate an 'ethnomedical system' and would seem to suggest that it is impossible to describe and analyse such systems while proceeding from biomedical assumptions about the nature of medicine (to which I will return in the final chapter).

Illness Just Happens

When I was fairly satisfied that I had a more or less complete list of illness terms and a general idea of what they referred to, I started to make some more systematic enquiries about etiology. I asked people which illnesses were common, what the symptoms were and what they thought were the causes. When I asked about causes people were often bewildered. Were they doctors? How were they to know what caused illness? Was that not what I should be telling them? They did sometimes have common sense explanations for simple ailments: they said that backache was caused by hard work, headache by drinking too much alcohol, or coughs by inhaling dust. The degree of elaboration in these explanations varied depending on a number of factors such as education, knowledge of traditional medicine, knowledge of biomedicine, etc. Most people simply said, though, that they did not know what caused illness, that it 'just happened', or it 'came from god', or it 'did not have a cause'. In discussions I tried not to make any suggestions and, except in discussions which were specifically about *ngang* or *bfaa*, did not ask about witchcraft. I waited to see what people would say about illness causation spontaneously, but nothing was forthcoming. After reading so many elaborate descriptions of 'indigenous etiology' in Africa this was disappointing. I mentioned it to Lawrence.

[5.2] 'It's interesting that people don't seem to have any idea about the causes of their illnesses. When they tell me that they have backache or cough and I ask what's causing it they just say they don't know.'

Lawrence looked surprised. 'But how do you expect them to know the cause? Do they know about causes in other countries?' 'Well,' I said, 'if someone in Holland has backache and you ask him what's wrong, he will generally have some theory about it. I also found the same thing during my research in India. People always had some idea of what was causing their illness.'

'What kind of theory would they have in Holland?'

'I have a friend in Amsterdam who is troubled by backache. He says that it's caused by a draft of cold air coming through his bedroom window and reaching his back under the blankets when he turns in his sleep and his back becomes bare. He says that the cold enters his muscles and that it's that which causes the pain the next morning.'

Lawrence burst out laughing. 'That's all lies,' he cried. 'He's just lying because he can't know the cause.' He continued to laugh, until tears rolled down his cheeks.

I was surprised at this outburst. 'But most people in Holland would have at least some explanation of the cause of their illness,' I said.

'Ah no!' Lawrence retorted, still chuckling. 'White men are very funny, just inventing stories like that about things they can't know about.'

So to Lawrence this apparent lack of etiological knowledge was not unusual. In fact, he found the idea of elaborate explanations for simple ailments amusing. Maybe he was right. Maybe our obsession with finding elaborate causal explanations for even the most minor ailments, while at the same time shrugging off major disasters and unexpected fatal illness as coincidence, is a culture-bound preoccupation.

This seems to be supported by the fact that people who did

give elaborate explanations of relatively minor ailments were usually relatively well educated and Westernised, and their explanations were strongly coloured by biomedical imagery. A good example of this is provided by a young man with secondary school education, whom I had employed to collect information on a number of kwashiorkor cases in Nkambe, the nearby divisional capital. He was from an urban background and considered himself a member of the 'civilised' elite.

On one of my visits to him he told me that he had been to hospital to have the sugar content of his urine tested. I was surprised and asked him why that had been necessary, as he seemed quite healthy to me. He replied that he was worried about getting diabetes. He said that since he had been staying in Nkambe he had been drinking a lot of sweet drinks. Also, because it was so cold in Nkambe, and because he had not been playing as much football as usual, he had not been sweating, so the excess sugar was not being excreted. Or at least he was not sure that it was being sufficiently excreted, because he was not sure that his pancreas was functioning properly. So he thought it better to take the tests just to be on the safe side.

These were not the only tests he took either. Once a month he went to the hospital to have his blood tested for 'gonococcus'. He told me that last month the test had been positive and he had been given a course of antibiotic injections. A second test had been negative, but he was planning to take another course of injections anyway just in case there were a few 'gonococci still lying dormant' in his blood.

Like Simon Ngengeh's explanation of *ngang* in terms of 'hormones' and 'negative organisms', this is a relatively elaborate explanation, but it is entirely in a quasi-biomedical idiom: diabetes, the functioning of the pancreas, the sugar content of the urine, gonococci, hormones, organisms. Explanations of this kind were usually quite idiosyncratic.

The conversations I had with people about the causes of illness seemed to support the argument that the role of supernatural causation in Africa had been overestimated: when I asked people about the causes of various common illnesses they almost always replied that they 'just happen', that they were 'natural' or that they 'had no cause'.[7]

---

7. In Limbum the term that is used as a translation for the English 'to cause' is "gee", which means 'to make' or 'to do'. When it is used in relation to illness causation the term seems to imply the active involvement of a personalistic agent, and in this it differs from the English "cause" which may refer to natural, impersonal factors. This explains why people can speak of natural illnesses that have no cause, that have not been 'made' by anybody.

The Death of John Tanfu

John Tanfu died when he was just thirty-six, his skin and eyeballs yellow as a result of liver failure. He had fallen ill some six months previously and when his condition deteriorated he was admitted to a nearby Mission hospital. After a brief stay in hospital he was discharged, sicker than when he had been admitted. The diagnosis on his medical card read 'incurable liver cancer'. Friends and relatives were shocked. Could the doctors not see that he was not yet better? How could they discharge a man so obviously sick? For the Wimbum the idea of an incurable illness is totally unacceptable. It was madness to simply wait around helplessly for someone to die, especially one so young. So John was taken to a medicine man in a neighbouring village where he remained during treatment. His brother, Joseph, footed the bill.

In the meantime the family elders consulted a diviner. The diviner suspected witchcraft and accused Joseph. Then John died. The family consulted more diviners. In serious cases such as this people never rely on the judgement of a single diviner. Neither do they consult diviners who may know those involved or who may have heard rumours of accusations. The elders travelled to a number of distant villages and consulted five different diviners. All of them, so I was told, had accused Joseph of killing his brother through witchcraft. When the elders returned to Tabenken the news spread quickly. Groups of vigilantes formed and the hunt was opened on Joseph. In the meantime he had taken refuge in the Mission, however, and that was where he stayed until the funeral.

On the day of the funeral the cemetery behind the church was packed with people. John had been one of the leaders of the Catholic youth society in Tabenken and was to be buried in the cemetery and not in his compound, as tradition prescribed. The priest started to pray as friends lowered the coffin into the grave. As he droned on someone suddenly screamed 'He is here!' and everyone except the priest opened their eyes. During prayer Joseph had arrived and was sitting on a nearby grave smoking a cigarette. 'You see,' the man standing next to me said, 'a witch always has to come back and witness the funeral of his victim. This act confirms that he has eaten his brother. That he is sitting and smoking adds insult to his deeds.' A man ran up and kicked Joseph so that he fell from his perch. He stood up and was immediately surrounded by a hostile crowd.

'You have killed your brother and now you have come to confirm that he is dead,' someone shouted.

'It was my brother,' he said defiantly, 'why should I not eat him if I choose?'

A man threw him to the ground and as he tried to stand up again someone threw a stone. Others followed and soon everyone was looking for stones. The priest prayed on at the graveside. An opening appeared in the crowd and Joseph sprang to his feet and ran, the crowd in hot pursuit.

'What will happen to him?' I asked someone.

'They will kill him,' he said, 'or drive him from the village.'

Later I heard that he had managed to escape to the Mission in Nkambe.

When it's Difficult to Cure then it's Witchcraft

Witchcraft was quite obviously present in people's day-to-day lives, and it was in terms of witchcraft that various misfortunes were explained. In the days following some misfortune or serious accident I would hear people discussing the event everywhere: in the bars in the market square, in the men's societies, along the road where people happened to meet and stop to chat. It was in these settings that I heard numerous discussions of witchcraft.

In one case the crops of farmers in a certain area had been destroyed or damaged, first by a heard of cows which had wandered into the fields unattended, then by a plague of insects and shortly after that by a storm. This was seen as too much of a coincidence and a meeting of the whole quarter was organised to discuss the matter. At the meeting the farmers in question accused certain other women (no names were mentioned) of being witches and transforming themselves into cows, insects and wind to destroy their crops out of spite. This was a topic of discussion in the village for a number of days.

In another case, a woman had been seriously injured when a granary under which she had been sheltering from a sudden storm, collapsed on her. As in Evans-Pritchard's (1937) well-known example, people all agreed that the granary had probably been in need of repair, and that the rain had been very heavy, but they were also convinced that the fact that it had collapsed on her and she had been injured meant that 'there must have been something wrong in her compound'.

There were also a number of cases of fatal illness, like the one described above, in which a member of the deceased's family was accused of witchcraft. In one such case a woman in her forties was accused of having killed her brother (who had dropped down dead one day after being discharged from hospital after recovering from a serious illness) by witchcraft and was banished to another village.

These examples suggest two things. Firstly, people do not seem to distinguish between the death of an individual from serious illness and death caused by accidents which we would not refer to as illness. And secondly, although people do not attribute minor ailments to witchcraft, it does seem to play a role in the explanation of serious misfortunes, including serious illness resulting in death.

So why did people appear to deny that witchcraft was causally implicated in illness when I asked them about it? I began to suspect that they were deliberately being evasive because I was an outsider, a White man associated with biomedicine and the Mission. I was also initially uncertain as to whether it was a good idea to start enquiring about witchcraft explicitly after only having been in the village for a couple of months. It might be a delicate subject and if people thought that I was prying they might not be willing to discuss other subjects with me either. I consulted Lawrence.

[5.3] 'You know, I think that people sometimes think that sickness is caused by witchcraft, but that they don't say so.'

'It's like that with chronic sickness, or ones which can't be cured. Then they think it's witchcraft.'

'But they never say so.'

'They never say so.'

'Maybe they don't mention it because I'm a White man?'

'No, no. Even when I ask them. The problem is that they don't know the cause. They don't know exactly what is causing it.'

'So you think that if they think that a sickness is being caused by witchcraft then they will say so?'

'They will say so. But they only suspect witchcraft. Because it's difficult for them to cure they just say it is witchcraft. Any sickness which is difficult to cure is seen as witchcraft. If it attacks me and I get medicine and I'm cured then I don't believe it is witchcraft, but if I go to several doctors and I don't get cured then I put it down to witchcraft. It's generally like this: all sickness, we don't know the cause, but when it is difficult to cure they consider it as witchcraft.'

'Do *you* think it's caused by witchcraft?'

'It's their belief when it's difficult to cure. Even myself. If I have a certain type of sickness and I'm treating it and it cannot cure, then I believe it is caused by witchcraft. But even if it is caused by witchcraft and it is cured then I will not believe that it is caused by witchcraft any more.'

What Lawrence said to me above closely resembles Evans-Pritchard's description of Zande ideas about the role of witchcraft in illness causation: people only revert to explanation in terms of witchcraft when events take an unexpected turn. Illness does occur, it is just one of those things. But if it is treated it should subside; treatment resulting in cure is natural. If, in spite of extended treatment, it is not cured then it can only be because of witchcraft. Witchcraft is the ultimate cause which explains unexpected chains of events (Evans-Pritchard 1937).

Lawrence's statements on the matter seemed to be confirmed by a number of cases of illness and treatment that I encountered during my stay. I will describe one of them as an illustration.

During a visit to the medicine man Simon Ngeh I noticed that one of the patients in his crowded consulting room, a young woman, had large, open wounds on both her feet and ankles. They were so deep that I thought I could see the bones. When it was her turn to be treated I asked what had happened to her. Simon said that she had been burnt when she tripped and fell into the kitchen fire more than a year ago. Since then she had been to two hospitals and a string of medicine men for treatment but the wounds had refused to heal. The girl's father had consulted Simon and he had agreed to treat her on condition that she did not consult any other healer while she was being treated by him. The father agreed and the girl was brought to Simon's compound, where she had been residing for two weeks as an in-patient at the time of our first visit.

Because the wounds had not healed, despite a year of treatment, Simon had immediately suspected witchcraft. He had divined and discovered that one of the girl's uncles was responsible. He visited the uncle and told him that he was aware of what was going on and that if the man did not halt his nefarious practices immediately then he, Simon, would reverse the witchcraft and make it attack its perpetrator, inflicting him with the same wounds. The uncle had become scared and agreed to desist. Simon had then begun to treat the wounds. His treatment for all complaints consisted of massage, supplemented with herbs and Western pharmaceuticals. In the case of the girl's wounds he used mainly the latter, the type of drug and the dosage being determined by casting his cowrie shells.

He insisted, and the girl and other patients agreed, that since the uncle had ceased his witchcraft the wounds had improved, and indeed, on subsequent visits during the following weeks I had to admit that they did indeed seem to be healing.

The girl had received burns through an accident. The normal, expected course of events would have been herbal or hospital treatment leading to reasonably rapid recovery. The illness had not followed this course, however, and had taken an unexpected turn. This led to consultation of a diviner and accusations of witchcraft. It was only when this the ultimate cause had been eliminated that a cure could be affected.

The same pattern can be detected in the other cases briefly mentioned above. It is quite normal for untended cows to wander into a woman's corn field and destroy her crop, just as strong winds and insects are normal. What is not normal is that all three should cause so much damage to the crops of these women at one particular time. It is also normal for an old granary to collapse in a heavy rain storm, but it is not normal if a particular woman is taking shelter under it and she is seriously injured. Similarly, it is quite natural for people to die, but not when they become sick and die while still young, or just drop dead without apparent illness in middle age. So, just as Evans-Pritchard described for the Azande, witchcraft seems to explain an unnatural sequence of events which are natural *per se*.

On the Causes of *Ngang* and *Bfaa*

Witchcraft played some role in etiology, even though people did not mention it when I enquired about it specifically in relation to common illnesses. People did not attribute common illnesses or minor ailments to witchcraft, but serious illnesses which did not respond to treatment, or which took an unexpected turn, would lead to thoughts of witchcraft and the consultation of diviners. But what about *ngang* and *bfaa*? These are serious and often fatal illnesses which strike down young children for whom death is not natural, and yet they do follow an expected course. Let me recapitulate what has already been said in the previous discussions about the causes of *ngang* and *bfaa*.

In our first encounter, Pius [1.1] mentioned various causal factors relating to *ngang*, ranging from eating garden eggs to prostitution and cannibalistic witchcraft. During my enquiries about *ngang* related in Chapter 3, Freda Malah did not know the cause of dry *ngang* but she thought that wet *ngang* could be caused by weaning the child too soon and not feeding it properly, or by eating bananas in which flies had excreted. Fai Gabriel [3.1] also mentioned incorrect feeding. Simon Ngengeh [3.3] mentioned nutrition, heredity and a number of biological factors.

There was some discussion of the relation between *ngang* and twins. Isaac called *ngang* a family disease (which can imply either that it is hereditary or that it is caused by witchcraft). Fai Gabriel [3.1] spoke of the child who died of *ngang* being a twin, Manasas Yangsi [3.2] suggested that there was some connection between *ngang* and twins and Pius [3.4] claimed that there was no kwashiorkor without twins and no twins without kwashiorkor. However, most informants seemed to agree that the fact of being a twin does not necessarily make a child more susceptible to *ngang*, and failure to fix a twin will not lead to the child developing *ngang* but will result in it growing up to be a fool.

Not everyone had ideas about etiology, however. In the interview with the grandmother of Confidence (the first kwashiorkor case cited in Chapter 1) she claimed not to know the cause of her grandchild's *bfaa*. And Fai Nga Kontar said he did not know what was the cause of his child's *bfaa*, though he said the word meant 'mistake from the mother's compound'.

In the conversations in which the relation between *ngang* and *bfaa* is discussed (Chapter 4) there were also a number of remarks about the causes of *ngang* and *bfaa*. Various people related *bfaa* to suicide. Pa TaKwi [4.2] said that 'bfaa is when a person has killed himself'. Freda Malah [4.3] also related it to suicide, though she did not make any statement about cause. Lawrence [4.4] said that mistakes by the mother (such as incest or attempted murder) can cause her child to get the illness *bfaa*. Francis thought that mistakes could cause illness, but this illness would not be called *bfaa*, only the mistakes would be called *bfaa* according to him [4.5]. Manasas Yangsi [4.6] denied that incest could cause *bfaa*, but he did make a causal connection between bfaa and suicide, and confirmed Lawrence's suggestion that if a man visits the site of a suicide and is not treated then his offspring will have the illness *bfaa* .

In my enquiries about *ngang* and *bfaa*, I was kept constantly aware of the possibility of witchcraft as a causal factor. The question of the relation between *ngang* and *bfaa* on the one hand and witchcraft on the other has been touched on sporadically in a number of the fragments of conversation presented in previous chapters. In what follows I will draw some of these strands together, while at the same time making some comments about the conversations.

In the interview with Confidence's grandmother, I asked her whether she thought the illness could have been caused by witchcraft. She said she knew that some people said that it could be caused by witchcraft but suggested, not surprisingly, that food was a more likely cause. I say 'not surprisingly' because the form of the interview (the authoritarian question-and-answer format) and the content of the questions (about feeding the child milk and eggs) must have reminded them of their interviews with the health worker whom they had first consulted in Ngarum. That encounter is likely to have influenced their answers to my questions, both because my questions probably closely resembled those of the health worker and (if I may be allowed to speculate on the basis of my observations of many such consultations), the rhetorical and authoritarian manner in which those questions had probably been put to them had already convinced them what the right answers were. My status as the 'White doctor' must have enhanced this effect as well.

By contrast, in the discussion between Pius and Lawrence [1.1] there was no formal interview arrangement, I was relatively passive and they were the ones who started discussing witchcraft. As in many later conversations, the topic was broached early in the discussion. To recap:

16. 'Yes', Pius said. 'He's a good scientist. And a soothsayer, he's a good soothsayer. If there is something, if there is any mistake, he can refer and tell the patient or the mother who comes with a child before he gives medicine. He cannot just give the medicine like that. If there is any sign he will just tell you what happened.'

17. 'Whether sickness has been caused by witch?' Lawrence suggested.
18. 'Yes, by witch.'
19. 'Or by carelessness of not using correct food?'

Pius had just told us that his father was a good diviner. At the time of this discussion the precise meaning of what he was saying escaped me. But rereading this conversation after my enquiries about *bfaa*, mistakes and abominations, it became clear that it was to this that he was referring. If there has been a 'mistake' or abomination then Pius's father will see a 'sign' through divination and warn the mother that this is the cause of her child's illness.

The conversation also says something about the relationship between kwashiorkor/*ngang*/*bfaa* and witchcraft (that they were talking about this and not about illness in general is clear from the way Lawrence switched back to food as a causal factor). Lawrence interpreted 'sign' as a sign of the involvement of witchcraft. He suggested that a witch may have made use of the 'mistake' to cause the child's illness.

Finally, the performance nature of the encounter is clear. When Pius spoke about his father's divinatory skills he implied the possibility of witchcraft when he said: 'if there is any sign'. Lawrence immediately focussed on this and made the suggestion explicit. Was this just for my benefit? After all, he must have realised that if he did not make it explicit I would miss the allusion: at that early stage I could never have realised that Pius was hinting at witchcraft, and I suspect that Lawrence's question was only meant to make this explicit for me and not to provide new information for himself. This is confirmed when we see that, as soon as Pius agreed that this is indeed what he meant, Lawrence switched back to his role as medical researcher and suggested that the hypothetical child's illness could also be a result of careless feeding, thus effectively preventing Pius from continuing to speculate about 'mistakes' and witchcraft. I was about to ask him to expound on what he meant by his reference to witchcraft, but just as I opened my mouth Lawrence cut me short with his question about food, and the discussion went off in another direction. But not for long. After a detour through food habits and *bfaa* the discussion petered out and I had the chance to ask Pius directly whether he thought that kwashiorkor could also be caused by

witchcraft. He did not need much prompting, as this was his
favourite subject.

80. 'Is kwashiorkor also caused by witchcraft?'
81. 'Yes cannibalism.'
82. 'Cannibalism?' I was surprised.
83. 'Yes,' Pius said, laughing wildly, 'the practice of eating
    humans.'
84. 'How does that work?' I asked.
85. 'Pardon?'
86. 'How does witchcraft cause kwashiorkor?'
87. 'Well, it's another way of eating human being. When they see a
    very fat child they will just take a...a...' he stuttered from excite-
    ment. 'If it is in the body and see what they are holding. Anyway,
    if they go to a native doctor he will cure it. But he will just pre-
    tend, take something behind it...cure that child.'
88. I was not sure what to make of this answer, and tried to pose
    the question differently. 'So what kind of people cause kwash-
    iorkor by witchcraft?'
89. 'Eh...sometimes...well I hope so, because this kwashiorkor
    mostly comes from the mother. And sometimes through prostitu-
    tion. You know, prostitutes are with diseases. They have diseases
    and people don't know. You go and contact one and get a disease
    and give it to your wife. Then she will begin to suffer.'
90. Here Lawrence intervened in an attempt to create consistency.
    'Now among the Wimbum people, a man who can cause witch-
    craft to eat the child and cause kwashiorkor, would this be a rela-
    tive of the child or someone from a different family?'
91. 'It could be someone who brings human flesh and gives it to
    your child without you knowing. Not only from the family,' he
    paused. 'That flesh is sold in the market...'

I asked Pius whether kwashiorkor is caused by witchcraft, as
he had suggested earlier. He agreed and to my surprise said
that it is caused by cannibalism. When I attempted to find out
how cannibalism causes kwashiorkor he became very incoherent.
I tried again but he reverted to his earlier explanation in
terms of prostitution. Lawrence intervened, as he had done previously, by displaying his own cultural knowledge for me
in the form of a question to Pius. This put Pius back on track
again and his answer to Lawrence's question was also an
answer to mine. Kwashiorkor can be caused by someone giving

human flesh to the child. After this Pius and Lawrence went off into a long discussion of cannibalism and witch markets. No more mention was made of kwashiorkor, and I did not intervene because I found the subject fascinating.

In a conversation with Fred and Mathias [4.10] I asked whether *ngang* can be caused by witchcraft and Fred replied categorically that it cannot (30–1). And then he went on to explain that witchcraft can play a role in causing *ngang* (45–7).

According to Andrew Nfor [4.7], when adults die of *ngang* and are swollen then witchcraft is involved. He said that the cause may have been that the victim himself was a witch. Simon Ngengeh [4.8] affirmed this: a person who dies a bad death is a victim of witchcraft, either his own or someone else's. When I asked Fai Nga Kontar ([4.9] 6–7) whether it is possible for someone to die a bad death because he has made a mistake, he replied that this will not be called *bfaa*, people will say that the person had made witchcraft. Fred Ngiri ([4.10] 41) also said that if a person dies with a swollen stomach then witchcraft will be seen as the cause.

Most traditional healers were, at least initially, quite emphatic in their denial of a possible connection between *ngang* and witchcraft, though some of these emphatic statements were later contradicted. Most people did seem to make some connection between *bfaa* and witchcraft, especially if they related *bfaa* to bad death, and most agreed that a child could not be responsible for its own bad death through witchcraft.

But apart from these odd references there was no systematic discussion of the role of witchcraft in the genesis of illness in general and *ngang* and *bfaa* in particular, and my enquiries on the topic petered out...

Chapter 6

Witches, Cannibals and Seers

Inherited Women are Poisonous

One day I was walking through the village with Lawrence. We had just left the compound of a woman whom we had been interviewing about her child's recent illness, and were on our way to pick up a calabash of palm wine which we were going to present to Fai Gabriel, who was 'celebrating' the recent death of his sister. I asked Lawrence who was the husband of the woman we had just visited. Lawrence said that he had heard that her present husband was not in fact her real husband. Her husband had died and his brother had 'inherited' her. I went on to ask him a lot of questions about how such things were arranged. At one point he mentioned that it was 'poisonous' to have such a woman in the compound.

[6.1] 'What's poisonous?' I asked.

'The woman herself,' he replied, turning round briefly. 'In such cases, if you are not careful, one of your brothers will kill you by witchcraft. You see, like this man up here, he's one of them.'

'So you think some witchcraft is involved there?'

'Yes, witchcraft is always involved in such cases. If the woman is very beautiful many people in the compound will be fighting to own her. If she is finally given to you then the others will be jealous.' He paused. 'They will bring in a lot of witchcraft.'

'So if the woman is ugly and no one is interested in her then you have nothing to fear?'

'Exactly,' he said, smiling. 'They will not mind.'

'So it's better to inherit an ugly woman?'

Lawrence chuckled. 'Well, we wouldn't like that either.'

'So who decides who will inherit the woman?'

'The compound head.'

'And if he gives the woman to you and the others are jealous, who will be affected by witchcraft, you or the compound head?'

'I will be affected.'

'So if they kill you with witchcraft it's so that they can take the woman from you?'

'No, the compound head will decide again. They won't take her by force. If he knows that they have used witchcraft then he won't give her to them.'

'So what's the use of them killing you?'

'It's just jealousy.'

'It's not because it improves their chances of inheriting her in the next round?'

'No. If they succeed in getting her then it is only because the compound head is dead or doesn't have strong power.'

'So if you inherit a woman and then you die, they will go to a diviner to find out whether there has been any funny business?'

'Yes, they will check very seriously, and if there is nothing, the compound head may decide to give her to you.'

'Does the woman have a say?'

'No.'

'If you inherit a woman like that but you already have a wife, isn't it possible that she will be jealous and use witchcraft?'

'She will try but she won't succeed.'

'Why not?'

'Because she has no power.'

'I thought that women were the worst witches?' Lawrence had previously told me that female witches were stronger than male witches.

'Yes, but she can never overcome the protective witchcraft of the compound.'

'But your brother can overcome it and kill you?'

'Yes, there are a lot of powers with your brother. He can poison you physically. But with witchcraft it is easier because he has a closer relationship with you.'

'Why does witchcraft only work inside families? Why are you never bewitched by someone from outside?'

'It's a natural thing to Africans. I can only use my witchcraft on my own family. But my witchcraft *can* touch you if you have some link with me. If you don't have a link it can't affect you.'

'What kind of link?'

'For example, if you have taken a girl from my compound and

haven't paid the bride price, and you refuse to pay it, then I can use my witchcraft on that girl's children. The children will be dying, or she will not be able to deliver.'

'So I can't use witchcraft to make the man who owes me money repay it?'

'No.'

'But I could if he married my daughter?'

'Very easily. If his children die or his wife doesn't deliver he will go to a diviner and the diviner will say "Money, money, there is something wrong in connection with money. That money must be sent back quickly. That is why the woman is not delivering."' Lawrence imitated the diviner in a deep voice. 'Then the next morning he will bring the money back very fast, with a calabash of palm wine as well.'

'That means that Michael Shey was being bewitched by a member of his own family?' My question referred to the man in whose house I was staying. He had moved to another village a few years previously because the house was bewitched and he did not dare to stay in it any longer.

'Yes, there's someone in the family doing that.'

'What reason could a member of the family have for not wanting him to stay in that house?'

'It could be that he was trying to usurp leadership of the compound and they had to use witchcraft to put him in his place. Or it could be that someone was trying to take over the leadership from him. In any case, the other man's power was stronger because he succeeded in driving him away from the village.'

In addition to calamities and misfortune, witchcraft also plays a role in the intrigues connected with inheriting women. If a man inherits a beautiful woman then his brothers may, out of sheer jealously or spite, use witchcraft to kill him. The man's first wife may be jealous of the new woman and also take recourse to witchcraft, but her witchcraft will not be effective because her kinship link with her husband is not as close as that between him and his brothers, and she will be thwarted by the 'protective witchcraft' of the compound.

It appears that witchcraft is only effective along lines of close consanguineal kinship, but does not directly effect affinal kin. This is clear in Lawrence's example of the unpaid bride-price and in the case of the man who owed me money. I could not force him to repay my money by using witchcraft against him because we were not related. If he were to marry my daughter then we would become related and I could use witchcraft against him, but only indirectly by directing it against his wife (i.e. my daughter) and his children by her (i.e. my grandchildren).

Witchcraft is an evil force used for the senseless destruction of life: jealous brothers strike a man down out of sheer spite because he has inherited a beautiful wife and his own envious first wife may attempt to do the same. It is also a disruptive force that is employed for the usurpation of political power and leadership in the compound. But witchcraft may also be employed as a regulatory power to maintain order and the status quo in the compound. The compound head maintains his position of leadership through his possession of regulative witchcraft power. A man's jealous brothers can only kill him and take his new wife from him if the compound head is either dead or does not have strong (witchcraft) power, and his jealous first wife's witchcraft will be neutralised by the protective witchcraft of the compound.[1]

Witchcraft and *Tvu'*

Witchcraft has a relatively prominent place in ordinary life. As we have seen, it was common for people to attribute various misfortunes to witchcraft, and people discussed this in public. I received a steady trickle of information on witchcraft and experienced various witchcraft-related incidents almost from the beginning of my stay, so that I had some general idea what it was all about before I started to make systematic enquiries. This is in contrast to my knowledge of *ngang* and *bfaa* which was only gradually constructed during my enquiries.

My enquiries about the two topics were also conditioned by different bodies of literature. My initial enquiries about *ngang* and *bfaa* were influenced by biomedical conceptions of kwashiorkor, whereas my initial enquiries about witchcraft occurred against the background of my reading of the anthropological literature on the subject. Another significant difference between witchcraft and the other concepts was that local scholars had

---

1. On witchcraft as an ambivalent political force in relations between villagers and the urban elite among the Maka in southern Cameroon see Geschiere 1988. For a more general discussion of witchcraft and the modern state in Cameroon see Rowlands and Warnier 1988.

already made studies of it (Tanto 1976, Mburu 1979, Njingti 1979).[2] I was able to make use of these studies to guide my own enquiries. Sometimes I referred explicitly in discussions to what I had read, usually it was just in the back of my mind, prompting a question here and there. Mburu's study came to my attention shortly after the discussion with Lawrence that I have just related, and Tanto's paper much later.

So far I have been using the English term "witchcraft", which is generally used as a translation of the Limbum term "tvu'". The term "tvu'" also means night, and I am not sure whether these meanings are related, but I have the impression this is merely a case of homonymy. Unlike "kwashiorkor", "ngang" and "bfaa", the terms "witchcraft" and "tvu'" are much less problematic as synonyms. Mburu says the following about this translation: 'Strictly speaking, the Wimbum have no definite word equivalent to the English "witchcraft". Loosely used, however, the Limbum "tvu'" refers to witchcraft. But we can rightly employ the compounded word *ngɛni tvu'* (a deed resulting from the use of witchcraft) to denote witchcraft. When properly used the word *tvu'* means witch-knowledge or secret knowledge' (Mburu 1979: 1).

He also distinguishes between potential witches and actual, practising witches: 'Everyone is said to be a witch but not everybody is believed to be an actual witch, i.e. a practicing witch' (Mburu 1979: 1). And further:

> A witch, for the Wimbum, is one who possesses witch-knowledge. Witch-knowledge itself is the ability everyone has developed and with which one can read and interpret signs from natural phenomena for good or bad ends. Thereby, the achievement of such knowledge is rendered mysterious in the sense that other people lacking this knowledge find it difficult to understand how such an achievement is possible... The Wimbum believe that the development of this kind of knowledge takes different directions with different people and that the extent to which it is developed in each person differs markedly. Some people are said to have developed this knowledge by virtue of their birth. Meanwhile some acquire such development later in life through learning or initiation. (Mburu 1979: 2–3)

This appears to be contradictory. First he says that everybody is a witch, though not all people actually practice, but then he speaks

2. Tanto, Mburu and Njingti are Catholic priests. Their studies of witchcraft were part of their training at the local Roman Catholic Seminary.

of people who lack witch-knowledge, and of people who only learn it later in life, which implies that not everybody is a witch. This probably reflects the contradictory answers of different informants which Mburu has tried to condense into one coherent account. But his study did guide my own initial enquiries, which began as an exploration of the meanings of "tvu'".

[6.2]   'What does the word "tvu'" mean?' I asked Lawrence one day. 'Does it refer to the person, or to the activity, or to the knowledge?'

'It just means witchcraft. If it is a man producing witchcraft we say *ngwɛɛ tvu'*, witch man.'

'Is it the knowledge which someone needs to make witchcraft which is called "tvu'"?'

'Yes, when he knows something for making witchcraft then....' He hesitated. 'Well, we call the action that he produces *tvu'*.'

'In Mburu's thesis it says: "When properly used the word "tvu'" means witch-knowledge, or secret knowledge." Is that is correct?'

'Yes, it's correct, because you use the knowledge in making the act. If you don't have the knowledge then you are not *ngwɛɛ tvu'*.'

'Where does *tvu'* come from?'

'Well, it's not easy. You can't say: "I'm going to learn it." I think you have to be born with it.'

'Mburu says that some people use their special knowledge for making witchcraft and others use it for good things like treating people.'

'That's how it is. Some use it in protecting their family. In the olden times they would say that some people had used witchcraft to bring smallpox to the compound and others then used their witch power to see how they had brought it.'

'Is that also *tvu'*?'

'Yes, you would say that the compound head is *ngwɛɛ tvu'*. He has used his *tvu'* in a very good way, to protect his family.'

'So if you are *ngwɛɛ tvu'* or you use *tvu'* then it's not always bad?'

'It's not bad.'

'Can you call someone like Simon Ngeh *ngwɛɛ tvu'*?' I asked, referring to a traditional healer we had visited on several occasions.

'Yes.'

'*Do* you call him that?'

'Yes, because he does abnormal things.'

'So if I call him *ngwee tvu'* it wouldn't be wrong?'

'Errrr...' Lawrence fell silent. 'In some ways it's wrong, because that word alone describes a man as a bad man. But if you use it in another sense then it is good. If you said "If you weren't *ngwɛɛ tvu'* then you wouldn't have seen this danger coming", then he would be very happy.'

'Why do some people use *tvu'* for good things while others use it for bad things?'

'You know, people are not the same. You can use insecticide to make food grow properly and help the country, and you can use it to poison people. That's also how people use their witchcraft.'

'Can a witch make somebody who is not a witch into a witch?'

'Yes, I think that some witchmen can make children who are still growing into witches, because it's easy to convert children in any direction. But I doubt that it can happen with adults.'

In this description *tvu'* (or witchcraft) is both an activity and an ability or characteristic of individuals. Lawrence agreed with Mburu that it is a form of knowledge, but I have the impression that he was not convinced and only agreed because of the author-itative status of Mburu's text. This was confirmed when I asked him whether *tvu'* is knowledge and he answered that it is action.

Lawrence also said that it is a form of power, as he did in the previous discussion. Evil witches may use it to bring illness to the compound, but the compound head can use his own power to see what is happening and take steps to protect his family. It is a morally neutral power which can be used for either good or evil purposes depending on the person who possesses it. But taken by itself the word "tvu'" does have negative connotations. Strictly speaking the traditional healer Simon Ngeh is a witch (*ngwɛɛ tvu'*), but Lawrence thought it would be wrong for me to simply refer to him as such, and if I did so I would be implying that he was a bad man. It would only be correct if I used the term in such a way that it was clear that I was referring to the use of *tvu'* for a good purpose. When Lawrence said 'Errrr... In some ways it would be wrong,' he sounded quite shocked, as though he was imagining the stunned silence in Simon Ngeh's crowded consulting room after I had, in my innocence, just referred to him as a witch.

Lawrence thought that it is not possible to learn *tvu',* it is something you have to be born with. He disagreed with Mburu, who writes that it can be acquired through learning. But Lawrence did claim that it is possible for witches to convert children into witches. On a later occasion he also denied Mburu's claim that everyone is born with *tvu'*.

Someone who possesses *tvu'* is *ngwɛɛ tvu,'* a witch, and someone who does not have *tvu,'* who 'knows nothing about witchcraft', is *ngwɛɛ jaja*. The word "jaja" means something like innocence. I did not encounter anyone who agreed that everyone possesses *tvu'*, and that a distinction can be made between actual and potential witches, as Mburu claims. People tended to make a different distinction, between active and passive witches, between those who participate in witchcraft activities and those who do not participate but can see what the others are up to.

Those Who See Things

Those who possess *tvu'* are also referred to in Limbum as *ngaa yɛ buu* (people who see things). For example, diviners can 'see' the more indirect causes of misfortune. In my first encounter with Pius he said the following about his father:

'Yes he's a good scientist. And a soothsayer, he's a good soothsayer. If there is something, if there is any mistake, he can refer and tell the patient or the mother who comes with a child before he gives medicine. He cannot just give the medicine like that. If there is any sign he will just tell you what happened.'

In discussions about illness or misfortune I often heard people say 'there must have been something, otherwise it wouldn't have happened...' or 'when it happened they checked but there was nothing...'. When Lawrence told me about the compound head's decision about who to give the woman to when a jealous witch had killed the 'brother' who had inherited her first, Lawrence said that the compound head would consult a diviner, and only 'if there is nothing they may decide to give her to you'. Here it is obvious that he was referring to witchcraft, but usually such statements were made without any explicit reference to witchcraft or *tvu'*. When the granary collapsed on the woman who was taking shelter from the storm people said 'There must have been something in her compound otherwise it would not have happened.' When Mathias explained to me why falling into a latrine

16 Pa TaKwi divining with cowrie shells

is related to *bfaa* he said 'The *ndap ngong* is a forbidden place, the latrine is a place where bad things are dumped. People say that just the fact of falling into the latrine means that there must have been something. It could be that even if you didn't fall in you would still have been trapped in another way.'

When people used the expression 'there must have been something...' it was often in connection with 'mistakes', (*bfaa*), but the statement also implies that witchcraft is the ultimate cause. I will come back to this later when I discuss personal responsibility for misfortune (see pp. 197–9 and pp. 231–2).

It is 'those with eyes' who are able to see whether 'there is something', or, in other words, what the ultimate but hidden causes of misfortune are. But they can also directly observe the nefarious activities of evil witches, and in particular the practice which people talked about most: cannibalism (*ye bee*, literally 'eating people'). In the first encounter with Pius he spoke of human flesh being sold in the market ([1.1] 91) and Pius and Lawrence talked about the diviner's ability to 'see' what the witches were up to. Pius said that his father could observe the witches' nocturnal activities while he slept.

Cannibals and Witch Societies

When I asked Pius whether kwashiorkor could be caused by witchcraft, he said that it could be caused by cannibalism ([1.1] 80, 81). He said that the witch need not be related to his victim and that a stranger may offer human flesh to a child. He added that this flesh was sold in the market. From the exchange between Pius and Lawrence which followed it became clear that both the sale and the consumption of human flesh by the witches is invisible to all but those who participate, and those, like Pa TaKwi, who can 'see'.

Whenever I simply asked people what witches do, the answer was almost always that they eat people (*ye bee*). The accounts of this activity were always remarkably detailed and relatively consistent when compared to accounts of *ngang* and *bfaa*. But those I asked always stressed that they did not really know what happened and were only telling me what they themselves had heard from others. In other words they had never actually witnessed this cannibalism, as having done so would imply that they were also witches and had probably also participated. With regard to this form of witchcraft Mburu writes: 'This set of people is by far the most dreaded. In fact, when the word witchcraft is mentioned the Mbum man's first thought is of this craft which is greatly feared' (Mburu 1979: 5). He continues: 'Eating people is generally only practiced on very close relatives. Thus, as it normally happens, when a member witch is to provide or pay back what he owes the others, he is expected to offer one of his own kinsmen... The Wimbum believe that without any connection a member of a family cannot eat a man from another family' (Mburu 1979: 6–7).

One day a neighbour, Tangwa, a man in his early fifties, called round with a calabash of palm wine. We were drinking and chatting when Francis, a sociology student from the University of Yaounde who stayed with me in Tabenken for two weeks to make a study of witchcraft, joined us and started questioning Tangwa in Pidgin about witchcraft. Tangwa described the witches' activities exactly as do the quotations from Mburu above. Then Francis asked him what would happen if a person refused to pay his debt to his fellow witches.

[6.3] 'He will pay with his own head if he can't repay them,' Tangwa said.

'But what if the person ate human flesh without knowing that he was eating it?' Francis asked.

'If you're there together with them eating then you know. If you're not one of them then you can't take that meat.'

'Okay, so if you want to go and pay for the meat you've eaten what do you do? Do you take money to the witch market?'

'You've eaten a man,' Tangwa said, his voice becoming louder, 'so you can only pay with another man. They will say: you have eaten my brother, now you have to pay with a man.'

'You have to take a full man?'

'Yes, a full man.'

'Are you and they going to eat him together?'

'You're both going to eat. It's a *njangi* where...'

'Can you give a fowl instead?' Francis interrupted, looking slyly at me.

'A fowl,' Tangwa shouted indignantly as he leaned forward. 'Is a fowl a man? If I give you a man are you only going to give me a fowl in return?'

'So if you bring a fowl and they refuse what are you going to do?'

'I'm only telling you how I see it. I would refuse to take the fowl and tell you to bring me a man.'

Tangwa was in agreement with Pius that people are not eaten individually but collectively. Whereas Pius spoke of a witch market (*ntaa tvu'*), however, and said that it was at such places that human flesh was bought and sold, Tangwa referred to the gathering of witches as a *njangi*. "Njangi" is a Pidgin term which refers to what are basically subscription societies. The members meet and drink palm wine and corn beer one afternoon every eight-day week and each contributes a sum of money. They function in the same way as a savings account and members can withdraw their savings at certain times. They may also borrow money from the society. In the towns and cities the *njangis* become 'ethnic' or 'cultural' societies, with people from the same area or village meeting every week in order to keep in contact with their 'countrymen' and maintain their cultural identity: in cities like Bamenda and Douala there are Wimbum *njangis*.

But there are all kinds of weekly social gathering based on the *njangi* model. For example, in Tabenken there are numerous 'cow societies'. The members meet every week, drink palm wine and contribute small sums of money. Then just before Christmas they use the money thus saved to buy a cow which they then slaughter and share among the contributors. The club that American Peace Corps volunteers formed to stimulate the development of fish ponds and rabbit breeding in order to supplement the protein content of the local diet, is known as the rabbit and fish society; its members also meet once a week, drink wine and save money. On the occasions when I attended nobody mentioned fish or rabbits at all, and drinking and paying your contribution were the main interest. The meetings of *Mfu'*, the men's warrior society, *Samba* the men's dance society, *Bongabi*, the women's dance society, and even *Ngwerong*, the regulatory secret society, all follow the same model, with members taking turns in 'providing' palm wine or corn beer for the day's drinking, and often also fowls or goats which are slaughtered and consumed in the society house.

Tangwa compared the witches' cannibalistic gatherings to these *njangis* and societies, (or rather he would have if Francis had allowed him to finish what he was saying). They are based on reciprocity, and if the person whose turn it is to provide fails or refuses to do so then he himself will fall victim to the witches. Tangwa also confirmed what Pius had said earlier about it not being possible for non-witches to accidentally eat human flesh. To participate you must be one of them.

It was unusual that Tangwa spoke in the first person singular ('I would refuse to take the fowl...') and did not keep stressing that he did not really know but was only repeating what he had heard. People were usually at great pains to avoid the suspicion that they had first-hand experience of these cannibalistic gatherings.

I broke off my discussion with Lawrence, with which I started this chapter, at the point where it became explicit that witchcraft requires kinship connections, and just before the topic of cannibalism was broached. I did this in order to facilitate my presentation of the non-cannibalistic aspects of witchcraft. Let us now pick the discussion up again at the point where we left off.

[6.4] 'So witchcraft can only work in families?' I asked.

'Yes, there has to be a family connection.'

'In some countries people speak of witches affecting people who are not members of their family,' I told him.

'Without any connection?' Lawrence asked.

'Yes.'

'There are different kinds of witchcraft,' he said. 'The family witchcraft is Wimbum witchcraft. Then we also have a national witchcraft, the one we call *munyongo* or *kupey*. That's a type of witchcraft in which you go into a certain society to get a lot of money. You have to give them people from your family and then they give you money. That's a different kind of witchcraft. I don't really understand it, I've only heard people talking about it.'

'What do you call the family witchcraft?'

'We just say *tvu'*.'

'Where do the words "kupey" and "munyongo" come from?'

'*Kupey* is French, it's mostly practised in francophone Cameroon. I think that *munyongo* is from the South West Province. Here we have *tvu'*, which is the family witchcraft.'

'Does *kupey* involve eating people?'

'I'm not sure whether they eat them.'

'Does *tvu'* also mean having to give someone?'

'If I help to eat your brother then I will have to give my brother as well and if we eat someone's father then I will have to give my own father, and you will have to give your father.'

'How do they eat them?'

'They change them into animals and eat them like that.'

'Why do people come together to eat other people?'

'Just for eating.'

'Why not just eat fowls or goats?'

'Because it's very sweet meat. It's the sweetest flesh.'

'But they transform the victim into a goat or a fowl.'

'Yes.'

'But then they're just eating goat or fowl.'

'Yes, but it's sweeter than normal goat or fowl.'

'But then why not just eat the person without transforming him?'

'Because it's difficult to just slaughter a person and eat him.'

'If "kupey" is from French what was the Limbum word they were using before?'

'We didn't know that before. It's only since people have been travelling to other parts of Cameroon. We only knew about *tvu'*.'

'If someone suddenly gets rich it may be that he was giving people to the society?'

'Yes, that's how some people automatically become rich. Then everybody will say 'That is not real money, that is *kupey* money'. Everybody has to see how you have become rich. They have to see that you have worked hard and earned your money. If you suddenly become rich and they can't explain it then they will suspect.'

'And if you get rich suddenly but no one has been dying will they still suspect?'

'They will believe that one day they will start dying.'

'And they will be people from your own family?'

'Yes. But I've heard that some people get rich in that way and then when they're supposed to pay with people from their family they refuse and the society kills them. But the money remains in the family. The family will be proud of the man, because he has refused to offer his family. The death is always very abrupt. You may be killed by a vehicle or you may fall into a stream.'

'And the people who have been given to the society, do they also die abruptly?'

'Yes. They don't die of a long illness but of wind shattering the house or something like that.'

Whenever people in Tabenken talked about *tvu'* as cannibal-ism they spoke of witches (*ngaa ye bee*, those who eat people) catching a victim, turning him into a goat or a fowl and tying him somewhere while the feast is prepared. When the time has come the goat/victim is slaughtered and eaten by the witches. The catching and tying of the victim does not occur literally, and he remains in his compound. But when he has been caught and tied he becomes seriously ill and remains ill during the time that he is tied. He will die at the moment that the witches slaughter the goat.

Descriptions of people being turned into goats and tied somewhere seem to involve a logical contradiction, somewhat like Levi-Strauss's parrots or Evans-Pritchard's cucumbers: a person is turned into a goat and tied somewhere where his friends and relatives will not find him, but at the same time he is still at home, in human form and bedridden. It is not simply a case of him suddenly having a mystical animal double (which, people said, was a completely different phenomenon), neither have the witches taken an already existing goat to represent their victim, nor is it just a figure of speech, a way of saying they have captured their victim's 'soul' or 'essence'. No, people insisted, they have *turned* him into a goat: the person who is sick in bed both is and is not a goat. When the goat is killed the per-son does not die because the goat has been killed, as in the case of animal doubles, he dies because he was the goat and has him-self been killed.[3] If someone falls seriously ill and does not respond to treatment a diviner will be called in to 'see' whether 'there is something' behind the illness. He will be able to see whether it is a result of the person having been tied somewhere. He will see where he is tied and, if he is clever enough, may be able to rescue him before he is killed. In that case the sick person will recover rapidly. If he is not rescued in time he will die. Lawrence said that people who have been given to a society die suddenly, whereas other people said that they died gradually, like John Tanfu.

Most people I spoke to described the workings of cannibalistic tvu' in this way. But there was no clear description of the work-

---

3. In their discussion of the concept of *tvu'* in Ndu, Probst and Bühler did state that the witch is believed to steal 'the victim's *riong* (meaning "life", "breath", "soul")'. This results in death or illness 'depending on how much of the *riong* has already been consumed' (1990: 449)

ings of *kupey* and *munyongo*. Lawrence distinguished between two types of witchcraft which require the provision of human victims: 'Wimbum' or 'family' witchcraft, which is called *tvu'* in Limbum, and *kupey* or *munyongo*, which he also referred to as 'national' witchcraft. Most people agreed that when human victims were required you could only provide relatives. However, I had often heard stories of motor accidents being attributed to *kupey*. If there was an accident and the passengers were killed but the driver survived then people would say that the driver must have been due to provide in his *kupey* house. This implies that non-kin can also be provided, but if I jokingly suggested to friends that I could also become rich by offering them to my *kupey* house, they insisted that this would not work. If it worked like that there would be an orgy of providing and the few remaining survivors would become rich. And in any case, how was I to offer them to my *kupey* house in payment of my debts when they did not 'belong' to me? After all, I could not just take a fowl or a goat from another person's compound in order to repay an ordinary debt, so it was only logical that I could only repay a witchcraft debt with someone who was 'mine'. They stressed that you could only repay debts with goods that belonged to you.

In conversation [6.4] above Lawrence claimed that only relatives may be provided, but his statements are ambiguous when examined more closely. He introduced the distinction between 'family' and 'national' witchcraft in answer to my remark that in some countries people do not see witchcraft as operating along lines of kinship. He implied that *kupey* ('national witchcraft') does not require relatives as victims (which is why he opposes it to 'family witchcraft' in the first place). When he described eating brothers and fathers he was clearly referring to *tvu'* and not to *kupey*. But then later on, when he was clearly talking about *kupey*, he stated that only kin can be provided. If that was not the case then the man in his example would not be confronted with the dilemma of sacrificing his relatives or loosing his own life; he could simply provide a stranger in payment of his debt to the witches.

Kupey appears to have been introduced in the Wimbum area relatively recently, which is why it is still sketchy and people tend to fill in their explanations with meanings derived from *tvu'*, which it resembles, and to which it is no doubt related, when I push them for a detailed description. Those who told me about *kupey* were generally younger and more educated or had travelled or worked in the cities or the plantations in the south. Old people who had hardly been outside the village had never heard of *kupey* or *munyongo*. Most people I spoke to said that *kupey* came from francophone Cameroon. There is a mountain near Nkongsamba on the Bamenda–Douala highway called Mount Kupey. People described *kupey* as either different and distinct from *tvu'* or similar and related to *tvu'*, depending on the features which were being emphasised and what they already knew about both.

Those who had heard of *kupey* agreed that people have to be provided, just as in the case of *tvu'*, but they were not sure whether the victims had to be relatives, and what exactly happened to them. Everyone agreed that, in the case of *tvu'*, the victim is always killed and eaten (unless of course he is rescued in time). With regard to *kupey* Lawrence was not sure whether the victims were eaten or not. In the southern plantation area people have no doubts as to the fate of the victims. Writing of the Bakweri of Buea in the South West Province, Ardener describes a person with *nyongo* (Lawrence called it *munyongo*) as: 'always prosperous, for he was a member of a witch association that had the power of causing its closest relatives, even its children, to appear to die. But in truth they were taken away to work for their witch-masters on... Mount Kupey' (Ardener 1970: 147). This closely resembles de Rosny's descriptions of *ekong* sorcery in Douala:

> *Ekong* is the most widespread sorcery in this part of Africa today. I could cite numerous tesitmonials to the reality of the *ekong* procedure, which consists in going to a sorcerer and offering money in return for human beings, whom the sorcerer will then undertake to deliver to you to make slaves of... *Ekong* is essentially bound to wealth and money. Prosperous persons are suspected of maintaining slaves, to work for them on invisible plantations. (1985: 58, 60)

Perhaps the most important difference between *tvu'* and *kupey* is the motive. In *kupey* victims are provided in return for money or other material reward, whereas in *tvu'* relatives are apparently consumed simply for gastronomic pleasure. Human flesh is 'very sweet meat...the sweetest flesh', Lawrence said. The fact that they are first transformed into an animal apparently does not alter the taste of the flesh: 'After all,' Mathias told me when I discussed the matter with him, 'what they are eating is not a goat, it is human flesh.' Transforming the victim into an animal simply makes it easier to slaughter him, according to Lawrence.

People generally agreed that the idea of providing victims to cannibalistic societies had always been part of Wimbum culture, but that doing this in return for money was relatively new. It is this element of financial gain which is the central characteristic of *kupey* and *munyongo*. Though there were some differences of opinion as to how quickly you became rich, most people agreed that you do not provide a victim one day and then wake up the next morning rolling in money. What happens is that you become rich relatively quickly, so that people cannot figure out exactly how you have done it. Stories abound of small traders or petty customs officials who, in the course of a couple of years, amassed large fortunes which, given the limited scope of their enterprise, or their relatively low position, could not be easily explained. This then leads to rumours of *kupey*, which will be confirmed if relatives of the person in question have been dying, or start falling inexplicably ill. Ardener states that by 1953 the belief in *nyongo* among the Bakweri had 'taken such a hold that no one would build a modern house for fear of being accused of possessing *nyongo* (1970: 147), and that 'in this atmosphere, *any* conspicuous material success became suspect' (148).[4]

Lawrence said that he had heard that it is possible to trick the *kupey* society by promising to provide relatives. On the basis of this promise the person receives an advance but then refuses to provide his relatives. The witches take his life in payment instead and the wealth and prosperity that, in the normal course of events, would have fallen to him are transmitted to his family. The person thus offers his own life to ensure the financial well being of the rest of his family. In such cases the *kupey* activities of the victim would be positively valued and he would be considered a hero. People often mentioned this trick when telling me about *kupey*.

The notion of personal material gain flowing from the possession of *tvu'* is also present in another form of witchcraft: that associated with the witch markets.

---

4. In this connection see Geschiere 1988 and Rowlands and Warnier 1988 on witchcraft as a social-levelling device.

Witch Markets

During my first encounter with Pius he and Lawrence described how the witches buy and sell human flesh at a market. Later he introduced the Limbum term "ntaa tvu'" (witch market). After talking about those who trade and eat human flesh Pius suddenly mentioned ntaa tvu'. Lawrence laughed and obligingly translated the term into English as "witch market" ([1.1] 147–8). They then both made use of my lack of knowledge of Limbum to take 'time out' and discuss local 'gift markets' (*ntaa bsaa*).

It is not clear who took the initiative for this 'time out'. Pius merely said '*ntaa bsaa*' ([1.1] 149). Maybe he wanted to exclude me from the conversation for some reason, or perhaps he was simply introducing another Limbum term into the English discussion, as he had done with "ntaa tvu'" two lines earlier. On that occasion Lawrence merely repeated what Pius had said and translated it, but in this instance he reacted with an informative question in Limbum. Did Lawrence think that this was a topic which should not be revealed to me, or did he just want to make some enquiries backstage before presenting his findings to me? His first question in Limbum gave me the impression that he did not know what a gift market was, but from his following discussion with Pius, and because of the way he explained it to me shortly after, it is clear both that he was familiar with the concept and that the time out was not meant to hide something from me. It appears, rather, that he was not familiar with the term "gift market" (and indeed, this was the only occasion on which I actually heard the term used). He asked Pius what he meant by a gift market and when Pius answered that it is a place where people 'collect things' (151) Lawrence clearly knew what he was talking about (152). Thus it seems that Lawrence simply used the 'time out' to enquire about the meaning of a strange term.

What is *ntaa tvu'*? (In what follows I will assume that *ntaa tvu'* and *ntaa bsaa* are the same thing). It is a place, a 'market', where people go to 'take things'. Pius said that the biggest such market, which he referred to as *kop bfu* (*kop* = forest), in the Wimbum area was situated in the forest on top of the large mountain situated between Tabenken and Binka. There are others. Lawrence said that the Ndu people take their 'things' from the market in Kaka, a village near his native Ndu. Apparently those who visit these markets are witches (151, 160). What kind of 'things' do they take

from the market? Lawrence made another backstage enquiry: can
you take things which will cause other people's deaths? (158).
Pius said that you may bring sicknesses (159). When Lawrence
translated this for me he added that they may also bring food
(160).

With this translation the discussion switched back into
English. There then followed another exchange in which
Lawrence appeared to be questioning Pius, whereas they in fact
alternated in telling (me?) the same story. What they described is
probably not very clear to someone who knows absolutely nothing about *ntaa tvu'*. I know it was not very clear to me at the time.
They mentioned people taking things and running, a terrible
wind, people being beaten and followed by the devil, dancing
(161–73). What it was they were describing only became clear to
me later, after subsequent discussions. The first of these was with
Lawrence, a full nine months later, when I explicitly questioned
him about witch markets.

[6.5] 1. 'What's *ntaa tvu'*?' I asked.
    2. 'That's a witch market,' he said.
    3. 'What happens there?'
    4. 'It's somewhere where all things are found. They are all there
       tied in leaves. You can go there and bring something home, like
       food, sickness, troubles. You don't know exactly what is wrapped
       in the leaves. Then in that market there is something like a *juju*, or
       satan. He is the one who has placed all the packages wrapped in
       leaves. He is the one called *nyvurka'*. They say that he plays the
       drum and sings and people are dancing. Then those who have
       come choose their own bundle and take it and run. If you escape
       you are free but if the *nyvurka'* catches you then you are dead.
       Then when you get home with your leaf you open it. If you have
       brought food then the area where you stay will have a lot of food,
       if you have brought disease then that area will be affected with
       diseases. When you take the leaf you don't know what is in it. If
       you have brought dance then the dance which starts in that area
       will be very good and will become famous. So, that's *ntaa tvu'*.'
    5. 'Is it an actual place?'
    6. 'Yes.'
    7. 'Where is it then?'
    8. 'In Ndu we say it is in Ngwa.'
    9. 'What do Tabenken people say?'

10. 'Well, Pius told us it is on top of that hill.'
11. 'Is there only one *nyvurka* there or are there more?'
12. 'It's only one.'
13. 'Can you see him?'
14. 'Yes, if you go there you can see him.'
15. 'So if there is a *ntaa tvu'* on top of that hill then I can go up there and have a look, and perhaps take a leaf bundle?'
16. 'Yes, if you are one of the witchmen.'
17. 'Oh, so you have to be a witch?'
18. 'Yes, ordinary people can't go there.'
19. 'What does that mean? Does it mean that if I go there something will happen to me?'
20. 'Nothing will happen to you but you won't see it, it's invisible.'
21. 'So only witches can see it?'
22. 'Yes. If you go there and they are having a meeting you will not see them. They will be there but you won't see them.
23. 'So if there's a lot of sickness in an area it may mean that someone has been to *ntaa tvu'*?'
24. 'Yes. That is why when there is an epidemic the landlord of the area will say that any person who is involved will die. If you are not a witch and not involved then you will not die.'
25. 'What else do they wrap in those leaves besides food and sickness?'
26. 'Money.'

About a month after this conversation with Lawrence I broached the same subject during a visit to Mathias, Fred and Susan. I had gone to Mbot to discuss some practical matters with Susan, who also worked for me as an assistant. When Mathias, her husband, came home from work we had lunch, which she always insisted I ate whenever I visited her. After lunch we went across to Fred's house where the following discussion took place.

[6.6] 1. 'What's *ntaa tvu'*?' I asked.
  2. 'It's where the wizards go and gather,' Fred answered.[5] 'It's like a society where they bring together the people they're going to eat.'
  3. 'So that's where they go and eat people?' I asked.

---

5. Some people used the terms "witch" and "wizard" as synonyms, others distinguished female and male witches by calling them witches and wizards respectively.

4. 'That's where they make their arrangements,' Fred said.
5. 'About two weeks ago,' Mathias said, leaning forward in his chair, 'we had a seminar in Nkambe and there I heard a very funny story. There was a man who was not a wizard and he was married to this woman. Whenever they had a child the child would be strong and then it would just die. This happened three times. Then somebody who attended that market came and hinted to the husband. He said that it had become too much, that he had come to tell him about the actions of his wife, about the cause of the deaths of so many of his children. But the man didn't believe that his wife could do such a thing, because she had wanted children. So the other man said: If you want to see her I will give you some medicine so that you can see. So he gave the medicine to the husband. When the time came he saw a kind of dance. Because of the medicine he was able to see the witches and wizards dancing seriously. Then he saw the wife, properly dressed, because the wife used to be a very active somebody there, with the heads of the children, because she had already killed a good many. So this story shows that maybe they do have a gathering place.'
6. 'There is medicine that can make you see?' Susan asked.
7. 'Yes,' Mathias answered. 'If you take that medicine and you go there and you are not careful then they can finish you, because you're not invited. If you are given the medicine you are usually protected by the one who gave it. But if he allows you to be seen by them you will not be safe.'
8. 'What's the place that people go to and take packages which they can only open when they get home and which contain money or sickness?' I asked.
9. 'That's *ntaa tvu*,' Mathias said, 'but it's usually somewhere else.'
10. 'Yes,' Fred added, 'its somewhere else. People here believe it's somewhere else.'
11. 'So that's different from the *ntaa tvu*' where they go to eat people?' I asked.
12. 'It's the same thing,' Fred said. 'Its in Ngwa sub-division, there is a group of people, dancing, and all of them are wizards. When they go out it is said that they go out and collect things. When they are coming back they are dancing. If there is a wizard who tries to disturb them they will kill him. It's only once a year.
13. 'It's like a dance,' Mathias added.
14. 'Then what's *njincang*?' I asked.

15. 'That's *ntaa tvu'*,' Mathias said. 'Those who go and collect things and then come back by witchcraft and open the leaves.
16. 'Is that the same as *ntaa tvu'*?' I asked.
17. 'It's the same,' Susan said.
18. 'Yes, it's the same,' Fred agreed. 'In *njincang* they go and collect things. You can go there and collect corn or food, but you may also take a leaf which is full of sickness and spread it in the area.'
19. '*Njincang* is the proper name for those who go to gain,' Mathias added. 'I think that everybody who goes there is aiming to bring back something good. But you can't make a choice, you just take your own package and come away.'
20. 'Does the word "njincang" refer to the people or the place?' I asked.
21. 'It is the place,' Mathias said.
22. 'It's a place known only by those who go there,' Fred added.
23. 'So only witches go there?' I asked.
24. 'Yes,' they all said.
25. 'If I want something can I also go there?' I asked.
26. 'How can you go there?' Fred asked, laughing. 'Those who go there go in the form of birds or insects or wind. They don't just go there like that. And they say that when you take something from there it isn't safe to come back. People are following you, you can be attacked and killed.'
27. 'Who follows you?' I asked.
28. 'The people there,' Fred said.
29. 'So there are people there?' I asked.
30. 'Yes,' Fred said. 'They chase you, and if you are caught then you are finished. You are killed as the price for the things that the others have collected.'
31. 'What do they do with you?' I asked.
32. 'They kill you and eat you,' Mathias said.
33. 'What kind of people stay there?' I asked.
34. 'Witches,' Mathias said. 'In most cases we hear that they come from Ngwa area, so it could be that it is situated there.'
35. 'Do they speak Limbum there?' I asked.
36. 'No, they speak Yamba,' Fred said.

In this conversation I introduced the term "njincang", which someone had told me was a synonym for "ntaa tvu'". Mathias and Fred confirmed this, though not everyone agreed, as the discussion with Tobias which follows shows (I will come back to the relationship between *ntaa tvu'* and *njincang* later).

[6.7] 1. 'What's the difference between *ntaa tvu'* and *njincang*?' I asked.
 2. '*Ntaa tvu'* is simply a market for the witches. *Njincang* is a place where wizards go to get something. If you want to get something you go to *njincang*. *Ntaa tvu'* is where the witches go to make market the same as we make market.'
 3. 'Which is the place where they have things wrapped in leaves?' I asked.
 4. 'That's *njincang*.'
 5. 'So what exactly do they do in *ntaa tvu'*?'
 6. 'That's where you go and exchange things.'
 7. 'What kind of things?'
 8. 'Well, the witches know. They take food or anything. And when you take from there it multiplies and you have a lot.'
 9. 'So when people bring sickness do they bring it from *ntaa tvu'* or from *njincang*?'
 10. 'Sickness normally comes from *njincang*, because in *njincang* the leaves are tied, and they are not the same. They tie bundles so that when you go there you pick your own. Then when you reach the stream you open your leaf and see what is there. When you see bad things you throw them in the stream. A wicked person will bring the bad things home. It could be sickness, or anything which is bad for the community.'
 11. 'Is *njincang* a place?'
 12. 'It's a spiritual place.'
 13. 'Do people live there?'
 14. 'I think so. If no one lives there why should people go there?'
 15. 'What kind of people live there?'
 16. 'Witches.'

People usually described *ntaa tvu'* as an actual place. Pius said that it was on top of the Tabenken-Binka mountain ([1.1] 151–7), Lawrence ([6.5] 8) and Mathias ([6.6] 34) thought that it may be situated in Ngwa, to the east of the Wimbum area. People often said that witchcraft came from Ngwa and that they thought that *ntaa tvu'* was situated there. But although they described *ntaa tvu'* as a real place, people generally agreed that it was not easily accessible to ordinary people. Pius said that it existed parallel to the ordinary market but that it was invisible to all except the witches who participated ([1.1] 100–21). He also said that it was situated in the forest at the almost inaccessible summit of the Tabenken-Binka mountain. Lawrence said too that it was invisible to all except the witches ([6.5] 15–22), as did Mathias, though he asserted that ordinary people could see it if they used 'medicines' ([6.6] 5–7). According to Fred the witches do not go there in human form, but transform themselves into insects, birds or wind ([6.6] 26). Tobias referred to it as a 'spiritual place' ([6.7] 12). So it is a real place, but it is either far away (in Ngwa), inaccessible (on a mountain summit) or close by but invisible.

There was also some agreement about *ntaa tvu'* being inhabited. Pius spoke of 'the devil' following those who go there ([1.1] 163, 173). At one point he suggested that it is inhabited by other people (161). Lawrence said that 'a *juju*, or satan', which he also called *nyvurka'*, is responsible for placing the leaf packages ([6.5] 4). Mathias and Fred said that it is inhabited by people, witches ([6.6] 26–36), as did Tobias ([6.7] 13–6).

It is dangerous to visit *ntaa tvu'* because the inhabitant or inhabitants chase and try to kill those who come to take the packages. Once the intruders have laid hands on a package they have to run for their lives, and if they are caught they are killed (Pius [1.1] 161, 173, Lawrence [6.5] 4, Fred [6.6] 26). Those who are caught may be eaten (Fred and Mathias [6.6] 30–2). If the inhabitants are witches and those who take packages are also witches then this seems to mean that different (regional?) groups or categories of witches are involved.

In describing *ntaa tvu'* people often mentioned dancing. Pius said that someone dances when the person runs off with the packages ([1.1] 173) and Lawrence said that the *nyvurka'* plays the drum and sings while the people dance ([6.5] 4). Mathias and Fred said that the visiting witches dance ([6.6] 5, 12).

In all three of these conversations *ntaa tvu'* is described as a place where people go to take 'things', such as food, money, sickness, troubles, dance, fertility and the ability to do well at school. People usually said that these 'things' were wrapped up in leaves (Pius [1.1] 151, 158–60, 175–7, Lawrence [6.5] 4, 26, Mathias and Fred [6.6] 8–19).

Although people spoke of the trips to *ntaa tvu'* as though they actually took place, and they described the packages as if they were real rather than merely metaphorical, I did not have the impression that they thought that witches literally removed cash, food or any other physical object from them. Rather, it seems that the packages contain the potential or power through which these goods or capacities are actualised. If the package contains 'money' then the person who has taken it will gradually, but relatively rapidly, become rich, and if it contains 'corn' then the recipient will have abundant harvests. People often said that the packages all looked the same and that those who took them did not know what was inside until they opened them, by which time it was too late to change. Once they have returned safely they stop by a stream to open the packages and see what they have taken. If it is something good they will keep it and benefit, but if it is bad they cast it in the stream and it will effect the whole area ([6.7] 10). If a witch finds that his package contains sickness and throws it in the stream then the whole area will soon be affected by an epidemic.

People sometimes spoke in discussions of *ntaa tvu'* and sometimes of *njincang*. As in the case of terms like "ngang" and "bfaa", the relationship between "njincang" and "ntaa tvu'" is fluid and depends on the context in which the terms are being used. Sometimes they are used as synonyms, on other occasions they appear to be unrelated. Pius described a market where witches buy and sell human flesh ([1.1] 95–123). He also mentioned a 'gift market', which Lawrence called *ntaa tvu'*, where people go and take things like food and sickness ([1.1] 145–77). Was he referring to one market or to several? When I asked Lawrence about *ntaa tvu'* he said that it is the place where people go to take things ([6.5] 4). He did not mention cannibalism and neither did I ask him about it.

When I put the same question to Fred and Mathias they described *ntaa tvu'* as the place where the witches eat their victims, but they did not mention the packages ([6.6] 1–5). When I asked them they said that it is the same thing: *ntaa tvu'* is the place where the witches eat their victims and go to collect things ([6.6] 8–13). I then mentioned *njincang* and they said that this is the same as *ntaa tvu'* ([6.6] 14–19). This is confusing. They described a place where witches live, and where other witches go to take things. If the latter are caught by the former then they are killed and eaten. But it is also apparently the place where the latter go to hold their society meetings and consume the relatives they have provided. Is this really one and the same place? Though they explicitly said that it is, an examination of the conversation suggests that they are talking about two different places: when the term "ntaa tvu'" is used the emphasis is on eating kin ([6.6] 1–12), whereas when "njincang" is used the emphasis is on taking packages ([6.6] 14–30).

Tobias insisted that *ntaa tvu'* and *njincang* are different, though the exact nature of the difference remains unclear. The witches go to both places to 'get something' ([6.7] 2). They go to *njincang* for the leaf packages ([6.7] 3–4) and it is from there that they take sickness and spread it in the community ([6.7] 9–10), but from *ntaa tvu'* they take food and other things which then multiply ([5.10] 8).

Tobias insisted that *ntaa tvu'* and *njincang* are different, although from his description I gain the impression that they are the same, whereas Mathias and Fred explicitly said that they are the same but spoke about them as though they are different. There is no simple answer to the question of the differences or similarities between *ntaa tvu'* and *njincang* and descriptions varied from one informant to another, as they did in descriptions of *ngang* and *bfaa*.

The Witchcraft of the White Man

Some time after I had had these discussions, Father Robert, the priest who had written a thesis on witchcraft, came to Tabenken to spend a few weeks' leave with his mother in the village. I visited him one afternoon in his small but modern house to drink beer and discuss my research. We talked about Wimbum 'tradition' and this led on to a discussion about traditional medicine and divination. From there it was a small step to the topic of witchcraft.

[6.8] 'What do you think about the claim that certain sicknesses are caused by witchcraft?' I asked.

'Yes,' he said, pausing to think. 'The case of witchcraft is something for which I wouldn't give my head, but I can't disprove it either. You see, I fall short of defining witchcraft. I have done research on witchcraft and written a paper on it, but I haven't been able to define it adequately. Do we mean by witchcraft everything that we can't understand? If it is that then okay, there are many things we don't understand. We can do many things without understanding where we got the power to do them. We could define witchcraft in that way. But then there is a problem. Take the phenomenon that they call transformation, in which a person incarnates into an animal or a fly or the wind or some element of nature. Somebody changes into another form and is then capable of doing things. Now I think that a lot of things which are referred to as witchcraft are just psychic powers, which can be explained in the field of science, like psychokinesis for example. If someone here were to do that then he would claim that it is a gift from God. Sure it's a gift from God. But these are psychic powers which are given to many people and some people discover them and others don't know that they have them. So witchcraft could be some such psychic power. Psychology has not yet been able to discover all the powers that people are capable of. No, if that is witchcraft then I agree that it exists.'

'What about this business of eating people?' I asked.

'That is something that I couldn't possibly explain. But I would refrain from saying, downright, that it is impossible. I have already mentioned psychokinesis: it is possible to do things from a distance. It's a psychic power. But when you talk about eating people it becomes problematic. I have tried to find out exactly what people mean when they talk about eating. Does it mean that you have caused a person's death from a distance, that you have broken him into bits from a distance? If you have tried to destroy his soul from a distance, as some have tried to explain it to me (you have not had any contact with him and he is walking upright though he is just a carcass, that is what they say), if that is it then I would like to know exactly what you have done to his soul, whatever the soul is, because as far as I know the soul is immaterial, so you couldn't actually affect it physically. So there must be something else they are trying to talk about but they fall short of the words necessary to explain. That's why it is difficult for me to understand. So I can't reject it and I can't embrace it.'

'If it were true would you explain it in terms of some devilish involvement?'

'Oh sure, I believe in the devil and demonology, in the power of the devil. If it is true, even psychic phenomena can be used for evil. If you use supernatural powers for doing evil, for destroying people, then I would say that it is the influence of the devil. The devil is not going to appear and say: Here am I, I am the devil. But he works through people. We meet devils through the people we meet. Through people we meet God and we meet the devil. Oh yes, oh yes!

But the Christian has no need to fear even if that were true (I don't say that it is true and I don't say that it is not true) because it is the power of the devil that was given to him by God, and the power of God is greater than that of the devil. So if you have God on your side then there is no other power to fear. That would be my advice. But I wouldn't make any effort to disprove the existence of witchcraft or to prove it. I have tried at one time because of my studies, to find out what exactly it is. A lot of what people refer to as witchcraft is just fear: fear of the unknown, loneliness, all kinds of fears. But when you want to pin it down and speak of witchcraft as such then they don't know what it is. At best I would say that it is the entrance of the devil in the world of human society. And that entrance can be overpowered by the influence of Christ.'

'In Mburu's thesis on witchcraft he defines the word "tvu'" as some kind of special knowledge. Would you agree with that?'

'I would say that he is probing at a definition. He used my paper, and in that paper I shied away from giving a definition because I couldn't get one from the people. They can go around it and give a description, but when you pin them down then they can't define it. In the last instance it is things we can't explain. I think that is what influenced Mburu when he referred to it as sacred knowledge. It is not gnostic knowledge but some form of psychic power.'

'*Tvu*' is one of those concepts that has a core of meaning which is relatively clear and on which most people can agree, but the further you get from the core the more confusion there is,' I said. 'Yes, it's like that.'

'Do you think that "clairvoyance" would be a reasonable translation, if you had to choose a single term?'

'Yes, it would be one of many possibilities. I think that if you insist on a definition that you will have to accept a very descriptive definition, and it will also be a very long one. It is clairvoyance, it is psychokinesis, it is psychopathology, etc. It is something that one individual can do and another can't, or that one individual can do and another can't understand. For example, a person here may see an aeroplane flying and not be able to understand how it works. Then he will call it *tvu' bara*': it's the witchcraft of the White man. We can't understand it so it's witchcraft.'

'Yes,' I said. 'Once I was typing and someone came to visit me. He just stood there shaking his head and muttering 'na White

man witch, na White man witch'.'
'Exactly.'
'This all means that "witchcraft" is a very inadequate translation of the Limbum "tvu'"?'
'Yes, it's a very incomplete translation. *Tvu'* is actually a compendium of all kinds of concepts. Even the ability to write. When my grandmother was still alive and I wrote to her and she got my cousin to read it she would call it *tvu'*: how could he be there saying what I said without having seen me? She couldn't understand it so it was *tvu'*. In a broad sense *tvu'* refers to things that they can't understand. But when you proceed from the word "witchcraft" and you are looking for a local word which is more or less equivalent then you can use "tvu'".'

This discussion brings to light another aspect of tvu', namely *tvu' bara'*, which people translate as 'White man witch' in Pidgin, that is to say 'witchcraft of the White man'.[6] It was quite early in my stay in Tabenken that I first heard the expression 'White man witch'. During sessions of palm-wine drinking people would often ask me about The Netherlands, how far it was from Cameroon, how long it took to get there, and so on. When I described the flight and told them it only took six hours from Douala to Amsterdam, people would shake their heads and exclaim 'na White man witch!' (it's witchcraft of the White man).

So *tvu'* is also involved in machinery and technical processes which people do not understand. Mathias asked me whether people in the West considered science and technical innovations to be the result of witchcraft. He said that Africans thought that people who achieved something unusual, who are gifted or talented, or who invent things 'have witch'.

Any discussion about *tvu'*, or about various technical matters, from aviation to motor cars and tape recorders, often led to bitter

---

6. According to Jeffreys (1962) and Nkwi and Warnier (1982) the term "bara'" refers to the Fulani. People in Tabenken translated "tvu' bara'" as "White man witchcraft", but "bara'" is as indeterminate as the other terms being considered in this study. There is evidence that the term was used to refer to the Fulani in the past. For example the horse, probably first introduced by them, is called *nya bara'* (*nya* = animal). The pineapple, which people told me was introduced by the Germans, is called *mru' bara'* (*mru'* is the raffia palm, whose fruits resemble pineapples). The English language is called *libara'* in Limbum (*li* = language). Only English (and not French, German or Fulani) is referred to as *libara'*. The word "bara'" also refers to that which comes from outside and is seen as sophisticated, complex, difficult to understand. Sophisticated urban *evolués* are sometimes referred to by villagers as *bara'*.
7. Here I do not pretend to adequately discuss the ethnographic literature on African witchcraft, but simply want to mention to a few points which bear on my descriptions above.

complaints about the difference between the ways in which Africans and White men utilise their *tvu'*. White men, they said, used it for constructive ends, for development and the good of society, whereas Africans were motivated by jealousy and greed and only used their power for destructive ends, to bring disease or to eat kin. This is an opinion that I not only heard from illiterate old men who had never been outside their village, but from a wide range of people, including sophisticated urban intellectuals.

The encounter with Father Robert has served to introduce the concept of *tvu' bara'* into the discussion and to link indigenous conceptions of witchcraft to Christian notions of evil. It also serves as a convenient conclusion to my presentation of the concept of *tvu'*.

Father Robert remained undecided as to whether *tvu'* 'really' exists. He refused to tie himself to a definition, indeed he insisted that it was impossible to define, and offered only the vague description that it includes things which some people cannot understand and abilities that some people have and others do not. Although he stated that "tvu'" is as good a term as any as a translation of "witchcraft", our conversation clearly shows the inadequacy of this translation. While cannibalistic banquets, flying to meetings, causing diseases and spoiling crops are the kind of phenomena we might associate with the term "witchcraft", such things as writing and aviation obviously are not.

The different denotations of the two terms become clear when we consider the conversation as a whole. In the first part we use the term "witchcraft" and in the second part the term "tvu'". Though in both parts Father Robert emphasised that they both refer to things that people do not understand, he used them differently. In the first part he related the enigmatic phenomena associated with witchcraft to the activities of the devil, which is to say they are evil, whereas in the second part he relates *tvu'* to morally neutral phenomena such as aviation and writing. This is also related to the way I questioned him. Initially my questions were about cannibalism and devilish involvement; in the second part of our conversation I questioned him about *tvu'* as a form of knowledge.

Here, also, meanings are fluid and contingent. What *tvu'* is depends on what you are talking about and to whom. It also depends on the context in which the discussion takes place and the form which it takes. The same applies to witchcraft. When I talk to Father Robert "witchcraft" probably means something closer to pre-industrial European witchcraft than when I speak to Lawrence, because Father Robert has read the literature whereas Lawrence only knows the term as a translation of "tvu'".

Tvu' and the Ethnography of African Witchcraft[7]

In the preceding sections of this chapter I have discussed the meaning of the Limbum term "tvu'" as it was used in the conversations I recorded. As in the case of "kwashiorkor", "ngang" and "bfaa", I started with an English term and gradually moved over to what appeared to be the Limbum equivalent. This shift to vernacular terms was a result of the realisation that the English terms were inadequate because their meanings only partially overlapped those of the Limbum terms.

There are, however, important differences between the extent to which "kwashiorkor" and "witchcraft" have been integrated into Limbum discourse. "Kwashiorkor" belongs to the technical vocabulary of biomedicine and has only entered local discourse to a relatively limited extent. "Witchcraft" (and the Pidgin "witch"), on the other hand, is a common term with which everybody, even non-English speakers, is familiar. This means that when people spoke to me in English or Pidgin they used the term "witchcraft" to talk about *tvu'* in way that they could not use "kwashiorkor" to talk about *ngang* or *bfaa*. As far as they were concerned they were talking about *tvu'*. I had to find out in which contexts "tvu'" is used in Limbum discourse in order to learn what meaning "witchcraft" has for the Wimbum when they speak English or Pidgin.

As I have shown above, witchcraft, as my informants spoke about it, sometimes bears little resemblance to that which is referred to by the same term in other cultures. It is fundamentally different to pre-industrial European witchcraft and it also seems to differ in important respects from the witchcraft described by ethnographers in other parts of Africa. In the literature witchcraft and sorcery are often by definition, evil, disruptive, destructive or anti-social forces. For example, Mayer writes

---

7. Here I do not pretend to adequately discuss the ethnographic literature on African witchcraft, but simply want to mention to a few points which bear on my descriptions above.

that 'witchcraft is always immoral. At best it is disapproved; at worst it inspires horror' (1982: 56–7). This view is widely held by writers on the topic (see Firth 1982: 39, Parrinder 1958: 14, Douglas 1970: xxvi), though some writers have described African witchcraft as a morally neutral force (Harwood 1970, Geschiere 1978, 1983, Probst and Bühler 1990). Similar generalisations have been made about European witchcraft (Larner 1982: 48, Marwick 1982: 15).

In his *Witchcraft, Oracles and Magic among the Azande* Evans-Prichard distinguished between witches and sorcerers. He described the former as possessing an innate mystical power which they use to cause harm to others. This power has its source in a physical substance in the witch's belly. Sorcerers, on the other hand, are ordinary people with no innate capabilities who use magical substances to cause harm. Witches may not be aware of their power and cause harm unintentionally. Sorcerers are always conscious agents (Evans-Pritchard 1937: 8–9). Witchcraft has been similarly described in the ethnography of many other African societies (for example Middleton and Winter 1963, Marwick 1982, Harwood 1970, Douglas 1970).[8]

The Wimbum do not view *tvu'* as evil by definition, they do not describe it as a physical substance situated in the belly and they do not believe that witches can be unconscious agents.

But at the same time *tvu'* often also shows some marked similarities with descriptions of witchcraft in other cultures. These similarities take the form of family resemblances (Wittgenstein 1958: 66, 67), which is what makes the use of the term possible. This becomes clear as soon as any single ethnographic description of witchcraft is taken and compared with my own presentation, and this applies particularly to the complex of witchcraft forms which have been described for cultures which are relatively close to the Wimbum. For example, in his ethnography of the Maka in the forests of southern Cameroon Geschiere describes the Maka concept of *djambe*. The Maka translate this term into French as "sorcellerie". Geschiere translates it into English as "witchcraft", but he avoids an unequivocal definition, and stresses that this translation is far from adequate. The *mindjinjamb*, pos-

---

8. The usefulness of the distinction between witchcraft and sorcery has been questioned by Turner (Turner 1967), but writers on the subject have tended to ignore his criticism entirely, or to refer to it briefly and then ignore it anyway. Arens seriously considered Turner's arguments, only to reject them as exaggerated in his enthusiasm for comparison and generalisation (Arens 1980).

sessors of *djambe* (witches), fly to nocturnal meetings and eat relatives, and in this sense they conform to the stereotype of the European pre-industrial witch. But this covers only part of the meaning of the term. Rhetorical skills, a career in the city, successful cash crop harvests, can all be related to the possession of *djambe*. The *nkong*, or medicine man, is someone who puts his *djambe* to constructive use, he can 'see' things that ordinary people cannot. Geschiere noted that 'Because djambe has such a wide, fluid meaning for the Maka, it becomes difficult to use distinctions like good/evil or social/asocial in the exploration of the *djambe*' (1983: 111). He concluded that *djambe* has a much wider meaning than our concept of witchcraft, and suggests that a more accurate translation would be 'energy', 'force' (p. 114), or 'hidden power' (p. 104).

This closely resembles Bohannan's description of the Tiv concept of *tsav*. Bohannan states that 'the past literature on the subject has, probably wisely, considered the word untranslatable', and he continues that '*tsav* deals with ideas which we usually discuss in English in terms of "power"' (Bohannan 1958: 2–3).

Not only is the meaning of *djambe* indeterminate, it is also inconsistent: elements from neighbouring groups are adopted and interpretations in terms of *djambe* vary depending on the situation (Geschiere 1983: 104).

In these and other respects *djambe* closely resembles *tvu'*. Geschiere describes *djambe* as a morally neutral force (p. 102), as unsystematic and mixed with notions from neighbouring peoples (p. 104), as inconsistent (p. 105). People with *djambe* are said to have eyes, they are people who can see things (p. 105). Those who use their *djambe* always do so as conscious agents (p. 105), and in their destructive activities they are motivated primarily by jealousy (p. 105). Rumours about witchcraft tend to crop up in connection with unexpected events (pp. 105–6), and *djambe* can operate in two directions: a person may be sick because he is the victim of someone else's *djambe*, or it may be a sign that he himself is a witch (pp. 108–9). The Maka also associate success in the modern world, in education or business, with *djambe* (p. 112). *Djambe* is ambivalent. It is related to both achievement and destruction, strength and danger. The closer its source in kinship terms, the more dangerous it is (pp. 116–7).

But at the same time it is also very different from *tvu'*. The Maka describe the *djambe* as a creature, a grey mouse or a crab, living in the belly of the witch (Geschiere 1983: 104, 1978: xxvi). This bears some resemblance to the 'witchcraft substance' described by Evans-Pritchard among the Azande, and to Bohannan's description of *tsav* as a material substance growing on a person's heart (1958: 3). No one ever described *tvu'* to me as a living creature or material substance.[9] In an appendix to the original Dutch edition of his book Geschiere also describes various kinds of witchcraft (here he uses "witchcraft" instead of "djambe") which bear no relation to the *tvu'* and witchcraft that people described to me, such as 'mammy water' and magical rings from French mail-order firms (Geschiere 1978: xxx–xxxiv). These are known among the Wimbum, as indeed they are known throughout Cameroon and other African countries, but they were not referred to as *tvu'*, at least not to my knowledge, in Tabenken, and were associated with medicines rather than with witchcraft.

But despite the wide variety of meanings which the Maka seem to give to the term "djambe", Geschiere tends to interpret *djambe* primarily in terms of political power (as Bohannan did with *tsav*). Indeed, Geschiere's interest in *djambe* stems from his interest in political power and leadership, and the influence which social change and the central state authorities have had on the traditional egalitarian society of the Maka. He encountered *djambe* in this context, and it is primarily in terms of this interest in political processes that he tries to interpret it, and perhaps this is part of the reason why *djambe* is primarily a political force in his interpretation.[10] In similar fashion, Probst and Bühler (1990) tend to relate the Wimbum concept of *mshεp* (medicine) primarily to political processes rather than to health and illness. My interest in *tvu'* stems from an interest in indigenous etiology and so I tend to interpret *tvu'* in terms of its relation to illness and misfortune.

I will come to a further consideration of my interpretation of *tvu'* in the next chapter, but before doing so I want to stress that I am neither saying that *djambe* is more political and less etiological for the Maka than *tvu'* is for the Wimbum, nor that it all arbitrarily depends on the idiosyncratic interests of the ethnographer who happens to attempt an interpretation and that all interpreta-

9. Though Probst and Bühler claim that the Wimbum in Ndu localise it in the stomach area (1990: 449) and Mbunwe-Samba says the same of the Wimbum in Binshua (1989: 13).

10. See, in this connection, Rowlands and Warnier (1988), who place witchcraft in Cameroon within the context of the modern state and, following Bayart (1981, 1986), interpret it as a form of popular political protest.

tions are equally acceptable. Ethnographic description must bear some resemblance to the way in which local people see and interpret their own culture otherwise it would not have been possible for the ethnographer to discuss such things with them in the first place. Rather, it should be accepted that ethnography can, and does, produce different readings of the same culture depending on the approach and the interest of the ethnographer. This is not a problem, as the heated discussions about controversial re-studies would have us believe, but follows from the fact that ethnographic knowledge is not simply collected during fieldwork but produced as part of an ongoing praxis of which the ethnographer and the fieldwork process are part. Ethnographers may 'read' the same culture differently and write about it differently, as long as there is enough overlap, enough family resemblances, with the interpretations of the people themselves and of other ethnographers to keep the dialogue going.

Chapter 7

Illnesses of God and Illnesses of People

Illnesses Which are Made

One day Lawrence and I paid a social visit to Tangwa, one of my neighbours. We had been sitting outside his house, eating kola nuts and chatting for quite a while when I enquired about the health of his children. I asked him how he decided on suitable treatment when they were ill. The conversation shifted to illness in general and at one point he and Lawrence told me about a certain illness which could not be treated in hospital but which was only amenable to traditional treatment.

[7.1] 1. 'Are there any other sicknesses like that, sicknesses which are common but can't be treated in hospital?' I asked.
   2. 'Any sickness can be like that,' Tangwa answered. 'Sometimes you go to the hospital with a small wound and they're unable to treat it. Then they send you home to make some country fashion [perform a ritual]. They say that you know about your sickness and they send you home.'
   3. 'How do you mean: know about your sickness?' I asked.
   4. 'That is, you must have stolen something,' Lawrence said. 'Or done something as a result of which someone has made medicine which has caused that sickness to attack you. So you have to go home because you know the cause of your sickness.'
   5. 'So it's caused by some kind of witchcraft?'
   6. 'Yes, medicine or witchcraft,' Lawrence said.
   7. 'Is there a difference between sicknesses being caused by medicine and by witchcraft?'
   8. 'No, no difference.'
   9. 'So if someone makes medicine to make you sick you also use the word "tvu'"?'
   10. 'They don't directly call it *tvu'*,' Lawrence said. 'They say it's a

177

sickness made by man. You say *a yang gee*, which means: the sickness has been made or caused by somebody.'

11. 'Stomachache is the most common sickness caused like that,' Tangwa added.

12. 'If someone is sick because he is being eaten do you also call it *yang gee?*' I asked.

13. 'If I'm sick because I'm being eaten then we say *yang gee* because that's a sickness which has been made,' Lawrence explained.

At the point where this conversation began I was enquiring about illnesses which people thought were amenable to traditional treatment but not to biomedical treatment. What I had in mind was simply different kinds of treatment being effective for different kinds of illness, so Tangwa's answer surprised me.

What he said is similar to what other people had told me in connection with bad death. When a person is about to die and his stomach swells it means he will probably die a bad death. As we have seen, this may be because witches are trying to 'spoil his death', but it may be that he is responsible for his own bad death, that he 'knows of his death, he knows the cause of his death' (Simon Ngengeh [4.8] 12). Tangwa used the same expression in our conversation to refer to illness which cannot be cured in hospital. Did he mean the same as Simon Ngengeh? Lawrence interpreted Tangwa's remark for me by saying that if your illness cannot be cured in hospital it may be because someone has caused it through the use of medicine, as punishment for something you yourself have done wrong ([7.1] 4). So, unlike Simon in his remark about bad death, Lawrence and Tangwa did not seem to think that the sick person himself would be a witch. Lawrence did not mention witchcraft explicitly and referred only to medicine.

However, witchcraft was very much in my mind at that moment, given the way in which people spoke of a dying person knowing the cause of his death because he was himself a witch. So when Lawrence said 'you must have...done something' (4), I immediately assumed (as my next question made clear (5)) that he meant that the sick person himself must have been involved in witchcraft activities (and perhaps I associated his mention of stealing with the taking of packages from *ntaa tvu'*, the witch market). Lawrence then distinguished between medicine and witchcraft as a cause of incurable/chronic illness (6). They are different kinds of cause, and the term "tvu'" will not be applied to the use of medicine (7–10), but both are referred to as *yang gee* because they are 'made or caused by somebody' (10).

In descriptions of African etiologies in the literature a distinction is usually made between illnesses which are caused by people and illnesses which come from God/natural illnesses. There is often also a third category of illnesses: those caused by the ancestors or by spirits (see for example Janzen and Prins 1981, Ngubane 1976). These categories may appear to coincide with those of naturalistic and personalistic etiologies referred to earlier, but this depends on how the category of illnesses of God/natural illnesses is interpreted. In much medical ethnography it is assumed that Africans traditionally believe in a personalistic 'High God' but that illnesses that are attributed to Him are not thought to be consciously caused, i.e. they 'just happen' and are therefore naturalistic rather than personalistic. In what follows I will briefly consider how what I have said above relates to this distinction before going on to present some conversations in which the role of god and the ancestors in illness causation is discussed.[1]

All the illnesses in which witchcraft is implicated appear to fall in the category of illnesses caused by people. But do the people themselves see illness causation in terms of this distinction, and, if so, is it only the illnesses caused by witches that make up the category of illnesses caused by people?

Shortly after the discussion with Tangwa and Lawrence above, I raised the same issue with Mathias and Fred.

[7.2] 1. 'What's *yang gee*?' I asked.
   2. 'That's sickness which has been caused by somebody,' Mathias answered.
   3. 'Caused how?' I asked.
   4. 'Caused by witchcraft,' Fred said.
   5. 'It's not always through witchcraft,' Mathias added. 'I can bury some medicine so that when you pass over it you get sick.'
   6. 'So if you make someone sick through medicine then you don't call it witchcraft?' I asked.
   7. 'No, it's not witchcraft,' Mathias responded.
   8. 'But then how do you make somebody sick through witchcraft?'

---

1. When I use the word "god" I only use a capital G when it explicitly and unambiguously refers to the Christian God. In all other cases I use a lower case *g*.

I asked.
9. 'That's best known to those who have the witchcraft in them,' Fred said, shrugging.
10. 'But ordinary people must have some idea?'
11. 'It is generally believed that if you are not a witch you are not easily effected by them,' Mathias said.

When I asked Mathias and Fred about *yang gee* Fred mentioned witchcraft, though Mathias immediately added that it includes illness caused by medicine. He agreed with Lawrence that the use of medicine to cause illness is not referred to as witchcraft (6–7). Mathias remarked that people believe that witches can only affect other witches (11). This would imply that the victims of witchcraft are by definition themselves witches. I will come back to this later when I examine the notion of personal responsibility (see pp. 197–9 and pp. 231–2).

I also raised this distinction explicitly in a discussion with Lawrence.

[7.3] 1. 'In connection with the causes of illness, do people make a distinction between sicknesses which are natural and sicknesses which are caused supernaturally?' I asked.
2. 'Mmmmm...well,' Lawrence hesitated. 'Their distinction is just when the sickness is hard to treat.'
3. 'Hard to treat?' I prompted.
4. 'Yes, then they start to make distinctions.'
5. 'What kind of distinctions?'
6. 'Well, if I have leg pains and I have been treating them for three months and my legs are still not well then I will go to *ngwɛɛ sɛng* [a diviner]. He will say that my legs have been made like that by people. From there I will start thinking that the sickness was caused by somebody.'
7. 'Would that be somebody who is still living?' I asked, wondering whether he was referring to witches or ancestors.
8. 'Yes, somebody who is still alive.'
9. 'Would it never be caused by someone who is dead?'
10. 'You mean like my father or mother?'
11. 'Yes.'
12. 'Yes, some people say that. They say that there was something in the compound which you should have done before your father died. So after he is dead he will be crying that it hasn't been done.

Then you will be attacked by sickness.'
13. 'What kind of things haven't been done?'
14. 'It could be that you were supposed to do some traditional things when he was still alive and you didn't do them. So when he's dead he'll be crying that he didn't get his fowl. Then you go to *ngwɛɛ sɛng* and take a fowl and stand on the grave and say all those things, as if you have made a vow, then you give the fowl and the sickness will stop.'
15. 'Are there any other things like that which can cause sickness?'
16. 'I can only think of, for example, if you have a farm and somebody comes and says that the farm belongs to him, then later that man can cause you to have sickness.'
17. 'Through witchcraft?'
18. 'Yes.'
19. 'Do people also think that sicknesses are caused by god?'
20. 'Yes, the type of sickness which people think is caused by god is easily treated.'
21. 'What kind of sickness is that?'
22. 'Like if I have leg pains and I can't walk and they carry me to a traditional doctor, and he starts treating me and after a week I am well, then I will say that sickness was caused by god. That's because it was easily treated.'
23. 'So if you get sick and you take medicine and get better then you think it comes from god?'
24. 'Yes.'
25. 'What about when you get a serious illness and die?'
26. 'If you are not cured then many people will say that it has been caused by somebody.'
27. 'Why do people say that illnesses which cure easily are caused by god?'
28. 'Because if it's caused by somebody you can't treat it easily.'

The distinction Lawrence made in this conversation is the same as that described in much of the medical ethnography of Africa, between illnesses caused by people, illnesses caused by the ancestors and illnesses of god/natural illnesses. It has always struck me as strange that illnesses which are placed in the same category are described as 'natural' and as 'coming from god', expressions which would appear to suggest very different kinds of cause. If a disease occurs 'naturally' then how can it be caused by a personalistic supreme being? And why should God want to cause simple ailments which are easily cured? Illnesses which people referred to in English as 'natural' or as 'coming from god' are called *byang nyvu* (singular *yang nyvu*) in Limbum. At this point I thought it was necessary to find out exactly what people meant when they talked about *nyvu*.

Illnesses Which Come From *Nyvu*

I usually questioned Lawrence or Tobias about a new topic to achieve some general idea of the related issues before discussing it more systematically with them and with other informants. I started my enquiries about *nyvu* by sounding out Lawrence.

[7.4] 1. 'What Limbum word do you use for god?'
     2. 'We say *nyvu*.'
     3. 'Are there different kinds of *nyvu*?'
     4. 'Yes.'
     5. 'Can they cause sickness?'
     6. 'Well, the traditional gods cause a lot of sickness. Any of them. When people know which god it is and they take a fowl and sacrifice it then the sickness stops that same evening.'
     7. 'If people are sick and they go to the hospital for treatment do they still think that it's caused by god?'
     8. 'Yes, if it's cured fast.'
     9. 'Why do these gods cause sickness?'
    10. 'Because, in Limbum we have *nyvu ro*, which is the god of water. Now if you go to a water source and you are just digging and spoiling it and the quarter head says it's god's place but you just continue digging then the gods of the water will cause you to get sick.'
    11. 'It's a sort of punishment?'
    12. 'Yes.'
    13. 'And if I'm just sitting here and I get sick, like you did yesterday with that fever, is that also caused by god?'
    14. 'Yes, I must have done something somewhere.'
    15. 'So you can't just get sick for no reason?'
    16. 'That is how it was traditionally. But these days young fellows believe that you can be running or working and then get backache because of that. Or you can travel under the hot sun and get headache. But in olden times if someone was travelling and

became sick then they said that he had travelled in a bad place. Or if a mother had killed and burned one of those green frogs, which you're not supposed to do, then because of that her child would become sick.'

17. 'But if god makes you sick because you did something wrong and you go to hospital and get medicine and are cured then how will you know that you are being punished for doing something wrong?'

18. 'Young people don't care about that. If I get sick in Ndu and I go to Douala and get treated then I will be less worried about coming back to Ndu to repair what I have done wrong. But in those days people didn't travel like that, they just stayed in their village, so when they were sick they knew that it was caused by this.'

19. 'When people get sick do they always first think that it is caused by god and only start thinking of things like witchcraft when they don't get better?'

20. 'Yes.'

21. 'Do people ever suspect witchcraft when they first become sick?'

22. 'No.'

Lawrence always insisted that the Wimbum were traditionally polytheistic and that monotheism had been introduced by the Christian missionaries. So when I explicitly asked him about *nyvu* (pl. *mnyvu*) he unvaryingly claimed that the term did not refer to a supreme being or 'High God' but to various lesser gods or deities, which he referred to as 'traditional gods'. In this conversation he only mentions *nyvu ro*, which he translates as 'god of water' (*ro* = stream), but on other occasions he told me of many more, such as *nyvu kop* (*kop* = forest), *nyvu la'* (*la'* = compound), *nyvu ngong* (*ngong* = land, world), *nyvu nse* (*nse* = ground), etc.

In the foregoing conversation he seemed to view these *mnyvu* as personalistic agents who consciously intervene in human affairs with the aim of maintaining the traditional order. If a person violates some norm or custom then the *mnyvu* can cause illness as a warning or punishment. He gave an example of *nyvu ro* causing a person to become ill because he has spoiled a water source ([7.4] 10). Once the sufferer becomes aware of the cause of his illness he has to sacrifice a fowl to the *nyvu* involved and he will recover almost immediately (6).

But what if, for no apparent reason, a person becomes ill with some minor ailment, which people call *yang nyvu* in Limbum and 'natural illness' or 'illness of god' in English? In our discussion I mentioned an acute fever which had kept Lawrence bedridden the previous day (13), and he replied that he 'must have done something somewhere' (14), in other words he was not ill for no reason, but was being punished for some wrong which he had (perhaps unwittingly) committed. He went on to say that, traditionally, all illness had a reason. And when he spoke of 'reasons' he meant the violation of some traditional rule, such as killing certain kinds of animals (16), which is also considered to be a form of *bfaa*.

This implies that people traditionally attribute *all* illness to personalistic causes: they are caused by people through medicines or witchcraft or by the *mnyvu* as punishment for violations of tradition. According to Lawrence the really naturalistic explanations of minor ailments (walking in the hot sun causing headache or hard work causing backache) are relatively recent introductions to the traditional system (16). The modern world not only provides new explanations of illness which enable 'young fellows' to violate traditional norms or neglect their obligations in the village, it also provides them with an alternative health-care system which treats minor ailments effectively without asking any awkward questions. The modern system also enables them to leave the village and work in the plantations or the city, thus reducing their material dependence on the village and the influence of the elders and the traditional system of social control on their actions (18).[2]

It was some months before Lawrence and I had another discussion about *yang nyvu*.

[7.5] 1. 'The natural sicknesses which people say are caused by god, how do they refer to them in Limbum?'
  2. 'They say a *yang nyvu*.'
  3. 'So most sicknesses must come from god?'
  4. 'Yes, and when they say *yang nyvu*, then it is people who cause that sickness through god. God doesn't cause sickness.' Lawrence paused. 'So when I think about it I don't know exactly

---

2. See in this connection Geschiere's description of the way in which the Maka villagers in southern Cameroon attempt to maintain the influence of traditional reciprocal values on urban *evolués* through the use of *djambe* (witchcraft) (Geschiere 1988).

what they mean when they say *yang nyvu.'*
5. 'How do you mean: people cause sickness through god?'
6. 'I mean the elders of the compound...' he hesitated. 'If you are sick, like me when I broke my leg, then they will say: It's going to be well, it's god's sickness. Now, when you go deeply into it it's not the heavenly father, because they don't believe in that traditionally. They have *nyvu ro, nyvu kop,* etc., and the sickness coming through these gods comes from people. So I don't know exactly what they mean.'
7. 'But how does it come from people?'
8. 'The way I explained.'
9. 'Through witchcraft?'
10. 'Yes.'
11. 'So in the last instance *all* sickness is caused by witchcraft?'
12. 'That's the way I see it. When you give the gift then the sickness is stopped. It is caused by witchcraft through that god.'
13. 'So witches use gods to cause sickness?'
14. 'Yes.'
15. 'So witches must be more powerful than gods?'
16. 'Yes, according to tradition they are more powerful. And with sickness they don't know...let me see...' A long silence followed. 'Yes...er...when they say: this sickness is caused by god, then it's just a casual type of sickness like headache, which bothers you for a couple of days and goes away when you take some tablets. But if it becomes serious, like two or three months, and you treat it but it does not finish, then, if a diviner comes and says it is being caused by god, then they may ask which god and he may say: the god of the land. Then when you give a goat to that god and the sickness stops then it has really been caused by witchcraft.'
17. 'So general headache comes from god?'
18. 'Yes, not from witchcraft.'
19. 'Why does god cause it?'
20. 'It's just a Limbum expression. They say it like that because they don't know the cause. If they don't know the cause then they say it's caused by god. If I have a headache for four days and it finishes then they say it's god's sickness. But if it becomes chronic and lasts for six months then they will start saying a lot of things: that it was caused by the ancestors, or a god, or whatever. So the way I see it there are short illnesses which are treated easily. They are god's sickness. Then the long sickness, which people say is caused by god and is cured if you give a goat, is caused by

the compound heads through a god. Or it's caused by ancestors. That's my idea about it.'

In studying this conversation some of the ambiguity in the meaning of "yang nyvu" becomes apparent. In conversation [7.4] Lawrence imputed personalistic characteristics to the 'traditional gods', the *mnyvu*. In the latter discussion, however, he appeared to interpret "nyvu" differently. He still insisted that the traditional system is polytheistic ([7.5] 6), but when people speak of *yang nyvu* they refer to illness caused by people through god ([7.5] 4–6). As in the previous conversation, he attributed all illness to personalistic causes, but in this conversation he said that in the last instance *all* illness is caused by witchcraft (11–12).

He might have talked to others about the matter after our previous discussion and become convinced that people were behind the illnesses attributed to the *mnyvu*. In extended discussions we had had some months earlier he never once suggested that the *mnyvu* were merely the passive instruments of people (i.e. witches), whereas this time he volunteered the information right at the start of our discussion, but he was confused, and he admitted it (4,6).

His confusion might have stemmed from the ambiguity of "nyvu". This ambiguity emerged as soon as people were forced by my enquiries to talk about the exact meaning of the term "nyvu" rather than simply using it pragmatically in relation to specific occurrences. Early Christian missionaries adopted the Limbum term "nyvu" as a translation of "God", so "nyvu" has come to refer to the Christian God.[3] The term is also used, however, to refer to what Lawrence called the traditional gods: *nyvu ro, nyvu kop,* etc. Finally, when people refer to minor ailments and acute predictable illnesses which respond to treatment, they call them *byang nyvu*, which they translate as 'natural illness' or illness that 'just happens' or 'illness of god'. So, theoretically at least, the word "yang nyvu" may imply very different kinds of cause. It may refer to illness caused by God, illness caused by one of the 'traditional gods' (whether personalistic deities or ultimately witches), or natural illness which just happens, without apparent cause.

Later on in conversation [7.5] Lawrence introduced a distinction between two types of *byang nyvu*. First there are illnesses

---

3. Though some local Christians insist that the Wimbum were traditionally monetheistic, and that "nyvu" has always referred to one supreme God, even before the arrival of the Christian missionaries.

17 Tobias drinking his morning coffee

attributed to the *mnyvu* which are, in fact, inflicted by witches as punishment or warning. These illnesses can be protracted, but as soon as the sufferer realises his mistake, admits his guilt and makes a sacrifice, recovery is immediate. Then there are natural illnesses, simple ailments and illnesses which respond in a predictable way to treatment, and of which people do not know the cause. These are also *byang nyvu*, but this does not imply any conscious intervention, it is 'just a Limbum expression' (16–20). This suggests that the categories illnesses of people/illnesses of god are not mutually exclusive, but that the categories illnesses of people/natural illnesses are. So, the usual grouping together of natural illness and illness of God as though they were the same thing does not apply here.

Are the *Mnyvu* Really Gods or Are They Just People?

By this time I was working regularly with Tobias. We met on two or three mornings a week to drink coffee and discuss the various topics I was working on. When I discussed *nyvu* with him I did not start off by asking him what he believed, because as a serious Catholic he would have told me about the Christian God. I started the conversation by asking him what other people traditionally believed about god.

[7.6] 1. 'What do people traditionally believe about god?'
2. 'People believe that a god exists. In my family we have a house we call *ndap ngong*, it's just like a small church. The *ndap ngong* behind here is the one for the whole quarter. With every season they always come there with food and make sacrifices to the god of the area and the *bkvubshi* [ancestors].'
3. 'Is that god one almighty God, like in Christianity, or is it a lesser god?'
4. 'Well, according to them it's a small god. They have something which is like a symbol of god, in the form of a stone, where they make sacrifices while calling god's name.'
5. 'Is that *nyvu la*' ['god' of the compound]?'
6. '*Nyvu la*' is just a place where the people of that compound gather to install something. They come there to make an oath, that as they live together nobody should steal from the other or chase after the other's wife, etc. They come together in a certain place

18 *Ta ngaa nyvu* in front of the *ndap ngong* in Kieku

and make the laws. Then they kill a fowl in that place. Then each
time the compound head goes to that place to make sacrifices.'

7. 'Does *nyvu la'* refer to the god or the place?'

8. *'Nyvu la'* means the god of that place.'

9. 'So there are different gods?'

10. 'Yes. That *ndap ngong* is where we have *nyvu ngong*, the god of
the earth. *Nyvu la'* is just the god around the compound.'

11. 'Does every *ndap ngong* have its own *nyvu*?'

12. 'Yes, there are four in Tabenken.'

13. 'Does that mean that there are four different *mnyvu ngong*?'

14. 'There are different *mndap ngong* making sacrifices to the same
nyvu ngong. They all believe in *nyvu ngong*. For example, you can
have different Catholic churches in different areas but they still
all pray to the same God. It's just like that.'

15. 'Are the *nyvu la'*, *nyvu kop*, *nyvu ro*, etc. all under the *nyvu
ngong*?'

16. 'They are gods within a certain area. They are different gods.'

17. 'So they are different to *nyvu ngong*?'

18. 'Yes.'

19. 'Is there a hierarchy?'

20. 'Yes, the others are smaller, *nyvu ngong* is the highest. The god
of the compound, god of the stream, god of the farm, etc. are all
under *nyvu ngong*. He is the general god.

21. 'Now when I discuss the causes of illness with people they
often say that sickness comes from god. Does that mean that it is
those gods which cause the sickness?'

22. 'That is what people traditionally believe, that when you are
attacked by sickness it is caused by god. You may go to the
stream and do a wrong thing there, then the *nyvu ro* can cause
you sickness. Or you may do a wrong thing in the forest –
because there are certain things which are traditionally forbidden
in the forest. In this forest behind here you are not allowed to
shoot anything, you are not allowed to cut wood there with a cutlass. If you go there and violate these rules then the *nyvu kop* can
give you sickness. And when they talk about *nyvu kop* it may
mean the people of that forest, the people who own that forest:
the so called *ngaa yɛr lir* [those with eyes] or *ngaa tvu'* [witches]
who are watching that forest, who keep watch over that forest.
When they see you doing a wrong thing there they can give you
sickness. If they give you sickness like that and you go to a diviner then he will say: "What did you do in this forest?" You will

have to bring a fowl and they will kill the fowl and eat it before you are released from your sickness.'

23. 'Is it the *nyvu kop* or the *ngaa tvu'* who make you sick in such cases?'

24. 'The *nyvu kop* can't make you sick. It's the people who are watching the forest.'

25. 'Then what does *nyvu kop* have to do with the sickness?'

26. '*Nyvu kop* has nothing to do with the sickness, it's only those watching the forest who give you the sickness, the wizards watching the forest. With a forest like this there are people watching it, and there's a *nyvu kop* there. Like the *ndap ngong*, there are people there watching it. If you go against the laws the people watching it will give you sickness, not the *nyvu ngong*.'

27. 'But then why do people always say that sickness comes from god...'

28. 'No,' Tobias interjected.

29. '...when it's the *ngaa tvu'* who actually cause it?'

30. 'Definitely *ngaa tvu*,' Tobias emphasised.

31. 'But then why do they say it comes from god?'

32. 'No, it's *ngaa tvu*'. But generally, with other sickness, when you haven't violated any law, you can just have sickness normally. You can have sickness normally, but not caused by god.'

33. 'So if you do something wrong in a forest or near a stream and get sick then it's not *nyvu ro* or *nyvu kop* who cause the sickness...'

34. 'No, it's not the *nyvu ro*....'

35. '...but the *ngaa tvu*'?'

36. 'Yes...I think that the *nyvu la'*, *nyvu ngong*, *nyvu kop* are good gods, but that the people who are guiding these gods, the people who are like the soldiers of these gods, are the ones who give illness, not the *mnyvu* themselves.'

37. 'Do you think that these ideas have changed a lot because of the influence of Christianity?'

38. 'It's tradition, even though it has changed. And even though people are Christians they still attend those places, because they cannot ignore them completely. As a family unit they cannot ignore it. Even though they are Christians. Take the *ndap ngong*. Every year they bring *chop* [food] and *mimbu* [palm wine] and gather there. As a member of that family you have to contribute, even though you are a Christian, otherwise you will be looked upon as a bad man of the compound.'

39. 'So you also contribute?'

40. 'Yes I also contribute. If they want wine or *chop* or fowls you give.'
41. 'Do *you* contribute yourself?'
42. 'Yes.'
43. 'Do you only contribute or do you also believe...?'
44. 'No, I only contribute, I don't believe.'

Tobias, like Lawrence in conversation [7.5], described a plurality of traditional gods, and he only said that one of these gods is higher than the rest, that is that there is a hierarchy, with a 'high god' and various lesser deities, when I pushed him (15, 19). Likewise, as in the conversation with Lawrence, it is not clear what the *mnyvu* really are. They do not appear to be personalistic beings or deities, as I had thought after my first discussion with Lawrence, and although Tobias did say that they cause sickness if you do something wrong, he immediately added that when people talk of *nyvu kop* (*kop* = forest), for example, they really mean the people (*ngaa tvu'*) who 'own' or 'watch' that forest (22). He repeatedly emphasised that the *mnyvu* or 'gods' do not cause illness, only the *ngaa tvu'* (23–36). The terms "nyvu kop", "nyvu ngong", etc. seemed simply to refer to witches (*ngaa tvu'*) who watch over or guard particular areas. Or perhaps to the areas themselves, including their watchers. At one point Tobias said that *nyvu la'* is just a place where the people of that compound gather...' (6). I often heard people say that *nyvu la'* (or *nyvu kop*, *nyvu ro*, etc.) is 'just a place'.

I cannot help having the impression that, like Lawrence, he was moving back and forth between different fields of meaning to which the term "nyvu" is related. Tobias described *nyvu la'* as a place (6) and he said that *nyvu kop* is only people watching the forest (26), but he also described the *nyvu la'*, *nyvu kop*, etc. as 'good gods' (36). He described *nyvu ngong* as being related to the *ndap ngong* in the same way that Catholics worship the same God in different church buildings, suggesting that *nyvu ngong* is like God (14).

When I asked him about illness which people say comes from god (21) Tobias gave the same example as Lawrence: *nyvu ro* or *nyvu kop* cause illness to punish a person for doing something wrong near a stream or in a forest. He also immediately added, as did Lawrence, that when people speak of *nyvu ro, nyvu kop*, etc. they really mean people (*ngaa tvu'*) (22). But when he insisted that *nyvu kop*, etc. play no role in illness causation, and that when they are mentioned in this connection it is really the *ngaa tvu'* who are responsible, he suggested that the terms "nyvu kop", etc. do refer to entities separate from the *ngaa tvu'* (23–36). He left open the possibility of a category of illnesses that happen without any reason, that will happen even if you have done nothing wrong (32).

This conversation revealed Tobias's ambivalence toward 'tradition' and Christianity, or, rather, the dilemma facing him: on the one hand he is a pious Catholic who is supposed to reject 'paganism' and belief in witches. But on the other hand he is a compound head and, as such, is compelled to participate in various activities forbidden by the church, such as the celebrations in the *ndap ngong* which he mentioned (38). If he totally rejects tradition he will come into conflict with those who are dependent on him for traditional services and his authority as compound head may suffer; if he participates in these traditional activities he risks conflict with the church. The response to this dilemma is what the local church authorities call 'neo-paganism' (Njingti et al. 1986).

When I asked Tobias about people's traditional beliefs he enthusiastically expounded on the *mnyvu*, the *ndap ngong*, the *bkvubshi* (ancestors). Hearing him insist that it is not really the *mnyvu* who cause illness but the *ngaa tvu'* I had to conclude that he was honestly telling me what he really thought himself. But when I explicitly asked him (43) he said that he participates but does not believe in the traditions of the *ndap ngong* (44). If he claims that the *mnyvu* (including the *nyvu ngong* of the *ndap ngong*) are really *ngaa tvu'* (as he emphatically did), and if he completely accepts the existence of the *ngaa tvu'* (as he stressed he did in many discussions), how can he participate in the *ndap ngong* while not believing?

This ambivalence is also expressed in his avoidance of the first person singular. I asked 'do *you* think that these ideas have changed...?' (37), and he replied '...even though people are christians *they* still attend...' (38). I asked him 'So *you* also contribute?' (39) and he replied 'If they want wine or chop or fowls *you* give' (40). In many discussions people dropped into the second person or third person plural whenever they were discussing activities or beliefs which were proscribed, or with which (I suspect) they thought I might disagree.

Gods, Witches and Personal Responsibility for Illness

Tobias suggested that we visit Pa Andrew Nfor, who was a good friend of his, and ask him to tell us what he thought about *nyvu*. Pa Andrew was president of the local traditional healers' association and I had already discussed *bfaa* with him (see [4.7]).

[7.7] 1. 'Tell me about *nyvu*,' I said.
2. 'God is god,' Andrew said emphatically, 'and he is there because everybody knows he is there. Everybody knows there is god and he is the living and almighty god. Then the *nyvurka'* is Satan.'
3. 'Is there only one *nyvurka'* or are there many?' I asked.
4. 'There are many, but there is only one god,' Andrew said.
5. 'Then what about *nyvu ro, nyvu kop*, etc.?'
6. 'They are just people. *Nyvu kop* is just the *nyvurka'* in the forest. They are not really gods.'
7. 'So *nyvu kop* is really a person?' I asked.
8. 'Yes,' Andrew said.
9. 'If it is not a person then it could be a place that their grandfathers had used to be there like that, so that when they die the people who know how to transform still go back to that place to renew,' Tobias added.
10. 'Can god also make people sick?' I asked.
11. 'Yes, he can make people sick,' said Andrew.
12. 'For what kind of reason?'
13. 'God created people and he said that they must be sick and must die. He can make a person sick to show his power, so that the person will think about god and realise that there is someone who is higher than him.'
14. 'So when people say *yang nyvu* they mean sickness that is caused by god?' I asked.
15. '*Yang nyvu* is a normal sickness which just comes, but we attribute it to god because he is the almighty. Then there is other sickness which is caused by *mnyvumka'* [sing. *nyvurka'*] and *ngaa tvu'*. Then there are sicknesses caused by yourself.'
16. 'Yourself?'
17. 'If you act evilly, say like a *ngwɛɛ tvu'* travelling somewhere, then you can be affected and you become sick.'
18. 'We were talking about the *mnyvumka'*,' Tobias intervened. 'The witch may want to transform himself and be affected by medicines and become sick. He may pass some medicines which affect him, then when he comes back he falls sick.'
19. 'But then it's not caused by yourself, it's caused by the medi-

cine,' I protested.

20. 'It's caused by the medicine,' Tobias insisted, 'because *you* have gone out like a *nyvurka*'. If you didn't go out you wouldn't have been affected. If you go to steal from the bank and they put wires to cut your hands and they are cut then who has caused it? Are you not the one?'

21. 'But if I become sick how do I know what the cause is?'

22. 'If somebody is sick and his senses tell him that he hasn't done any wrong then he can know that his sickness comes from god. Even if he is dying then he should know that it is god who is calling him,' Andrew said.

23. 'But the man who has transformed himself to go to another place, when he becomes sick he will be afraid, he will suspect that while he was travelling he crossed some medicines,' Tobias added.

24. 'Can *ngaa tvu*' also cause sickness?' I asked.

25. 'Yes,' Andrew said.

26. 'How do they do that?'

27. 'They have their ways. They can cause you to be sick and you won't know what has caused it.'

28. 'If I get sick how will I know whether it is being caused by *ngaa tvu*' or god or whatever?'

29. 'If you are sick and it is caused by *ngwɛɛ tvu*' then you can go to a diviner and he will tell you that it is caused by *ngwɛɛ tvu*',' Andrew explained.

30. 'And the *ngaa tvu*' will always try to trap you before they make you ill,' Tobias added. 'For instance, you are in a compound but you are not a compound head. You have a daughter and she is to get married. Now the tradition is that you cannot be the one to drink the first *mimbu* [palm wine]. The compound head has to drink the first *mimbu*. But if *ngaa tvu*' want to make you sick then they will watch and if you dare to drink the first *mimbu* then they will give you the sickness. They take your mistake and use their power and cause you to be sick.'

31. 'Can they only cause you to be sick if you make a mistake?' I asked.

32. 'Yes,' said Tobias.

33. 'So if you don't make any mistake they can't make you sick?'

34. 'No,' Tobias replied, 'then they can't make you sick. They always follow in your footsteps and wait for you to make a mistake before they can cause you to be sick.'

35. 'So if I never make mistakes then there is no witch who can make me sick?'
36. 'There are some who can make you sick even if you haven't made any mistake, but such illness will not affect you. It only affects you very lightly. It won't be serious,' Andrew said.
37. 'Does that mean that if I am seriously ill as a result of witchcraft then I must have made some mistake?' I asked.
38. 'If you are seriously sick as a result of witchcraft then it must be that you have violated the laws of the compound. When you go to a diviner he will tell you to give something because you have violated the rules. Then when you give it and apologise for doing wrong you will be well.'
39. 'If you violate the rules of the compound and you become sick, who exactly is it who is making you sick?'
40. 'Your relatives in your compound.'

Andrew started somewhat differently compared to Lawrence and Tobias, by describing *nyvu* as the 'living and almighty god' and introducing *nyvurka'* as Satan (2). He said that there is only one god (4) and his interpretation of *nyvu* is in a Christian idiom. This is probably a result of his own religious background, but the contrast between his description and those of Tobias and Lawrence might also have been a result of my initial questions, because Tobias is, after all, as devout a Catholic as Andrew. I asked Lawrence whether there were different kinds of *nyvu* ([7.4] 3), (thus leaving the way open for him, as a self-confessed pagan, to elaborate on 'traditional religion') and I asked Tobias to tell me what people traditionally believed about god (thus effectively preventing him from telling me what he thought, or thought he was supposed to think, as a Christian). On the other hand, I simply asked Andrew to tell me about god. Tobias told me what he thought other people traditionally believed rather that what he himself believed (or perhaps they were his own ideas disguised as general opinion): if I had opened the discussion with him with a more open question his remarks may have resembled Andrew's more closely. Indeed, Andrew's answers may have been different if I had been with Lawrence rather than Tobias.

Andrew agreed with Lawrence and Tobias on the nature of the *mnyvu* by saying that they are 'just people' (6). Tobias added that 'If it is not a person then it could be a place...' (9).

Andrew also had another version of the role of god in causing illness. He said that god consciously causes illness simply to demonstrate his superiority and his power over people. He distinguished this from *yang nyvu*, though, which he described as 'normal sickness which just comes' (15). The distinction he made was similar to that made by Lawrence in conversation [7.5] between two types of illness which can be said to come from *nyvu*: natural illness which just happens without apparent cause and illness which is consciously caused by a personalistic God. His description differed from Lawrence's in that he seemed to be referring to the Christian God rather than the 'traditional gods'.

In addition to god, Andrew also mentioned *ngaa tvu'* and *mnyvumka'* as causes of sickness, and he said that the afflicted may themselves be responsible for causing their own illness ([7.7] 15), which brings us back to the theme that has already been mentioned a number of times: personal responsibility. Andrew said that a witch may go out (for some evil purpose) and become ill (17). Tobias was more specific, saying that a *nyvurka'* may be affected by protective anti-witchcraft medicines with which he has come into contact (18). When I suggested that the illness is therefore not caused by the person himself but by the medicines, or those who placed the medicines (19), Tobias disagreed and put the blame fully on the person himself. A person who goes out with the intention of doing something wrong is responsible for the harm that comes to him as a result of his actions: 'If you go to steal from the bank and they put wires to cut your hands and they are cut then who has caused it? Are you not the one?' (20).

Andrew said that people are aware of the wrong they have done and if they know they have not done anything wrong then they can be sure that their illness is a test by god or simply natural illness (22, see also 15), and Tobias added that the bad witch will always have a guilty conscience and suspect that he has been hit by protective medicines when he becomes ill (23). So, if you have done something wrong and you become ill then you are personally responsible for your illness, and if you have not done anything wrong then your illness must be natural (*yang nyvu*), and therefore mild or easily treated. A diviner will probably have the last say in attributing responsibility, though someone with a guilty conscience will hesitate before consulting one, for fear of being exposed.

Tobias and Andrew seemed to have forgotten that the *ngaa*

tvu' (witches) can also cause illness by providing relatives to their cannibalistic societies or by their visits to *ntaa tvu'*. Previously, when I was specifically enquiring about *tvu'* as a cause of illness, and particularly about the role of cannibalism and witch markets, people attributed almost all illness to the evil activities of this kind of witch. In the context of these later discussions about *nyvu*, though, they attributed most illness to *nyvu* (whatever that may be), and tended to emphasise the moral responsibility of the victim himself. In the conversation above I tried to bring the discussion back to the question of the *ngaa tvu'* (witches) causing innocent people illness through their evil activities (24, 26).

Tobias and Andrew spoke of the cause of illness primarily in personalistic terms: it is caused either consciously by god as a test of faith, or through witchcraft, either because the victim himself is an evil witch or because he is being punished by *ngaa tvu'* in the compound (i.e. elders) for breaking some rule. Tobias said that the witches (compound elders) 'will always try to trap you before they make you ill' ([7.7] 30). If you have not done anything wrong then they cannot make you sick. 'They always follow in your footsteps and wait for you to make a mistake before they can cause you to be sick' ([7.7] 34). This also applies to the illnesses said to be caused by the *mnyvu*. If you violate a certain stream or forest then you are given sickness as punishment by the *mnyvu*, who are in fact not gods but 'those who own the forest' ([7.6] 22) or 'those watching the forest' ([7.6] 26).

They said that the *ngaa tvu'* can only make a person sick (except perhaps for minor ailments) if he has done something wrong. In the illnesses in which god does not play a role, personal moral responsibility is central. According to Fred and Mathias the person afflicted by *bfaa* was being warned or punished because he had done something wrong ([4.10] 9, 11, 23–5), and Mathias said that if you are not a witch yourself then you cannot easily be affected by them ([7.2] 11). Lawrence also said that when he had a fever he 'must have done something somewhere' otherwise he would not have become ill ([7.4] 13–16). (See in this connection the discussion of the significance of remark 'there must have been something', in Chapter 4).

It is not clear whether people also include illness caused by cannibalism in this latter category, which would imply that these witches can only capture and eat someone who has himself done something wrong, though I suspect that they do not.

Illnesses can therefore be divided into two general causal categories: *byang nyvu* and *byang gee*. *Byang nyvu* include illnesses with no cause, natural illnesses which 'just happen', and illnesses inflicted by the *mnyvu*, the traditional gods. *Byang gee* include illnesses caused by cannibalism, self-inflicted illness, etc. (caused directly by witches) and illness caused by the the *mnyvu* (caused indirectly by witches hiding behind the traditional gods). Lawrence's description of different kinds of cause ([7.4], [7.5]) leads to a similar classification. *Byang gee* are all caused by people, but they differ both in the way in which they are inflicted and the reasons for the affliction. The illnesses that are directly caused by the witches are unjustified, destructive and motivated by evil and illegitimate intentions, such as greed and jealousy. Those that are indirectly caused, through the *mnyvu*, are justified because they are constructive and motivated by a legitimate concern to uphold traditional norms and values. The former are caused by evil witches, the latter by compound elders (who are also *ngaa tvu'*).

In a particular case of acute illness that does not respond to treatment, or chronic illness, relatives of the sick person will consult diviners and it is they who will decide on the ultimate cause of the affliction. This implies that it is the diviners who decide where the moral responsibility lies, who, that is, is to blame for the illness. They will decide whether the person is ill because he violated tradition, is an evil witch who has fallen into a trap of powerful protective medicines, has been wounded while escaping from the witch market (*ntaa tvu'*), or been beaten by a more powerful rival, or whether the sufferer is merely an innocent victim of evil witches or has perhaps been tied as a goat awaiting slaughter for a cannibalistic banquet. It is only in the last case that the victim would appear to be without blame, and in that case divination will point out those who are responsible.

He May Let You Carry the Cross to Test Your Belief

Like Tobias, my neighbour, Fai Gabriel, was also a devout Catholic and compound head. I often called in to see him or stopped to chat as I passed his compound. One day I asked him whether he could tell me about various aspects of 'tradition'. He agreed but asked me, as usual, to be more specific so that he could think about the matter beforehand and prepare. I said I wanted to know what Wimbum traditional religion was like before Christianity. He said he would think about the matter and I arranged to call in a few days later.

When I arrived he was waiting for me in his sitting-room with a calabash of palm wine and two glasses.

[7.8]　1.　'So how shall we begin?' Fai Gabriel asked once I was seated.

2.　'Maybe you can tell me what the Wimbum traditionally believe happens to somebody when he dies,' I suggested.

3.　He reflected for a moment. 'Most people believe that if a person dies it is the will of god. That's how they say it. Even what you witnessed today,' he said, referring to the man who had fallen into the stream and drowned after drinking too much palm wine. 'We say it's through his own carelessness, but people will say that if god didn't want him to die he wouldn't have taken so much drink and fallen into the stream. They say it was the time that god wanted him to die in that way. There are different ways of dying. You have bad deaths and you have good ones.'

4.　'Is this a bad one?'

5.　'Yes, it's a bad one. The bad one is that you die yourself. Nobody knows how you started before you died. In that case it will look like witchcraft. People will say that it was someone in the compound, or he was trying to demand something from somebody, or he wanted something, then the other person opposed him, being the same witchman, and pushed him in that way.'

6.　'Is that different to when people say that he died because god wanted it? Because at first you said that when someone dies it it's because god wanted it.'

7.　'Yes, they say it like that, they say it is the will of people. Now when you follow it deeply they will tell you it is god who directed the other witchmen to get this man. If god wants you to die you will not just die directly. He will send me to push you or get you by the neck.'

8.　'So if god doesn't want you to die then a witch can't kill you?'

9.　'They will say it is the will of god, but it comes through somebody, so that you die in that way. But people know that if a man dies at the correct time, taken by god, it should be a man of age. If you die old then people will say it is your time, that god has called you to come...' He fell silent and gazed into his glass. 'Originally we were all pagans. We never knew there was god. We believed that these *bkvubshi* [ancestors] were god... Even right

19 Fai Gabriel on Good Friday

now they still deal with them, except a few who know very well about god...'

10. 'Don't people also speak about lesser gods, like *nyvu kop* and *nyvu ro*?

11. 'Yes, you have *nyvu ro, nyvu kop, nyvu la'*. Now these *mnyvu* are the gods of certain areas. So when you commit a crime on the farm, like if you kill a crab or snake with no face, you have committed a crime. Then you have to bring a chicken to the man who owns that land, so that he will talk to the *nyvu la'* [*la'* = compound] and say that you have made a mistake by killing that animal... Then you will bring a fowl. It will be taken to that person, the owner of the land (*Ta ngaa nyvu*) and he will say to the god of that area: this is what the person has done. So there is not only one *nyvu*, there are different ones in different areas. You have *nyvu ngong*, which is the god of a whole area, like the village. Then there are other ones belonging to certain sections.'

12. 'So before the church came people believed in different gods?'

13. 'Yes. These *bkvubshi* [ancestors], and *nyvu ro* and *nyvu nkvù* [*nkvù* = farm], etc. You will see those stones,' he said, referring to the graves of his ancestors, in a grove somewhere in Kieku quarter, which he had promised to show me. 'It shows that before Christianity we never knew that there was only one god. They made those things to be gods. The god of the family. My grandfather really believed in that, otherwise you would not be able to see those stones.'

14. 'Do you accept the existence of the *bkvubshi* and the *mnyvu*, as well as that of god?'

15. 'I don't accept them. I know there is only one god. As a catechumen to a Christian I learned these things.'

16. 'Do you think the *bkvubshi* are there, or not?'

17. 'Well they are there, because when you die your soul remains. god made you to serve him, to love him in this world and to be happy with him forever in the next... So I believe that those *bkvubshi* are there with god...because their souls, they may be in purgatory or limbo, or in heaven, but their souls are alive. Their souls may be suffering or they may be enjoying.'

18. 'Do the *mnyvu* also exist?'

19. 'They live. When you check properly you see that the *mnyvu* are the gathering of *bkvubshi*.'

20. 'What do you mean, gathering?'

21. 'There are so many *bkvubshi*. With *nyvu la'* you have *bkvubshi*

from this compound, and this one and that one. The *bkvubshi* belong to a certain area. These *bkvubshi* make the *mnyvu* of that area. That is what I think.'

22. 'Does that also apply to *nyvu ro, nyvu kop*, etc.?'
23. 'Yes, if you have a stream down there and one up here then the *nyvu* from down there can't come and stay up here. It's just the gathering of *bkvubshi* from that area. It may be that a powerful section of those *bkvubshi* are living in that stream, or that *kop* [forest].'
24. 'Can god also cause sickness?'
25. 'Yes...the cross, the cross of Jesus Christ, people also bear that cross. There was no fault in him, in Jesus, but he bears the fault of people, to save them, to save them from hell. That is why he was crucified... Now there are many ways for people to carry this cross... He may let you to carry a cross, just to try you and see, to test whether your belief is sound or whether you are just temporary... You know, some people get sick and become well. Some are at the point of death but they never go to *ngambe* [diviner]. They believe there is only one god, that this sickness is caused by god and they shall be well. Even if they die they will be with god in paradise. They will still have that belief. A person may be a few minutes from death and suddenly become well. Then he is still a Christian. He never said there was no god. When such sickness is caused by god he is trying to see whether you are really a Christian, whether you are really bearing that cross to follow him... So there are some sicknesses that are caused by god through Christianity. God is testing them to see whether their belief is still firm.'
26. 'Do you think he also sends sickness to punish people?'
27. 'Yes, that's what I am saying. He can send sickness to punish people, whether you know there is a god or not. In addition to that, people can cause sickness, I think you know that, huh?'
28. 'You mean through witchcraft?'
29. 'No, not through witchcraft. Somebody could poison your food so that it causes sickness. Sometimes you may feel that it is caused by god, but meanwhile it is caused by your enemies...'

The tape recorder on the table between us clicked off because it had reached the end of the tape. I took a new tape out of my bag and replaced it. When I had turned it on again Fai Gabriel resumed.

'In the first place sickness is caused by carelessness, or because you are not financially fit [because of poverty], or through your enemies. Maybe your enemy has no means to kill you directly, so he will make poison that will work gradually.'

30. 'Can it be caused by witchcraft?'
31. 'I don't believe in that.'
32. 'But people generally do believe in it?'
33. 'Yes, they believe in it. But I don't believe in it because fault causes sickness. When you are at fault your mind is not steady, you are always fearful... If someone steals your radio and later he knocks his toe he will think it is caused by you. He has a guilty conscience and feels it was caused by you. He may fall sick and someone will ask: "What have you taken?" and he will say: "I took something from the doctor." That type of act is bad, it can cause you to be ill. Already when you are committing the act you are already a sick person, in mind and movement. So I think that most of this sickness, when they say it is caused by somebody, is caused by your own guilty conscience. Here they say that somebody is a witch because he is never sick. But I think he is a straightforward person, he has no fault. They may want to make you sick by putting leaves [harmful medicines] in the ground, but it will not work because you have no fault in you. Then they will begin to say you are a witch. But I think that most sickness comes because people invite it through their own faults.'

Fai Gabriel spoke about the role of god in illness causation. A few days previously a man had disappeared after spending an evening drinking in the market (this incident is described in Chapter 4). Shortly before I spoke to Fai Gabriel his body had been found in a stream along the path to his house. He had drowned, apparently after falling from a narrow bridge. Fai Gabriel mentioned this death and said that the man would not have died if god had not wanted him to (3). But he also suggested that, because it was a bad death (people will say that) witchcraft was involved. More specifically, that the man may have been a witch himself and come into conflict with other witches who turned out to be stronger and 'pushed him in that way' (5).

I failed to see how his death could have been the result of witchcraft and at the same time the will of god (6). Fai Gabriel thought that a person cannot die unless it is the will of god. If someone dies 'at the correct time', if he is 'a man of age' who has been 'taken by god' then it is a good death (9). A bad death is both the will of God and the will of people (did he mean witches?). God cannot kill directly but sends witches to kill the person (7). It was not clear to me whether this was what Fai Gabriel himself thought or whether he was just reporting what he believed others thought. When I asked him explicitly he said that he did not believe in witchcraft (30–1), but what do such explicit denials mean? Do they mean that he 'really' did not 'believe', that is to say that he found the possibility that witches exist unthinkable, or do they simply mean that he did not 'believe' in this particular context, i.e. in regard to this problem at this point in this discussion? Or was he perhaps afraid of affirming something which was contrary to his self-image as a Christian (cf. Tobias's dilemma in [7.6])?

Fai Gabriel agreed with Lawrence that the Wimbum were, by tradition, polytheistic. He mentioned the various *mnyvu* and related them to the punishment of abominations connected to the killing of certain animals (11), as had Lawrence ([7.4] 16), which is also a form of *bfaa*.

Fai Gabriel's own attitude to the *mnyvu* and the *bkvubshi* (ancestors) was ambivalent. He said that he did not accept the existence of the *mnyvu* and the *bkvubshi* (15), but this was another highly equivocal, even if categorical statement, as *mnyvu* and *bkvubshi* became mixed up with Catholic conceptions of souls and saints. He saw the *bkvubshi* as souls in heaven ('I believe that those *bkvubshi* are there with god...') or in limbo or purgatory (17), and the *mnyvu* as gatherings of *bkvubshi* (19, 23). All of which infers that he did think that both the *mnyvu* and the *bkvubshi* exist.

When I moved on to the topic of illness his remarks tended to agree with those of Andrew that it can be caused by god to test people's faith (24–7). But he clearly saw personal responsibility and guilt as the most important cause of illness. Even harmful medicines will have no effect on the person with a clear conscience (33).

Are the Wimbum Traditionally Atheists?

I started this chapter with the question: what do people mean when they talk about *nyvu*? The answer seems to be, at least to some extent, it all depends on who you talk to, what you talk about and how you put your questions.

As I have mentioned, early missionaries adopted the term "nyvu" to refer to the Christian God and local people have in turn adopted this usage. They also use the term "nyvu" to refer to *nyvu ro, nyvu kop, nyvu ngong,* etc., those Lawrence called the 'traditional gods'. Are these *mnyvu* personalistic gods or deities who act consciously (Lawrence [7.4]), passive beings or entities which are 'used' by witches (Lawrence [7.5]), groups of *ngaa tvu'* (witches) guarding certain places against violations of tradition (Tobias [7.6] 22), the places themselves (Tobias [7.6] 6, [7.7] 9), or gatherings of *bkvubshi* (ancestors) who reside in certain places (Fai Gabriel [7.8] 19, 23)? And how do these *mnyvu* relate to the illnesses which are called *byang nyvu* and which people say are natural and just happen without any cause?

Are the Wimbum 'traditionally' polytheistic? Lawrence rejected the idea of God as having been introduced by the Christian missionaries and insisted that the Wimbum traditionally believed in many gods. This view was echoed by Tobias and Fai Gabriel, both Catholics, who said that monotheism was introduced by the missionaries. Analysing the position of those who say that the Wimbum are traditionally polytheistic, and that the traditional 'gods', the *mnyvu*, are really only people (witches), the implication would seem to be that the Wimbum are in fact traditionally atheistic, the 'gods' being reduced, in the last instance, to the activities of people. But there are also those, such as Pa Andrew, who insist that the Wimbum have always been monotheistic. Such people distinguish between one traditional *nyvu*, who is simply the Christian God under another name, and the *mnyvu*, who are really just people (witches).

People use the term "nyvu" when referring to certain kinds of illness, which they call *yang nyvu*. In the conversations presented above there appear to be three ways in which people used the term "nyvu" in relation to illness causation: (1) illness caused by God as a test of faith, (2) illness caused by the *mnyvu* (however defined) as punishment and (3) illness that just happens and has no cause. Andrew and Fai Gabriel said that God causes illness to test his followers' faith, others, such as Pa TaKwi, whom I have not quoted in this regard, disagreed and said that God never causes illness because he is good. Lawrence, Tobias and Andrew said that the *mnyvu* cause illness as punishment, but they also said that this illness is really caused indirectly by witches. 'Natural' illnesses are not 'caused' by *nyvu*, they just happen,

20 Open-air Mass in Tabenken

21 Traditional dances have been integrated into church services

though they are referred to as *byang nyvu*. In fact, as far as I can
tell, when people are talking about illness without my questioning them about the meaning of "nyvu" they only use the term
"yang nyvu" to refer to minor illnesses which happen without
apparent cause – natural illnesses. It is only when they start to
reflect on the meaning of the term "nyvu" in *yang nyvu* because I
question them and force them to speculate that they start to talk
about the involvement of the *mnyvu* and God in *yang nyvu*.

Lawrence gave "nyvu" as an initial Limbum translation of
"god", and perhaps I placed more emphasis on this translation
than on other possibilities which were suggested, causing a lot of
confusion and speculation. The fact that people translated "yang
nyvu" as natural illness suggests that "nature" may be a more
accurate translation of "nyvu" than "god", at least in this connection. The Oxford English Dictionary gives the following meanings of "nature": 'Vital force or functions or needs... Physical
power causing phenomena of material world, these phenomena
as a whole...' I am not sure whether in this instance we should
interpret *nyvu* as an impersonal process or whether we should
see it more pantheistically, with *nyvu* being identified with, and
being the essence of, natural forces and substances. At any rate, a
more 'natural' interpretation of "nyvu" would clear up much of
the ambiguity in the way people speak about *nyvu kop, nyvu ro*,
etc. and make the way in which people talk about *yang nyvu*
much more coherent.[4]

Interpreting "nyvu" as nature rather than as god is also supported by the way in which people use the term in other contexts.
In Tabenken most women breast feed their infants for at least a
year and usually for almost two years. Bottle feeding is almost
unknown, and women said that they would not use formula
foods even if they could afford them because breast milk was
much better. When I asked them why they thought that breast
milk was better they said, in Limbum, that it was because it 'came
from *nyvu*'. When they spoke in English they either said that it
was 'natural' or that it 'came from god'.

I can only speculate on what made the early missionaries
decide to use "nyvu" as a translation for "God", but I suspect
that, on hearing of sacrifices to *nyvu ngong* (*ngong* = land, world)

---

4. This is related to the suggestion I made earlier, that it is possible to interpret the way is
which people speak about *nyvu* in such a way that they seem to be basically atheistic.

in the *ndap ngong* (= house of the land) they probably interpreted this as a pagan analogy to Christian ritual: the *ndap ngong* was a pagan 'church' and *nyvu ngong* to whom the sacrifices were made was a pagan god.

Perhaps Christian missionaries have been too keen to interpret secular indigenous customs as 'worship' (just as anthropologists often over-enthusiastically see symbols in ordinary objects and tend to interpret everyday behaviour as symbolic or ritual). One day I was attending the death celebration of a member of the warrior society *Mfu'*. The man had been buried in the yard of his compound. A raffia–bamboo pole had been driven into the ground next to the grave and his cap, cutlass and a framed photo had been hung on it. The members of *Mfu'* sat on wooden benches that had been placed on each side of the grave site forming a square around the pole. Only *Mfu'* members could sit there and drink palm wine, and they had to be wearing caps and carrying cutlasses. Non-members and relatives were seated beyond this inner square and they were strictly forbidden from entering it. The celebration had been going on for some time when Father John, the (European) parish priest arrived in search of one of his workers. He strode through the crowd and to everyone's surprise entered the inner square. He stopped in front of the pole and looked around until his eye fell on me. 'Huh,' he said, 'don't tell me that you also participate in this pagan worship of the dead?' Those present exchanged meaningful glances and could scarcely conceal smiles of amusement. It did not occur to Father John that we might simply be sitting and drinking and chatting about the deceased, just as one might do after a funeral in Europe, sitting in the deceased's lounge, drinking coffee with his friends and relatives, with his picture on the mantlepiece.

As I have mentioned, the meanings of key terms are also partially dependent on their place in the conversation, how they are introduced and the nature of the discussion which preceded or led up to their introduction. In discussion [7.8] with Fai Gabriel, when the term "bkvubshi" (ancestors) was used in the context of my enquiries about tradition he said that he did not believe in them, but when it was used again in relation to heaven and God he said he did believe in them.

I had a conversation about illness with another villager who told me that certain illnesses were caused by god as punishment. Later, during the same conversation we talked about religion and the church. I asked him again whether god could cause illness as punishment and he denied this emphatically saying that god could not do such a thing because he was good.

At the start of the conversation with Tobias [7.6] I purposely asked him what people *traditionally* believe about god. If I had simply asked him what *he* thought about god he would, being a devout Catholic, probably have given me an exposition of Catholic doctrine, no matter what he actually thought himself. In the discussion with Pa Andrew I simply asked him to tell me about *nyvu*, and he started telling me about the 'living and almighty god' and 'satan' ([7.7] 2). In these conversations, as indeed in all the conversations presented in this study, it was impossible to be sure whether the person I was talking to was telling me what he himself thought, what he thought other people thought, what he thought I wanted to hear, what he thought that I thought he should think, whether he was just pulling my leg, or whether there was something of all of these possibilities in what he said.

Given my assumption that data about genuine indigenous culture cannot be simply gathered, but that knowledge was produced between me and my interlocutors in an ongoing praxis, does it matter? Does such indeterminacy mean that what they told me is less 'genuine' or not really 'tradition'? And if so, what *is* genuine and what *is* tradition? Those who speak of 'the invention of tradition' seem to assume that it is possible to distinguish between genuine and invented traditions (Hobsbawm and Ranger 1983). Is what Tobias and others told me no longer genuine tradition because it was fluid and changed even while we spoke? Tobias did not think so. 'It's tradition, even though it has changed,' he said ([7.6] 38), and I tend to agree with him. The Wimbum (and of course not only the Wimbum) have never been isolated and change is an integral part of their tradition. They created and re-created their tradition even while they interacted with me. What I present in this book might be an idiosyncratic and momentary glimpse, but it does say something about how Wimbum people interpret their world. And, of course, there are similarities with neighbouring and more distant cultures. As in the case of witchcraft there are both fundamental differences and similarities with related ideas in other areas. These constellations of ideas can be seen as being related to each other through a series of family resemblances.

At the same time, however, we should be careful of generalising too easily from a single ethnographer's account of a single culture. Sometimes accounts of 'traditional religion' which ethnographers have given tend look more like culture-bound ethnographic constructions posing as tradition.[5] For example, Horton's descriptions of '*African* traditional thought' (1967) and '*typical traditional* cosmology' (1971) look suspiciously like projections of his own Kalabari ethnography (1962) onto African thought in general (and his descriptions of African traditional religion bear little resemblance to my descriptions of Wimbum religion).

Moreover some of the studies which have attempted to show that 'the African' traditionally believed in a 'High God' are, at least in part, projections onto a people by those who would like to believe that they have 'discovered some belief in the existence of God among the Africans' (Smith 1950: 33, see also Parrinder 1969, Mbiti 1970). This tendency to project Christianity into traditional African religion was criticised a long time ago by Driberg (1936). Traditional religion is described in such studies as though it had remained pure and not been influenced by Christianity, but by ignoring the influence of categories imposed from outside, the surreptitious introduction of these very categories is facilitated, and what is really a hybrid and very fluid product is then presented as a neutral description of traditional religion. This same process can be discerned in the study of ethnomedical systems, to which I will return in the final chapter.

Of course, many ethnographers have taken the diversity and fluidity of indigenous ideas into account and have not attempted to paint grand pictures of a coherent 'traditional cosmology', though they do generally tend to forget to mention the role of their own knowledge constituting role in the final product (see for example Buckley 1985).

---

5. I am aware that these few critical remarks do not do justice to the extensive ethnographic literature on African religion and are a simplification of a complex problem. However, an adequate discussion would take me too far from my main topic, and these remarks are merely intended to point to a tendency which I see as problematic.

Chapter 8

The Ancestors and Illness

Life after Death

One day Fai Gabriel said that he wanted to take me to the graves of his ancestors. We left his compound and followed a narrow path for about half a kilometre through coffee bushes and palm groves, until we came to an area of dense vegetation. There were many such groves in Tabenken, between compounds or in the middle of agricultural land. No one was permitted to cut wood or damage the trees in any way and if they did so illness would result. We entered the grove and the *Fai* had to force his way through the thick web of branches and leaves. After covering about twenty metres we reached a small clearing. In the middle there was a row of about seven narrow stones protruding from the ground. 'My ancestors,' the *Fai* said. He referred to each by name and discussed them as though they were living people, and he pointed out the spot where his own stone would stand when he died. These were not really the graves of Fai Gabriel's forefathers, however, as they were buried beneath the entrance to his compound. What were the ancestors then?

As in the case of *nyvu* I wondered whether people saw the ancestors (*bkvubshi*) as conscious beings and whether they were thought to cause illness. I considered it better to approach the topic indirectly, rather than simply to ask people what the *bkvubshi* were. As usual, I decided to consult Lawrence first, but he was not there. A few weeks previously he had received word that his sister, who lived in a village some fifty kilometres to the south of Tabenken, was seriously ill. He had gone to see her and I had not seen him since.

Then, one morning, a few days after my visit to Fai Gabriel, Lawrence turned up at my house. His leg was in plaster, from the toes right up to the hip, and he could only walk with crutches. He said that he had been drinking at the market in Ndu. It had become late and as he had left one of the bars two men had attacked him. They had beaten him up and as he lay on the ground they had kicked him. He said that they had also stolen his money.

Later, at the hospital, the doctor had told him that his leg was broken in three places and that it would take at least a year to heal properly. He would have to keep the plaster on for a few months and rest his leg, otherwise the bones would not set properly. He had said that he did not want to stay in Ndu and had come back to Tabenken so that we could continue with our work. I told him that it was not necessary, that I could manage without him and that he should take it easy until he was better, but he would hear nothing of it. He insisted on working, so I said that I would come to his house to discuss some of the topics we had been working on; that would enable him to rest his leg. I arranged to call in the next morning.

As I approached his house I saw him hobbling around the yard without his crutches.

'What are you up to?' I asked. 'The doctor said that your leg wouldn't heal if you didn't rest it. Where are your crutches?'

'I can't walk with those things in public,' he said, 'otherwise I look like an invalid.'

'If you continue to behave like that your leg will never heal,' I said.

'I will go to a traditional bone-setter,' he said. 'Then I will be walking normally in no time.'

He hobbled into his house and I followed him. We sat down at the table and I took out my cassette recorder. 'What are we to discuss?' he asked.

[8.1] 1. 'When someone dies do people think it's the end of him or do they think...'
    2. 'That he's still alive somewhere?'
    3. 'Yes, in the form of a spirit or something like that.'
    4. 'Yes, they say he has gone somewhere, they don't say he is finished.'
    5. 'Gone where?'
    6. 'To...er...some areas which they call...' A long silence followed and Lawrence stared up at the ceiling. 'I don't really know... They call some people *byir*. Those are dead people. Dead living people. Like ghosts.'

7. 'Are *byir* the same as ancestors?'
8. 'No, not ancestors.'
9. 'What are ancestors then?'
10. 'Ancestors are *bkvubshi.*'
11. 'What's the difference?'
12. '*Bkvubshi* are like our old grandfathers who died and come to act in the compound, like the carers of the compound. Or they try to make you sick, or give you things, good things. They make you sick if you haven't paid some debt, or you have been troublesome in the compound. Then the *bkvubshi* will come and make you sick. But if you have been good then they make you live happily.'
13. 'Do people first become *byir* before they become *bkvubshi?*'
14. There was a long silence. 'I think "byir" is the general word for those who are dead, and *bkvubshi* are really those who are related to the compound.'
15. 'Which people become *bkvubshi?*'
16. 'All people.'
17. 'Then what's the difference between *bkvubshi* and *byir?*'
18. 'Well...when you're making prayers to the ancestors you say *wa bkvubshi* [my *bkvubshi*], you never say *wa byir* [my *byir*].'
19. 'What's the relationship between the *bkvubshi* and god?'
20. 'It's that the *bkvubshi* take their power from god before acting in the compound.'
21. 'Can the ancestors make you sick?'
22. 'Oh yes, very seriously.'
23. 'Do they cause specific kinds of sickness?'
24. 'No, any sickness.'
25. 'What do you call sickness which has been caused by the ancestors?'
26. Another long silence followed. 'They don't have a special word for that. They go to a diviner and he will say that it has been caused by the ancestors.'
27. 'If someone is sick and takes treatment but doesn't get better then people start thinking that it has been caused by somebody, eh?' I asked.
28. 'Yes.'
29. 'Does that mean that if the sickness is caused by god or the ancestors and you take medicine that it will respond and you will get better?'
30. 'Mmmmm...with "somebody" they mean somebody who is still alive. If it is ancestors they will ask you to give a fowl. When

you do that then the sickness will stop.'

31. 'But I mean, for example, if the ancestors make me sick and a diviner tells me to give a fowl, but I don't give the fowl, I just go to the hospital and get treatment – will I get better?'

32. 'No, the sickness will continue seriously until you give the fowl.'

33. 'What is the connection between witches and *bkvubshi*?'

34. 'Witches are people who are alive and who use the names of the ancestors to act witchcraft.'

35. 'How do they do that?'

36. 'Let's say that the grandfather of the compound is dead. The person who has inherited the position will be acting and ruling the compound. When you are heady then, if he's a witch, he calls the name of that ancestor and produces the witchcraft. He calls the name of the man who has died and plays the witchcraft on you who is alive. So when you go to a diviner he will just say: "The ancestors say that you should pay this fine." Meanwhile it is the head of the compound who is using the name of the ancestor to play the witchcraft. So when you bring the fowl it is the old man who is alive who eats it, not the ancestors, who are dead.'

37. 'Are people who can see witchcraft being helped by the ancestors?'

38. 'Yes, according to the old men they are being helped by the ancestors.'

Lawrence said that people continue to exist after death. He distinguished between *byir* and *bkvubshi*. In this instance *byir* appear to be dead people generally, whereas the *bkvubshi* are a person's deceased relatives to whom he prays. They are the 'carers of the compound' who reward or punish the living as they see fit (12).[1] According to Lawrence the *bkvubshi* can cause illness as punishment. Like the *ngaa tvu'*, they do not cause specific illnesses and any illness which is chronic or does not respond to treatment could be caused by them. In such cases a diviner will decide on the cause and, if he decides that it was the *bkvubshi* he will also

---

1. People often translate the term "byir" as "spirits". I am not sure how adequate this translation is. The term refers to the dead and it is not easy to determine whether, when informants use the term, they mean people who are no longer in the realm of the living but who still exist as spirits, or people who once lived but have ceased to exist. Here I will only be concerned with the *bkvubshi*, as a discussion of other related concepts would be at least as long as that which I have devoted to *ngang, bfaa* and *tvu'* in previous chapters. I am primarily interested in *bkvubshi* as they relate to illness causation.

specify what penalty must be paid (this is usually a fowl or goat and palm wine which has to be given to the compound head or the elders). Once this has been done the sick person will recover (12, 21–32).

From Lawrence's description I gained the impression that the ancestors exist as powerful conscious agents: you can pray to them (18), they punish and cause sickness (12, 21–2) and they help old men to 'see' (37–8). But when I asked him about the connection between the witches and the *bkvubshi* he said that the witches 'use the names of the ancestors to act witchcraft' (34). A compound head who is a witch (*ngwɛɛ tvu'*) will use his power to maintain order and punish deviants in his compound. He does not do this directly but remains anonymous, hiding behind (the names of) the *bkvubshi*, so that when a person who is chronically sick consults a diviner, the diviner will, as neutral mediator, reveal the offence and establish the nature of the fine which must be paid to the compound head or the elders without revealing exactly who is inflicting the punishment (36). In this way justice is carried out impersonally through a neutral intermediary and conflict is avoided. This gives the impression that the *bkvubshi* are merely passive instruments of the *ngaa tvu'* who use them to mask their own activities (34, 36). This ambiguity is reminiscent of Lawrence's description of the *mnyvu* in the previous chapter.

Lawrence also said that the *bkvubshi* 'take their power from god' (20). What did he mean? He does not believe in a 'High God' and, as we have seen, what he described as the 'traditional gods' are (at least in [7.5]) largely the passive instruments of the *ngaa tvu'*.

I consulted Tobias on the same matter. Because he was a compound head he was expected to have some knowledge of these matters.

[8.2] 1. 'What do people traditionally believe about what happens to you when you die?' I asked.

2. 'Well, people believe that when somebody dies he goes and remains in the same place he was living, but in a different form. In a compound like this we have a compound head who has the cup. When there are troubles in the compound he gets *mimbu* [palm wine], puts it in the cup and goes to the burial place, where the ancestors are buried. He goes there and talks and pours wine.'

3. 'Is that the place where the stones are?'

4. 'Yes, those are the stones of compound heads. Not all who die in the compound have a stone. Each successive compound head who dies gets a stone. It is on such stones that the living compound head does the sacrifices. That is with *mimbu* and fowls.'
5. 'So the compound heads who die remain in the compound but in a different form?'
6. 'Yes, that is the belief.'
7. 'Is it only the compound heads who remain like that or everybody who dies in the compound?'
8. 'Anybody who dies in the compound remains. But they only give sacrifices to the compound heads. The rest are subordinate.'
9. 'Do they move around the village or do they just remain in the compound?'
10. 'They don't move around, they just stay in the compound.'
11. 'Is that what you call *bkvubshi*?'
12. 'Yes.'
13. 'Can they cause people to become sick?'
14. 'It is believed that if you do any wrong thing which is against the family tradition then they can cause illness. If you do something which isn't seen by human eyes, they see it, the *bkvubshi* in their graves see it, and when they see it they can punish you by giving you some sickness.'
15. 'Do they cause certain kinds of sickness or can it be any sickness?'
16. 'It can be any sickness. And when the sickness attacks and they go to a diviner then the diviner will prove it. Then you come home and make a sacrifice. You give a goat or a fowl or some small money to the man who has the cup [the compound head] so that he can make the sacrifice to them so that they will forgive you.'
17. 'Is there a connection between the *bkvubshi* and the *mnyvu*?'
18. 'You know, the *bkvubshi* work together with the gods, the *bkvubshi* are the people working together with the gods. In case of any demand, if the compound heads demand anything, the *bkvubshi* will have to seek that thing from god and send it to them, because the *bkvubshi* are nearer god. So if the compound is in chaos and they pray for help then the traditional priest [*Ta ngaa nyvu*] will make his sacrifices and pray to the *bkvubshi*. Then the *bkvubshi* will ask the god, the *nyvu ngong*, who will give what the people want.'
19. 'Do you personally think that the *bkvubshi* exist?'

20. 'No, no, I don't think so myself.'
21. 'Why not?'
22. 'No. I believe that when someone dies he either goes to heaven or to hell. And if he's a saint in heaven I pray to him.'
23. 'Aren't the saints just like *bkvubshi*?'
24. 'Yes, they are just like *bkvubshi*. *Bkvubshi* are correct people who are dead, with responsible traditional posts. They are exactly like saints.'

Tobias said that when compound heads die they remain in the compound in a different form, where they can be consulted in times of trouble by their successors (1–6). Everyone who dies continues to exist, but it is only the compound heads who are consulted and to whom sacrifices are made. They are called *bkvubshi* (7–12).

The *bkvubshi* can 'see' violations of tradition and inflict illness as punishment. Tobias agreed with Lawrence that this can be any kind of illness, and the fact that a diviner is consulted implies that it would be a chronic or unexpected serious illness (13–16).

When I asked him about the relationship between *bkvubshi* and *mnyvu* Tobias described a hierarchy, with the *bkvubshi* mediating between people and god. It is not clear whether he is referring to *mnyvu* or to God. In the conversation I detailed in Chapter 7 he implied that the *mnyvu* did not exist (at any rate not as conscious personalistic agents) and he described them as *ngaa tvu'* who guarded certain places, and even suggested that the term referred to those places ([7.6] 6, [7.7] 9). In the conversation I have just related he was talking about people praying to the *bkvubshi*, who in turn ask god, *nyvu ngong*, to give what the people are asking for ([8.2] 18).

This is a clear demonstration of the production of hybrid concepts in which traces of both traditional and Christian conceptions are visible. Tobias described how the *bkvubshi* mediate between people and god (18), but when I asked him whether the *bkvubshi* exist (19) he said that he did not think so (20), because when people die they either go to heaven or to hell, and some become saints (22). Then when I suggested that saints resemble *bkvubshi* (23) he agreed wholeheartedly that they are just like saints. They are 'correct people who are dead, with responsible traditional posts' (24).

As we have seen, people can communicate simultaneously

through different, often incommensurable discourses, leading to apparent contradictions in what they say. Christian and traditional discourses merge, and the terms which I am discussing are the points at which this merging takes place. They are therefore necessarily indeterminate. Terms which at first appear to be unproblematic translations have very different meanings, depending on the context (both internal and external to the conversation) in which they are used. The term "bkvubshi" can, then, be used to refer to ancestors (in the anthropological sense), to souls and saints (in the Catholic sense) and to *bkvubshi* (whatever they might be). What the term means in any given instance depends on who is using it, to whom he or she is talking and on what it is that they are talking about.

So Tobias could freely discuss the existence and behaviour of the ancestors with me, deny the existence of the *bkvubshi* quite explicitly, and then go on to say that they are the same as saints without realising the apparent contradiction (see also the discussion of Fai Gabriel's remarks on the *bkvubshi* in Chapter 7 ([7.8]).

How Can a Person be Alive When He is Lying in the Ground?

I wanted to discuss the same topic with Fai Nga Kontar. Because he was a non-Christian 'traditionalist' I thought that he might shed different light on the issue of the *bkvubshi*. Lawrence said that he would accompany me and I arranged to meet him along the path so that he would not have to walk too far in his plaster cast. Since his return to Tabenken some two weeks before he had stubbornly refused to use his crutches, and during the last couple of days he had been visiting a traditional bone-setter.

I sat on a slope overlooking the path and as I gazed in the direction of the market square Lawrence emerged round a bend in the path and strode powerfully toward me. 'You see,' he beamed, 'I told you that my leg would be fixed.' As we strolled to the *Fai*'s compound he told me that the bone-setter had removed the plaster cast two days previously and had healed the leg by massaging it with a bundle of chimpanzee bones, tied together with a leopardskin thong: a form of treatment which I had often seen and which never ceased to amaze me by its apparent success.

When we arrived the *Fai*'s compound he did not seem surprised at Lawrence's sudden recovery. He, like Lawrence, had

had no doubts about the outcome of traditional therapy. We sat down, and after some preliminary chat and kola nuts we got down to business.

[8.3] 1. 'What are *bkvubshi*?' I asked.
2. '*Bkvubshi* are as I have said: when a person is dead he is dead, he will never return.'
3. 'Does that mean that the *bkvubshi* are not alive.'
4. 'How can they be they alive? How can a person be alive when he is lying in the ground?'
5. 'I mean that when a person is dead and buried, does he stay alive and continue to exercise power in the compound?'
6. 'What people say in the compound is made by people.'
7. 'So the *bkvubshi* don't really exist?
8. 'There are no *bkvubshi*, in the sense that when you call your dead father he answers. You only dream about that.'
9. 'Why do witches do things that appear to be caused by the *bkvubshi*?'
10. 'If I do something wrong in the compound and I get sick, and I hear that my father is the cause then it is bad. When people cause me to be sick then they say it is the *bkvubshi*. Or when you don't do as people want you to, they say you haven't been behaving as your *bkvubshi* wanted you to, and they cause you to be sick. Then when you give a fowl to the *bkvubshi* everything will be all right.'
11. 'When you are dead will there be nothing left of you? Won't you be able to influence things in the compound anymore?'
12. 'When I am dead it will come out, but not made/caused [*gee*] by me. It is made by people who are alive.'
13. 'What will come out?'
14. 'They come and take me from where I am buried. *Wi tvu'* [witches] are *wi tvu'*. I will not see and people will not see. They come and stand there and take the ground from the grave to cause a person to be sick. Then when he goes to a diviner the diviner will say that the sickness is caused by the *bkvubshi*. Then he will catch a goat and give it to them and admit he has made a mistake.'
15. 'When they take the ground from the grave does the person lying in the grave know that they are taking ground to go and cause sickness?'
16. 'I'm lying in the ground. People who lie in the ground don't know. People who lie in the ground are dead.'

17. 'When they take the ground, is there some power in it that comes from the grave that makes the witchcraft work?'
18. 'Can the witches not destroy this house? Power is *tvu'* and power is people. I have told you that people do not remain when they are dead. It's people who say that you didn't fix you father's head. If you bring a goat, is it people or the *bkvubshi* who eat it?'
19. 'Then why do the *wi tvu'* [witches] take the ground?'
20. 'They needn't take the ground. When they reach the grave they can still act on the mistake you made, then you have to confess and give something. They don't take the ground, they just call the name. They say: Ask your father whether that is what he told you to do before he died. Does he see that you are doing bad?'
21. 'So they just pretend to take power from the dead person?'
22. 'They make as if they have taken his power but it is not his.'
23. 'Why do they go to the grave, why not just do it from where they are?'
24. 'It is the same. They can stay in the house and do it. If they sit together and say something is going to happen to you it will happen. They take the name of the *bkvubshi* so you won't be able to blame them. They say that it is what the *bkvubshi* have said.'
25. 'Some people say that when you do something wrong you should take a fowl to the *bkvubshi*, why is that?'
26. 'It is as I have said. Have you ever seen *bkvubshi* eating fowls?'
27. 'Christians say that when people die they continue to exist. They go to heaven or to hell. What do you think about that?'
28. 'That if a person dies he goes to *mbe buu* [heaven]?'[2]
29. 'Yes.'
30. 'I think they speak the truth.'
31. 'I don't mean what the Christians think, but what you yourself think.'
32. 'I think so. I think so because of sickness which sometimes lasts for long. I didn't know, but I found out that when a person dies he goes to *mbe buu*. I died in hospital, eh! People were coming down steps like those of the Mission, wearing black coats. White men like yourself,' he said, pointing to me. 'They were very happy and singing.' He got up from his stool and went out through the bamboo sliding door. A couple of seconds later he emerged again, walking sideways, waving his arms and singing loudly. 'There

2. In Limbum translations of sections of the Bible and during the Christian mass the word "heaven" is translated into Limbum as *mbe buu*, which literally means 'up in the air' or 'up in the sky'.

were a million of them,' he said. 'Black men also... That day I said that it is true that when a person is dead there is really life after death.'

The *Fai* did not share Lawrence's and Tobias's ideas about the *bkvubshi*. He quite emphatically stated that people do not continue to exist after death, and that the *bkvubshi* therefore do not exist and cannot be communicated with. The things which happen in the compound and which are attributed to them are caused by living people: by witches.

As Lawrence and Tobias had already said, these witches are not cannibals but the compound elders who have *tvu'*, 'those with eyes' who maintain order and uphold tradition. When the *bkvubshi* inflict illness to punish someone and a diviner says that they are responsible this will give added import to the elders' authority, and prevent any further discussion of the matter. This will be particularly useful when the compound head is weak and lacks authority of his own, or when he has no other sanctions with which to bring young rebels with urban jobs into line. The way in which the *Fai* spoke about the *bkvubshi* (20) resembles the way in which people in the West sometimes refer to the dead. We could, for example, imagine a widow who is gradually losing control over her rebellious children invoking the authority of her dead husband by saying something like 'What would your father have said?'

But there is also confusion. When the *Fai* said that the witches take 'ground' from the grave and use it to cause sickness (14), I assumed that he meant that the witches need to take something from the grave (whether just the ground or the *Fai*'s power) in order to cause illness, and that this implied that he would not cease to exist completely. The *Fai* later rejected these ideas, though. The witches have no need to take anything from the grave as they are powerful enough to carry out their activities and remain anonymous behind (the names of) the *bkvubshi* anyway (18).

He was quite emphatic that there are no *bkvubshi* and that people do not exist after death (2, 4, 8, 12, 16, 18, 26). Yet, when I mentioned Christianity and the souls of the dead going up to heaven, he readily agreed (27–32). Does this mean that he sees things very differently to Tobias and Lawrence, or is it that he was better at keeping the different discourses separate? If I had only questioned him about 'traditional cosmology' he would not have mentioned Christianity and I would have concluded that he was a traditionalist.

A few days after this conversation I was walking back from an afternoon session of palm-wine drinking in the *Ngwerong* lodge, when Fai Nga Kontar, who had also been present, being one of its hereditary leaders, caught up with me. He invited me down to the market square to continue the afternoon's drinking with '*brasseries mimbu*' (beer brewed in the city). I agreed and as we walked he asked me whether I was satisfied with what he had told me about the *bkvubshi*. I said that it was still not clear to me whether or not the *bkvubshi* really existed, because although he had said they did not exist other people continued to claim that they did. 'Then they're lying. When you're dead you're finished, it's only people who take you,' the *Fai* declared, suddenly grabbing my arm with both hands, to illustrate what he meant.

A few days later Tobias and I went to see Pa Andrew. We chatted casually and drank palm wine for some time before I asked him about the *bkvubshi*.

[8.4]   1. 'I want to ask you about *bkvubshi*,' I said. 'Do you think that the *bkvubshi* are really there, that they exist?'
2. 'When somebody dies then he is dead. If he is a *nkvushi* [sing.] we know he exists, but we don't see him. He exists like a *ryir*,' Andrew answered.
3. 'Can you speak to the *bkvubshi*?' I asked.
4. 'Yes, you can contact them. If you are in difficulties and the *nkvushi* is your father or your mother then you can talk to them. You make a small sacrifice and call their names and ask them for help, then they will help you.'
5. 'Some people say that the *bkvubshi* don't really exist, that when you are dead you are finished and there is nothing left.'
6. 'That's not true. I know that when somebody dies he goes and lives like a *ryir*. If you had a relative who died many years ago, and you sleep and see him in a dream, then that means that somebody in the compound will die.'
7. 'Some people tell me that if someone in the compound becomes ill and he goes to a diviner and the diviner says that it is caused by the *bkvubshi* then it's not really the *bkvubshi* who have caused the sickness but the witches working through the names of the *bkvubshi*.'
8. 'If you go to a diviner and he says that your sickness is being

caused by *bkvubshi* then it is really the *bkvubshi* who are affecting you, not those people in the compound.'

9. 'Then why do some people say that it is the witches and that the *bkvubshi* don't really exist?'

10. 'The real *bkvubshi* are there, and the witches are also there. Sometimes the witches can use the names of the *bkvubshi* and come and harm you. The real *bkvubshi* exist but witches can also use their names to affect you.'

11. 'Do the *bkvubshi* move around or are they only here in the compound?'

12. 'They have their own special place where they live. They live just like we live in compounds.'

13. 'Can the *bkvubshi* make people in the compound sick?'

14. 'Yes, they can make you sick, if you violate the rules of the compound. They don't want to see any bad thing. If they see that then they can make you sick. Because they are dead they don't want to see bad things, things which will harm the compound.'

15. 'Do they cause certain kinds of sickness or can they cause any sickness?'

16. 'It can be any kind of sickness.'

17. 'If someone is sick and it is caused by the *bkvubshi* then how will the person know that it is being caused by them?'

18. 'When a person is seriously sick then he will have to go and consult a diviner. Then the diviner will tell him that his sickness has been caused by the *bkvubshi* because he has done something wrong. He will say that he has to do certain things so that the *bkvubshi* will forgive him. Then when they return the head of the compound will sit at the door or the place where they make the sacrifices and call the names of the *bkvubshi* and the *bkvubshi* will forgive him.'

The discussion continued and Andrew said something about witchcraft only affecting you if you have done something wrong.

19. 'If you violate the rules of the compound and you become sick, who exactly is it who is making you sick?' I enquired.

20. 'The relatives in your compound.' Andrew answered.

21. 'Not the *bkvubshi*?' I asked.

22. 'No,' Tobias said, 'not the *bkvubshi*.'

23. 'It's the witches of the compound,' Andrew added.

24. 'But then what's the difference?' I asked. 'Earlier you said that if you do something wrong then it's the *bkvubshi* who make you sick.'

25. 'The *bkvubshi* have their own part. Their part is when you do
    something that even the *ngaa tvu'* [witches] don't know about,
    something which is bad for the compound, then they can give
    you sickness,' Andrew said.
26. 'Are these good or bad witches?' I asked.
27. 'Some are good, because it's a way of punishing you so you
    won't act like that again. It's for your own good,' Andrew
    explained.
28. 'Like when a child breaks a calabash and you take a cane and
    whip him so he won't do it again,' Tobias added.
29. 'Are the *bkvubshi* stronger than the *ngaa tvu'*?'
30. 'Yes,' Andrew said, 'they are stronger. The *bkvubshi* can even
    affect the *ngaa tvu'*.'

In this conversation Andrew initially gave a very different picture of the *bkvubshi* to that of Fai Nga Kontar. For him the *bkvubshi* are invisible, but they exist as conscious personalistic agents
with whom one can communicate (1–8). They live just like people
in compounds (12). They cause illness as punishment if a person
violates the rules of the compound (14). Andrew said that if you
are sick and a diviner says that your illness is caused by the
bkvubshi then it is really caused by them (8). Yet he also stated that
the witches can use the names of the *bkvubshi* and act through
them (9–10).

Then, later, he went right over to Fai Nga Kontar's point of
view when he said that it is really the elders of the compound (i.e.
the witches) and not the *bkvubshi* who inflict illness as punishment (19–23). When I reminded him about what he had said earlier he said that the *bkvubshi* only punish those violations which
the *ngaa tvu'* have missed (25).

They Have Died, But They Still Live in Another Way

As I strolled down to the market one afternoon I heard a furious
thrashing noise high up in one of Fai Gabriel's avocado trees. I
looked up just in time to see the *Fai* leap out of the foliage and fall
to the ground. He then sprang to his feet and, flailing about wildly with his arms, he ran into the house. I followed him and found
him sitting in the kitchen with his shirt off examining multiple
bee stings. I ran back to my house to fetch a tube of anti-allergic

ointment. When I had applied a generous dose to the rapidly swelling stings, we sat chatting about the *Fai*'s war of attrition against the bees inhabiting his avocado tree and his luck at not having been seriously injured by his fall. After a while the conversation turned to the topic of death. As usual I had my cassette recorder at hand.

[8.5] 1. 'What happens to you after you're dead? Are you finished, or do you still continue to exist in another form?' I asked.
  2. 'You still continue, according to our tradition.'
  3. 'How do you continue?'
  4. 'Some time ago I took you up to my compound. I showed you different statues, the fathers of the compound. Though they are just stones, those are their statues. Now, something might happen in this compound. We always make a prayer, if there is an accident, or a child is missing or sick, or there is sickness. In the evening you will sit at the door with a stick. You will knock at the door calling the names of all your fathers, as I showed you up there. You will tell them: "Oh my gods, you Kimbi, or you Nfor [names of his forefathers], of this compound, I handle this cup [symbol of the compound head] by your own right, you gave me the cup, to be in this compound. I see no reason why this child should be sick, or why this should happen in the compound. I pray that you should take up your eyes and see what is happening and save us from all this." When you talk like that you are making prayer, talking to them, because they are the people who have been in the compound and who have given the chair to you and so that you are multiplying. They have seen that you are fit and the cup is handed to you. You are praying to them. They have already died, but they still live in another way.'
  5. 'What do you call them?'
  6. '*Bkvubshi.*'
  7. 'Do all people who die become *bkvubshi*?'
  8. 'Yes. There are just so many. But you don't pray to them all when something happens in the compound. You don't pray to little children. You only call on the compound heads, and ask them to show you your own fault.'
  9. 'So when you are dead they will call on you?'
  10. 'Yes, the next compound head will call on the rest, and lastly me.'
  11. 'What's the relationship between the *bkvubshi* and god?

12. 'Originally we were pagans. We didn't know about god, and we thought that the *bkvubshi* were god. Your own father and mother are your own god because they delivered you. Even right know they still deal with them, except a few who know very well about god. But traditionally, if you are one of the compound heads, you might not want to follow this up. But your son might be staying somewhere, he might have completed his studies but be unable to get a job, or his child may not be progressing at school. So he comes back to the compound and tells you this. Perhaps there are certain things which he himself has committed in the compound, offences, things which are not right. It could be that he is not affected but one of his children. So he has come back to you, the compound head, to tell you what has happened. He may bring a fowl. Maybe the grandmother died and there was no death celebration. He will say: "Get a fowl and talk to the *bkvubshi*. Tell them that I am staying out of the village but that I will make the celebration. But then they should let go of this child." So when your children come to you to do this on their behalf, you can't refuse. You shoulder that responsibility. If you refuse to follow it up they will rebel against you. They will pray to the *bkvubshi* and say that you are not ruling well. They brought a chicken that you could talk to the *bkvubshi* but you refused. So you are forced by the people of your compound to follow up this tradition.'

13. 'Can the *bkvubshi* also make people sick?'

14. 'Yes,' he said with emphasis, 'that is what is believed.'

15. 'Why do they do that?'

16. 'Well, as I am telling you, if you believe the *bkvubshi* are there and you promise them something but don't follow this up then you can fall sick. Let me tell you about my brother,' he said, and went on to give a long and detailed description of conflicts between himself and a younger brother which had lead to a split in the family.

The younger brother had left the family compound and gone to live in Nigeria, and since then had had a long spate of misfortune. He had then come back after many years and asked the *Fai*, as compound head, to forgive him. He promised the goats and fowls necessary for a reconciliation but had not fully complied with the requirements.

'So,' the *Fai* continued, 'now the diviners are telling him that the *bkvubshi* are asking him something. They are telling him that he didn't come fully back into the compound and that through this action, through these words, he can become sick. That is, he thinks he was deceiving me, not knowing that it is the *bkvubshi* who are dealing with him. So people believe that the *bkvubshi* can make you sick. If you are not doing the right thing in your own compound you always feel guilty. Let's say, if you move from your home with a mistake between you and your parents. If you get sick you will feel, you will remember your mother and your father. You will say: "Before I left I committed a certain crime against my parents. In case I die here, how will I telephone, how will I send a message?" Your conscience is judging you. This may get you sick. It's through your own mistake; not that the people are really fighting there to make you sick. It's through your own mistake, you believe that you have made a mistake and really you will get sick. But here we say like that, we say: "No, they are your own *bkvubshi*, you should now do something correct." With most sickness people here go to *ngambe* [diviners]. The diviners will refer you to your compound. You must talk about these *bkvubshi* in the compound, what you have done and what the *bkvubshi* are asking.'

17. 'Is a lot of sickness caused like that?'

18. 'Most sicknesses are caused through carelessness, and through faults. You know, if you have a fault and somebody says: "You will knock your foot because you insulted me", and if you really know that you did something bad to him then you will knock your toe. That is through fault. But if you always move plain, politely [never do anything wrong or cause offence], then people won't quarrel with you. People always fear the right person. They know that if you have not been quarrelling with people they will be kind to you. If someone wants to fight with you people will say: "No." So we can say that most sickness is caused by people through their *bkvubshi*. Because the *bkvubshi* don't want you to make a fault, they don't want you to make mistakes. Your father doesn't want you to misbehave. They want you to be peaceful. But if you misbehave then they will tell you: "This is not how we want you to act." God likes people to live as long as they can. God made you to love him and serve him and be happy with him as long as possible. But we have free will. God has made you with free will. You know bad and you know good. If you want you can do bad and if you want you can do good. But if you make bad then you know that you are making bad and if you

make good you know you are making good. If you want to die, okay, if you want to live, okay. But when you die god will ask you: "Why do you die? Why do you kill yourself? Why do you hang? Why do you take poison? You know this is a bad thing, why do you do it?"'

'Then there is also this: sometimes people die because they are financially poor. I may unknowingly eat some bad food that causes me constipation. I will feel it in my stomach, but I have no money to treat myself. This thing will remain for a long time and develop. The sickness may lead to death before I get money. If I had money I would have treated myself.'

'That is another way people die. Then another way is willfully. As I have said, you have free will. A person may be short-sighted because of his friends. They may have shops or cars, or be ministers or magistrates. They are of his age but he is still creeping on the ground with his feet. So he may take a rope and hang himself. But he knows that if he hangs and dies it is bad. If he does it he is careless. He doesn't think. He thinks he is the poorest person, so his death is caused by his own carelessness. It's not caused by god. It's not even caused by the *bkvubshi*. It's his own fault. I told you, there are good and bad deaths. This is a bad one.'

'Or a taxi driver. He knows the bend is there and he still uses too much speed, so he runs into a stream or a stick [tree] and all are dead. So it is caused by him. The death of the passengers is caused by the driver. That is not caused by god. God didn't ask him to drive at such a speed. He has given you the sense and the eyes to see. If somebody with a tipper [truck] who loads sticks [timber] takes people on the timbers [and] when he takes a bend the timbers crush the people then it's not caused by god. The tipper is for materials, it's not for people. It's caused by the driver. Death is not always caused by god, at least not in this early stage.'

Fai Gabriel saw the *bkvubshi* as conscious agents (4, 8). He said that people are still obliged to deal with them even if they do not believe in them. If you are a compound head you have to communicate with the *bkvubshi* otherwise people in the compound will complain (to the *bkvubshi*) that you are not a good compound head (12). This resembles Tobias's dilemma chronicled in [7.6].

Fai Gabriel said that the *bkvubshi* cause illness as punishment. He gave neglecting the death celebration for an old woman and also the case of his brother as examples of the kind of behaviour that would merit such punishment. In the latter case it is not clear who is the cause of his brother's misfortune. According to the *Fai*'s theory of personal responsibility it is his brother's own fault, but if we are to believe other people's interpretations of the nature of *bkvubshi* then the *Fai* himself, as compound head, would be the one who is ultimately inflicting the misfortune on his brother as punishment for violating compound rules and ignoring the *Fai*'s authority.

This is, of course, a very delicate matter and people's views often varied depending on whether we were discussing a hypothetical example or an actual case, and on whether or not the case involved themselves or others. Also, the *Fai*'s emphasis on the role of personal responsibility may have been influenced by his brother's disobedience and subsequent misfortune: his explanation of misfortune in terms of the victim's own moral responsibility lent support to his own authority as compound head and served to emphasise that his brother deserved his misfortune.

Ancestors, Witches and Personal Responsibility for Illness

The nature and ontological status of the *bkvubshi* is indeterminate in the same way as that of the *mnyvu*. They exist as conscious, active beings (Andrew [8.4]), and as less clearly-defined entities that are used (as an instrument or as a cover) by the *ngaa tvu'* (Lawrence [8.1]). According to Fai Nga Kontar [8.3] they do not really exist at all, but are merely the names of deceased elders behind which the *ngaa tvu'* can hide in order to remain anonymous.

As in the discussions about *nyvu*, it is impossible to distinguish 'traditional' meanings and interpretations from Western and Christian influence, because it is impossible to say what, if it existed, the traditional cosmology in its pristine state was like. And, as I have mentioned before, given the dynamic and open nature of Grassfield societies it is doubtful whether there ever was any such thing. The only thing of which we can be sure is that indigenous conceptions have changed and continue to change, and that the nature of this change is being influenced in the twentieth century by powerful Western discourses: biomedicine, Christianity and even anthropology (the anthropological literature is not entirely unknown among educated villagers).

There are numerous examples in the conversations presented here of the way in which new knowledge and new meanings are being produced in situations in which these discourses meet, and of the creative ways in which people manage to adopt and utilise different and often incommensurable discourses in the praxis of everyday life.

Whatever the nature of the *mnyvu* and *bkvubshi* people appear to ascribe to them similar roles in illness causation. They inflict illness as punishment for violations of tradition. These are not specific types of illness but can be any illness which is chronic or takes an unexpected course. The nature of the affliction leads to divination and the diviner then establishes the immediate cause (*mnyvu* or *bkvubshi*) and the ultimate cause (some violation of tradition or mistake). Personal responsibility for illness plays a prominent role in these illnesses: the afflicted individual is ultimately responsible for his own illness because of his mistake and subsequent failure to put this right immediately and thus avoid illness. Fai Gabriel placed particular emphasis on the role of personal responsibility in the genesis of illness, but it is a theme which is also present in the other conversations.

There are also differences between the illnesses ascribed to the *mnyvu* and those ascribed to the *bkvubshi*, however. The former are punishment for violations of norms and rules related to the natural environment (spoiling a water source, cutting trees in a forbidden grove, violating the *ndap ngong*, killing certain animals), whereas the latter are punishment for violations of social norms and obligations in the compound (failure to hold a death celebration, disobedience to a compound head).

The illnesses caused by the *mnyvu* and *bkvubshi* are not distinguished terminologically, neither from each other nor as a category separate from other illnesses, though, strictly speaking, they would probably fall under the category of *yang gee*, illnesses which are 'made'. This brings us to another common feature: in both kinds of illness the *ngaa tvu'* are always present in the background as ultimate cause. Whatever the nature of the *mnyvu* and *bkvubshi*, whether they are conscious personalistic agents or simply places and names, the *ngaa tvu'* seem to be the ultimate moral judges and causal agents. It then remains for the diviner, himself also *ngwɛɛ tvu'*, to point out the mistake and decide on the penalty.

When I discussed *tvu'* with people the immediate connotation was, as I have shown, negative. The first thing they told me about was cannibalism and witch markets. They described the *ngaa tvu'* as envious and evil and their activities as destructive. When they cause illness those afflicted are innocent victims and those responsible must be sought out and punished. But in discussions of *mnyvu* and *bkvubshi* the *ngaa tvu'* are good: the protectors of the natural environment and upholders of traditional values and customs. When they cause illness it is as benign punishment or as a warning (Tobias compared it to punishing a child who breaks a calabash so that he will not do it again).

In the former case the emphasis is on the evil nature of the witches and divination is directed at exposing the *ngaa tvu'* responsible, whereas in the latter case the moral responsibility of the victim is emphasised and the aim of divination is to keep the identity of the *ngaa tvu'* hidden while exposing the 'mistakes' of the victim.

It is now possible to extend the summary of illness causes beyond that presented in the previous chapter as follows:[3]

3. It should be noted that I have not discussed all forms of illness causation (just as I have not discussed all forms of witchcraft) which I encountered in in Tabenken. For example there were illnesses related to the activities of witches who transform themselves into animals and go out at night to carry out their witchcraft activities; there were illnesses caused by *rka'*, objects which a witch can shoot into a victim and which must be removed by specialised medicine men; and there was a form of witchcraft in which the victim dreams that he is being strangled. I have had to select in order to make as concise a presentation possible, but these other forms easily fall into the categories in the table.

	Type of Illness	Immediate Cause	Ultimate Cause	Reason	Ultimate Moral Responsibility
Not Caused by Living Humans	Minor, easily cured	hard work, hot sun, mosquitoes etc.	none	none	none
	serious/chronic	mnyou (gods or deities)	mnyou (gods or deities)	punishment or warning for violating natural resources	victim is to blame, gods are good
	serious/chronic	bkcubshi (ancestors)	bkcubshi (ancestors)	punishment or warning for violating social norms or customs	victim is to blame, ancestors are good
	various	various	God	test of faith	none
	serious/chronic	cannibalism, packages from the witch market, etc	witches	evil nature of witches	witches are to blame, victim is innocent
	serious/chronic	mnyou	witches	punishment or warning for violating natural resources	victim is to blame, witches are good
Caused by Living Humans	serious/chronic	bkcubshi	witches	punishment or warning for violating social norms or customs	victim is to blame, witches are good
	various	harmful medicines	witches and ordinary people	evil nature of witches or protection from witches	victim may be innocent or himself and evil witch
	acute, sudden	poison	people	evil intent	victim is innocent poisoner is to blame

Chapter 9

From Representation to Dialogue in Medical Anthropology

In this chapter I draw together some of the themes which have been developed throughout the book. I start with some of the theoretical issues raised in the in the first two chapters, in particular those of translation, dialogue and representation, which are all basically related to the question of the accuracy of ethnographic description. I will then turn to a discussion of the themes which have emerged relating to Wimbum culture. Finally I return to medical anthropology and round off the discussion, started in Chapter 5, on the idea of the medical system.

Language and the Ethnographer's Linguistic Competence

In a provocative article Maxwell Owusu (1978) criticises Western anthropology, and in particular the ethnography of Africa, which he finds to be largely inadequate (he singles out two 'classics', Fortes's Tallensi ethnography and Evans-Pritchard's work on the Nuer, for detailed criticism). He claims that anthropological 'theories' are eurocentric: they are 'well established, fairly orthodox Western views of society and culture, their origins and development, which are then applied to the whole of humanity' (p. 317). He agrees with Hsu (1973) that 'truly universally applicable theories of man can hardly emerge unless Western anthropologists break out of their near obscurantist 'mental bondage' and recognise and accept the significance and validity of competing non-Western assumptions and theories and contrary viewpoints about man and culture not in conformity with conventional Western orthodoxy' (Owusu 1978: 318).

Although I agree with much of Owusu's argument, I do not think that he goes far enough in his critique of conventional anthropology. The problem Owusu addresses is the accuracy, or rather lack of accuracy, of ethnographic description, and the source of the problem is the linguistic competence of Western anthropologists. In his critique of Western anthropology Owusu ignores its underlying assumptions and the realist and representational genre conventions. He does not seriously consider the possibility of adopting the non-Western 'contrary viewpoints' suggested by Hsu, rejecting, in fact, the very relativism which would make this possible (p. 331). Rather, he looks for a solution within the dominant paradigm.[1]

He criticises Western anthropologists for looking for, and pretending to have found, the '*real*, raw, exotic native' (p. 319). He does not doubt the existence of this strange creature, but merely says that Western anthropologists have not really found him because their tools (linguistic competence) have been inadequate. He describes the problems in contemporary African anthropology in terms of 'data quality control' (p. 313), 'data contamination' (p. 312), 'falsification', 'replication' and 'evaluation of objectivity' (p. 312). The problem is that 'we cannot without serious distortion of reality derive valid macrosociological theories or cross-cultural generalisations from our crude microsociological techniques' (p. 330).

He suggests that only indigenous ethnographers, working in their own culture and through their own native language, can give us a description that does no violence to the 'integrity of the cultural realities' of the natives (p. 317), because only they are able to obtain 'uncontaminated data' (he cites Schneider's American kinship studies as an example). But if native ethnographers are able to collect 'uncontaminated data' on their own societies and communicate their findings to their non-indigenous colleagues by translating them into the anthropological lingua

---

1. My criticism in this section is not so much directed against Owusu as against two attitudes or tendencies in (certain sections of) anthropology which continue to be renewed in different guises. One is the quest for 'accurate representations' of other cultures and the other is the stubborn idea that only insiders can produce such representations. The former is encountered throughout the literature and some of its expressions will be criticised in other sections of this chapter as well. Indeed, this whole chapter can be seen as a critique of the idea that accurate representations of cultures are possible at all. The latter idea is encountered mainly in more informal anthropological discourse, in seminars, conferences, discussions, etc. It takes the form of: only Africans can study Africa, only gay anthropologists can study homosexuality, only women can study issues relating to women, etc.

franca (and Owusu implies that this does occur, otherwise it would be impossible to 'falsify', 'replicate' or 'evaluate objectively' their findings), then it should also be possible for 'native informants' to provide the same service for partially competent foreign ethnographers. Or is it that only natives who have been academically trained (in Western-style institutions and in the very eurocentric discipline that Owusu is criticising) are capable of such a feat? Owusu seems to think so, stating that 'interpreter-informants' are 'often misguided' (p. 326), and warning of the dangers of 'paraliterate feedback', by which he means that they may come to accept the anthropologist's description of their culture, which would then be 'corrupted' (pp. 319–20).

Owusu doubts whether a 'true dialogue' that leads to 'real understanding' and 'genuine communication' between a foreign ethnographer and a native interpreter–informant is possible at all (p. 316). He is optimistic, though, of native scholars doing 'more realistic, and more reliable' work (p. 326) which will provide 'real understandings' (p. 327) of indigenous culture.

Will these 'reliable' and 'real understandings' involve taking villagers' conceptions of witchcraft and traditional healing seriously as 'contrary viewpoints' which are 'not in conformity with conventional Western orthodoxy' (i.e as incommensurable with Western science and biomedicine but none the less equally valid), thus leading to a questioning of the native scholar's own assumptions? Or will they merely involve elite, academically-trained native scholars reducing 'contamination' by applying Naroll's techniques for 'data quality control' (pp. 314–5)?

Owusu criticises the slender basis on which many anthropologists generalise about Africa but he himself makes sweeping generalisations about anthropologists who study Africa. Must we assume that just because an ethnographer is himself a native his ethnography will be better? Is the average sociological monograph 'more accurate' than the average ethnography just because the author is usually a native? I have my doubts.

And what are we to think of the work of scholars like Tanto, Mburu, Njingti and Mbunwe-Samba: are they ideal indigenous ethnographers in Owusu's sense, whose ethnography of 'Wimbum witchcraft' is a priori more 'accurate' than my own because they have written about their own culture, or are we to view them as cases of 'contaminating' 'paraliterate feedback' because their interpretations have been influenced by a very specific body of Western ethnographic literature (Parrinder, Mbiti, Mair) and (excluding Mbunwe-Samba) by their Catholic missionary background?

Of course Owusu is right in claiming that ethnographers *should* be competent in the native language. Fluency is always better than dependence on incompetent interpreters, and I have not the slightest doubt that the number of anthropologists who speak the language of their informants with the fluency of a native speaker is low. But Owusu goes too far. He demands 'a *prior* ability to speak and understand *several* relevant local vernaculars' (p. 313, my emphasis). This means in effect that ethnographers can only study their own society. If we assume that four or five years continuous residence in a society is required in order to be proficient in a vernacular (to say nothing of two or three vernaculars) that is usually not related to one's own language then it would be almost impossible for any ethnographer to acquire proficiency *prior* to doing fieldwork.

I fully agree with Owusu that the whole question of linguistic competence should be made explicit (how many anthropologists would dare to be publicly honest on this matter?). This is not the same, though, as closing the door to all except the privileged few who have previously established competence, thereby implying that ethnographers may only work in their own culture.

Owusu ignores one of the most important the reasons for doing ethnography in the first place: it is the *experience of difference*, both cultural and linguistic, which stimulates curiosity and leads to understanding. After all, 'what is ethnography if it is not the phenomenology of asymmetry, of otherness, foreignness?' (Tedlock 1987: 329).

This ethnography is the product of the difference resulting from my initial lack of understanding of local interpretations and competence in the vernacular. After all, had I been a native I would probably not have found the terms that are the subject of this ethnography problematic and therefore intriguing in the first place, and I would not have felt the need to spend so much time enquiring about their meanings. My enquiries were fruitful because as I did not initially know what people were talking about I had to construct my own, partially unique understanding. Yet the interpretation is not simply a result of my lack of understanding. It is, rather, a product of my enquiries, generated on the one hand by my anthropological knowledge and my ignorance of local language and culture, and, on the other, by my informants' interpretations of their culture and their attempts teach me the meanings of vernacular terms. Proficiency is necessary, but it has to be developed gradually *during* fieldwork and *through* fieldwork. Of course the ethnographer will make mistakes in his translations, of course he will retranslate texts as his competence increases, revise interpretations, change his mind. The natives will also change their minds and revise their interpretations (as a result of the contaminating 'paraliterate feedback' of which Owusu is so afraid). But that is what ethnography is all about, and it should therefore be explicitly presented rather than shamefully effaced from the final monograph.

Fluctuation, fragmentation and indeterminacy are only a problem as long as we continue to assume the pre-existence of an external objective reality or an underlying order capable of being gradually revealed by the application of proper research methodology or analytical techniques and then authentically represented in the final monograph through some form of literary realism. Once we accept that 'real' native culture does not exist out there in some pure or pristine form waiting to be discovered and represented by the ethnographer, but that ethnography is, above all, shared praxis, dialogue, performance and production, in which communication is often not unambiguous and complete but indeterminate and fragmentary, then the problem appears in another light.

Dialogue and Representation

This study can be seen as an attempt to make the nature of this shared praxis explicit. Because it is dialogical and because recent discussions about the possibility of a dialogical anthropology are closely related to what has been called the 'crisis of representation', I feel obliged to situate my presentation in relation to these discussions.

The whole debate about dialogue seems to centre on two questions. Firstly, can dialogical texts accurately represent actual dialogue in the field, and can they adequately represent indigenous thought and culture more generally (Tyler 1984). Secondly, can dialogical texts actually be dialogues rather than simply monological representations of dialogue, however accurate, because the ethnographer wields the pen and has ultimate editorial authority (Clifford 1983, Tyler 1984, 1987). I will consider these issues briefly in relation to my own ethnography.

Firstly, the texts I have presented are not meant to be mirror-image representations of the 'real' encounters in which I participated in the field. They are not meant to be representations of anything, and could not be, if only for the fact that recording and transcription have eliminated almost everything except the spoken part of the original encounter (other sounds, smells, gestures, facial expressions, tones of voice, etc. are reduced to a minimum), and the transcriptions have been translated, re-translated, selected and edited before ending up in the pages of this monograph. In the narrow sense of actual physical co-presence and verbal interaction they are no longer dialogues but interpretations of dialogues, though this does not necessarily make them any less dialogical in a broader sense of the term (see Tedlock 1987, Dwyer 1982).[2] Secondly, they are not meant to be privileged representations of 'native thought and culture' (Tyler 1984). They cannot be this because they have been partly produced by me against the background of my Western, Christian and anthropological conditioning. But of course they do bear some relation to native thought and culture because they were also partly produced by my informants. Thirdly, they are not meant to simply illustrate or embellish some thesis that I already had in mind, they are not merely 'souvenirs' (Tedlock 1983: 324). Finally, their presentation is not 'a matter of ethics or politeness ('giving a voice to our informants') nor a matter of literary theory (recognising multiple authorship)' (Fabian 1990a: 15).

Rather, they are intended to *evoke*. To evoke my confusion and puzzlement during discussions in the field; to evoke the pull away from those aspects of my official research topic which had been defined by experts beforehand as important and relevant; to evoke my informants' enticement toward topics which they (and increasingly, I) found to be both more important and more interesting; to evoke the dilemma of my position, between conformity to structures of relevance which were imposed on me (and through me on my informants) from above and acquiescence to

---

2. In referring to a chapter in Paul Radin's *The Method and Theory of Ethnology*, in which Radin discusses texts he had collected in the field, Tedlock claims that it is dialogical because 'Radin's discourse is in constant alternation with that of the texts, rather than taking the form of an introduction, footnotes, an appendix or a separate book' (Tedlock 1987: 326–7).

local conceptions of relevance which increasingly impinged on me from below. I now realise that the fact that I went so far with them was, at least to some extent, an act of resistance on my part: resistance to the conventions and objectivist assumptions of applied, problem-solving anthropology, resistance to the grant-giving agencies with their narrow, ethnocentric and scientistic conceptions of relevance. That I did not go further was a result of my own dependence on these same power structures and discourses.

But, and this is also what I have intended my presentation to evoke, I *could not* enter further into their world with them because I was not one of them and I was not fluent in their language. I had to keep interpreting what they were telling me in terms of what I already knew and expected, given my own Western background and the influence of anthropology and biomedicine on my expectations and perceptions. The bracketing of these assumptions which phenomenologically oriented medical anthropologists call for is impossible. Kleinman insists that 'health care systems' are not entities but conceptual models which have been reconstructed by the researcher in the process of medical ethnography (Kleinman 1980: 25–6) and I agree with him; but he none the less goes on to say that: 'In order to conduct such an ethnography, the investigator usually needs to *step outside* of the cultural rules governing his beliefs and behaviors, including his own health care involvements. Otherwise he risks *contaminating* his analytic model of the health care system with his largely tacit actor's model of his own health care system' (p. 26, my emphasis). Although the notion of an 'explanatory model' which a patient or healer holds in relation to a particular episode of illness is a useful concept because it makes it possible to avoid generalisations about 'indigenous etiology' or 'illness beliefs', Kleinman still assumes that these models exist in people's heads independently of his attempts to 'reveal' them through the use of 'ethnoscientific eliciting procedures' and that such procedures 'avoid *contaminating* them with the researcher's own beliefs' (p. 106, my emphasis). As if these procedures were neutral instruments which simply reveal people's ideas.

The kind of approach I have used here is aimed at overcoming the distinction between emic and etic, subject and object, method and data. I had to start from biomedical conceptions such as etiology, disease and kwashiorkor, and I had to keep coming back to them both because that was the only way in which I could comprehend what people were telling me in what was for me a meaningful way, and in order to ensure that my results bore at least some relation to the original research plan. This influence was not necessarily negative. For example, if I had not been carrying out parallel investigations into infant feeding along more conventional, biomedical lines, I would never have heard of *yang bobkɛ'* and the relation between bad breast milk and *ngang* and *bfaa*.

Similarly, I was constrained by the anthropological conception of 'traditional etiology' with its distinctions between naturalistic and personalistic, illnesses of god and illnesses of people, etc. These various influences and constraints are clearly visible in the conversations themselves as well as in my comments on them and in the way in which I have selected and presented them. This is not contamination but part of an anthropological praxis which does not recognise a radical break between 'data' and 'analysis' (Fabian 1985). The presentation of conversations rather than just interpretations of what people said is made necessary by the fact that they are part of the 'work of interpretation' (Tedlock 1983).

This ethnography is dialogical not just because it consists of a series of conversations. It is not just a question of literary form, it is also a means to enable us to reflect on the nature of fieldwork and the kind of knowledge which this produces (see Fabian 1990b).

Through the presentation of these conversations my influence on the topic becomes explicit. I started enquiring about kwashiorkor and infant feeding, but when informants presented twins and abominations as interesting topics which had nothing to do with kwashiorkor as it is biomedically defined I followed their lead. Still, I kept tacking back to the original topic. I explored *ngang* until it led to twins, and I explored *bfaa* until it led to bad death, then I came back to illness terms and etiology. Through a chance conversation with Lawrence about inherited women being poisonous I started a series of discussions about witchcraft, only to return to etiology and the anthropological distinction between illness of people/illnesses of god. This in turn led on to my enquiries about the nature of god and the ancestors.

Through the conversations I wanted to make explicit the limitations of my own competence in my informants' language, and the extent of their competence in my language. In this I have not entirely succeeded because an adequate presentation of conversations through an interpreter would not have been easy reading. The presentation of conversations enables those with whom I worked to appear as individuals rather than anonymous 'informants' and it also makes their role in the dialogue explicit. Lawrence, Tobias, Fai Nga Kontar, Fai Gabriel, Pa Andrew and the others not only contributed to the conversations which constitute this ethnography, they also helped me to interpret them. As Tedlock has pointed out, informants are not only producers of texts, they are also *interpreters* of texts (Tedlock 1987: 331). I do not give them equal status as 'co-authors' because I do not want to hide my role as autocratic editor and interpreter of their statements behind the romantic pretence of equal and multiple authorship.

The conversations not only give some idea of the way I worked; they also reveal the important and highly ambivalent role of Lawrence, my interpreter, assistant and friend. He was important because he provided me with access to Wimbum discourse and influenced the course of the research (putting on a long face when we had to conduct interviews in the more conventional part of the project, reacting with enthusiasm and interest at the discovery of each new strand of meaning of such terms as "bfaa" and "ngang"). His role was ambivalent because he both opened up new areas of research which led to new understandings and caused confusion by some of his translations and interpretations.

Lawrence was part of the constitutive praxis, a participant in the dialogue of which this ethnography is part. In this sense his role was radically different to that of Crapanzano's 'field assistant', Lhazen (Crapanzano 1980). Lhazen was necessary for Crapanzano's relationship with his informant Tuhami, but he was apparently neutral and invisible: 'Had he not been there, our relationship would have been awkward. Present, he could be ignored and was ignored' (p. 143). For Crapanzano the interviews he conducted were between himself and his informant, Tuhami. His interpreter, merely alternating as spokesman for both of them, 'was identified seriatim with each of us as we addressed the other' (p. 149). In the discussions and interviews which I conducted Lawrence could not be ignored and sometimes, as in the first encounter with Pius, I was the one who was largely ignored; in retrospect fortunately so, moreover. Had I been in control the encounter would certainly not have been as productive or as interesting.

Finally, dialogue is not necessarily limited to verbal interaction which takes place between the ethnographer and his informants during fieldwork. There is no reason for the dialogue to end when we leave the field. As Tedlock uses the term, dialogue can continue into the armchair and beyond.

> The armchair dialogue I have in mind here involves the interpretation of the discourse recorded while in the field. Again, this armchair dialogue is something we all do, listening, puzzling, questioning, and, as it were, talking back. It still partakes of the specific nature of the social sciences; it is still dialogical anthropology. But so far, we do it mainly *prior* to publication, rather then *in* publication. (Tedlock 1983: 324)

The intrusion of dialogue into publication becomes unavoidable once we accept that the separation which is conventionally assumed to exist between 'data gathering' and 'analysis' is untenable. The elision between fieldworker and author has been discredited and we must be prepared to situate our interpretations. Which brings us to the issue of accuracy.

In recent discussions about 'experimental' ethnography there has been much talk of a crisis of representation, and in particular, a crisis of 'ethnographic realism'.[3] Marcus and Fischer see this crisis as arising 'from uncertainty about adequate means of describing social reality' (1986: 8) and they point out that much recent experimental writing has been concerned with 'strategies for incorporating *more authentic representations* of the experience-near and experience-far concepts, which occur during the process of fieldwork, directly into the resulting ethnographies themselves' (Marcus and Fischer 1986: 31, my emphasis). They see these experiments as 'adapting and bringing anthropology forcefully into line with its twentieth-century promises of *authentically representing cultural differences* and using this knowledge as a critical probe into our own ways of life and thought' (42–3, my emphasis).

This emphasis on more authentic representations of other cultures is related to Marcus and Fischer's vision of anthropology as a cultural critique (How can we criticise something we cannot adequately represent?). Though in most recent 'experimental' writing in ethnography the more extreme objectivistic and posi-

---

3. See Marcus and Cushman 1982, Marcus and Fischer 1986, Clifford and Marcus 1986.

tivistic assumptions are explicitly rejected,[4] much of it still remains well within the bounds of representational discourse. As the quotations above illustrate, the 'crisis of representation' is seen as primarily a problem of 'accuracy'.[5]

It is not the accuracy of representations which is problematic but the very notion of realistic or accurate representations itself. As Tyler puts it:

> The problem with...realism...is not, as is often claimed, the complexity of the so-called object of observation, nor failure to apply sufficiently rigorous and replicable methods, nor even less the seeming intractability of the language of description. It is instead a failure of the whole visualist ideology of referential discourse, with its rhetoric of 'describing', 'comparing', 'classifying', and 'generalizing', and its presumption of representational signification. In ethnography there are no 'things' there to be the objects of a description, the original appearances that the language of description 'represent' as indexical objects for comparison, classification and generalization; there is rather a discourse, and that too, no thing, despite the misguided claims of such translational models of ethnography as structuralism, ethno-science, and dialogue [sic] which attempt to represent either native discourse or its unconscious patterns, and thus recommit the crime of natural history in the mind (Tyler 1986: 130–1).[6]

As Fabian has pointed out, the problem with 'ethnographic realism (as a literary convention) was not its realism (as an epistemological stance) but the surreptitious substitution of the former for the latter'. As a result 'a kind of knowledge that is *really* created by conventions of writing claims to be a reflection of that which is *real*' (Fabian 1990b: 761–2).

What is at issue in discussions about representation in ethnographic writing is not just a matter of style but what it is we are doing when we write. Writing is part of anthropological praxis, and in this praxis 'the Other is never simply given, never just found or encountered, but *made*' (Fabian 1990b: 755). In my pre-

4. They are still alive and kicking in anthropology more generally (see for example Spiro 1986), though, and in medical anthropology Browner, Ortiz de Montellano and Rubel 1988.

5. This was also the main focus of Owusu's (1978) critique of Western anthropology discussed above.

6. In various publications Tyler has criticised 'dialogical anthropology' and in particular the work of Tedlock. I think that he interprets Tedlock wrongly when he accuses him of presenting dialogue as a more accurate representation of native discourse, and his criticism is certainly not applicable to Dwyer 1982. I will not go into the details of this misunderstanding here.

sentation of conversations I have not attempted to avoid realistic representation but rather to problematise it.

Emerging Wimbum Themes

This study started with an exploration of indigenous conceptions relating to the biomedically defined syndrome kwashiorkor. The term "kwashiorkor" was translated into Limbum as "ngang" and "bfaa", but it soon became clear that the meanings of these terms only partially overlapped those of "kwashiorkor". At this point my project bifurcated and one branch was devoted to investigating indigenous interpretations of *ngang* and *bfaa* and how they were related to etiology more generally. The exploration of these interpretations led away from biomedically determined concerns to themes which seemed to have nothing to do with kwashiorkor. "Ngang" and "bfaa" appeared indeterminate and the more I attempted to reveal their 'real' meanings, to create some kind of order by placing them within an 'indigenous etiology' or 'medical system', the more indeterminate they became, and I started to realise that I was not revealing anything, but rather participating in the creation of something partly new and partly unique.

What I was discussing with people was, I increasingly came to realise, not a coherent system of knowledge about which there was general consensus. The terms whose meanings I was trying to discover were focal points in unstable and loosely articulated constellations of meaning. Each encounter with an informant was a unique performance, generating a fleeting and more or less idiosyncratic cluster of meanings which I transformed into a text through recording and transcription. This materialisation did not result in a fixing or stablisation of meaning, but rather led to new indeterminacies and the generation of new meanings, through translation, discussion with those involved, re-translation and re-interpretation: Tedlock's 'armchair dialogue' (Tedlock 1983).

As the conversations presented in this ethnography show, it would be impossible for me to generalise with any reasonable amount of certainty about what my informants 'believe' about kwashiorkor, *ngang*, *bfaa*, *nyvu*, etc., let alone make general statements about 'traditional religion' or 'Wimbum etiology'. In that sense I do not assume that what I have presented in this ethnography corresponds to any putatively objective cultural reality which exists outside the ethnographic process. Having reached the end of my ethnographic presentation, it seems that the only general statement which I can legitimately make is, somewhat paradoxically, that no general statement is possible. One possible strategy would then be to let the conversations, and my commentary on them, speak for themselves.

Does this mean that I have fallen prey to the spectre that constantly seems to haunt Ernest Gellner – and, apparently, 'human thought' in general: relativism (Gellner 1985)? Have I, by focussing on dialogue, slid into 'atomistic nihilism where it becomes impossible to generalise from a single ethnographer's experience', thus rendering my text 'of no particular ethnographic interest' (Marcus and Fischer 1986: 68)? I do not think so. Naive relativism, nihilism, solipsism are not the only alternatives to objectivism (Bernstein 1983, see also Geertz 1984). No general conclusions can be drawn but, as I will show, the conversations do say something about Wimbum culture, not as a 'seamless web', but as certain 'partially consistent themes'. They 'capture...some of the "lines" or patterns that, inferred from present adult discourse, lend an intelligible form to quickly changing social practice, thereby making accessible some of the terms in which... [the Wimbum] have understood their fellows' motives and made sense of themselves' (Rosaldo 1980: xi).

The fragmentary, partial and open nature of ethnographic knowledge does not imply that 'anything goes', or that the number of acceptable interpretations at any given moment is infinite. There are criteria in terms of which interpretations and descriptions can be judged to be more or less adequate. But these criteria are historically and culturally contingent.[7]

As I pointed out in Chapter 2, this ethnography is partly an autobiographical narrative of discovery, but that does not make it solipsistic, nor does it mean that it bears no relation to indigenous conceptions or interpretations. In a dialogical anthropology the interpretive community in which the adequacy of ethnographic interpretations is decided should also include those who, as informants, were also co-producers.

I assume that the ethnographer's interpretations of another culture should be accessible and acceptable to the people who belong to that culture in a meaningful way. This only seems fair.

7. See Fish 1980, Bernstein 1983, Taylor 1979.

After all, when foreign ethnographers describe and interpret our culture we judge the adequacy of their ethnography by the extent to which we can relate it to our own interpretations of our culture. The English may find Biku Parekh's (1974) ethnography of their culture exaggerated, but they do recognise it as meaningful and they can relate it to their own understanding of their culture. The extent to which this is achieved may, of course, be debatable: Geertz claims that the Balinese recognise and agree with his interpretation of their cockfight (Geertz 1973), other anthropologists have their doubts (Shankman 1984). On the other hand, we can be reasonably sure that there are not many Amazonian Indians who would be able to discuss meaningfully Levi-Strauss's dissection of their myths.

The point here is not that local people are not 'clever' or 'educated' enough to understand anthropological analyses when they become too complex or abstract, but that such analyses constitute a discourse that is analogical in Tedlock's sense. This anthropological discourse comes to replace native discourse, and it is then claimed that the former is somehow 'equivalent or proportionate, in a quasi-mathematical sense', to the latter (Tedlock 1983: 324). This 'created object that rises *above* or comes *after*, increasingly claims to describe rules or laws that lie *under* or come *before* what the natives do or say' (Tedlock 1983: 327).

Most Wimbum would recognise the topics discussed in this ethnography and the more general themes which emerge from them as meaningful in relation to their own concerns and interpretations of their experiences, particularly those relating to illness and misfortune. I could discuss these themes with most people in a meaningful way, something which I could not have done with, say, an interpretation of illness in terms of humoral pathology (see, for example, Lawrence's reaction to my friend's explanation of his backache in terms of a cold draught). They might not agree with all my interpretations but they are familiar enough for them to understand and relate to their own interpretations, and they could easily say what they disagree with and why. Also, I was able to formulate very low-range generalisations and feed them back into the discussions and communicate with people about them (e.g. my idea that twins who are not 'fixed' are prone to *ngang*, or that witchcraft could cause *ngang*, or that "nyvu" refers to an impersonal nature rather than a personalistic High God). Not everyone would agree with my interpretations (Father Robert would certainly not agree with my suggestion that the Wimbum were traditionally atheist), but we could communicate about them in a way we would both find meaningful. To that extent, my descriptions and interpretations of what people tell me, although they are *my*, perhaps idiosyncratic, descriptions and interpretations none the less are, or become, part of *their* discourse as well.

In this ethnography I have been concerned with the meaning of certain terms which became central in the discussions I had with a number of people about illness. I have attempted to explore the fields of meaning in which these terms are embedded and the way they are related to each other in people's discourse. I have emphasised their indeterminate and ambiguous nature, situating them as the products of an ongoing dialogue and examining both their unique and intersubjective aspects. But in spite of the indeterminacies, or perhaps because of them, it is possible to distinguish a number of constellations of meaning in which these terms form focal points, and to discern a number of lines or partially consistent themes which run through the various discussions.

"Ngang" is highly indeterminate. It refers to an illness, mainly in children, but statements on what the exact symptoms are, what causes it and how it relates to kwashiorkor vary significantly from one informant to another: some people distinguish between wet and dry *ngang*, or early and late *ngang*, others disagree; some suggest a connection between *ngang* and the treatment of twins, others say they are not related; sometimes "ngang" seems to be a synonym for "kwashiorkor", on other occasions there is no semantic overlap whatever.

The same applies to "bfaa". Some people say it is a synonym for "ngang", others claim the terms are not related at all; some say that it is a synonym for "kwashiorkor", others say that it only refers to 'mistakes'. There are those who distinguish two homonyms, one referring to the illness which resembles kwashiorkor, the other referring to mistakes and abominations, and there are those who claim that there is only one term and it refers to two closely related aspects of the same phenomenon: a physical illness caused by an abomination.

Then there is "yang bobkɛ'". Literally the term means children's illness and seems to be a synonym for "ngang", "bfaa", and "kwashiorkor" in conversations relating to pregnancy taboos and weaning.

Though indeterminate, these terms are related to each other across the various discussions through a series of family resemblances in the meanings which people attribute to them. This is partly a result of the fact that Tabenken is a geographical point at which a number of regional variations meet (the word "bfaa" is more common in Ndu to the south, whereas the word "ngang" is more common in Nkambe to the north). But it is also partly a result of my initial interest in kwashiorkor which, though gradually receding into the background, formed a line running through most of the conversations about *ngang, bfaa* and *yang bobkɛ'*: after all, it was this interest, and my search for Limbum translations of "kwashiorkor", that led to the discussions about *ngang, bfaa* and *yang bobkɛ'* in the first place. In this sense these terms can be seen as constituting a single, partially consistent constellation of meaning.

Another key term relevant to the way in which people talk about and interpret illness is "mcɛp", or "medicine". "Mcɛp", is a polysemic term related to a wide variety of objects, which all seem to have in common an active property or force: they are all 'charged objects' (Geschiere 1983).

A third constellation centres on "tvu'", or "witchcraft". The more specifically I enquired about witchcraft in relation to *ngang, bfaa*, etc. or as a cause of illness generally, the less it seemed to play a role. When I explicitly enquired about etiology people appeared to interpret most illnesses as naturally caused, saying that they 'just happened'. But later on, when I started to talk to people about witchcraft and *tvu'* they mentioned numerous ways in which witchcraft played a role in illness causation. This led to the emergence of a more or less distinct constellation centring on "tvu'".

But "tvu'" is highly ambivalent, referring to both an evil destructive force and a morally neutral, regulative power, depending on how people talk about it and in what context. In discussions about witchcraft the negative meanings were usually emphasised: witches were evil, deliberately causing illness or disruption through their cannibalistic activities and their visits to the witch market (*ntaa tvu'*) or simply through sheer malice. But in the context of discussions about nyvu and the ancestors (*bkvubshi*) witches were good, causing illness to warn or punish people for wrongdoing.

The emergence of witchcraft as a significant cause of illness brought my enquiries back in line with the anthropological literature: in particular the distinction which is usually made in descriptions of African etiology between illnesses of people and illnesses of god. This led on to the discussions about *yang nyvu* and the nature of *nyvu*.

"Nyvu" then became the centre of another constellation, which also included the terms "mnyvu", "god", "God" and "nature". As in the case of the other terms being discussed here, it is impossible to say with any degree of certainty what "nyvu" 'really' means. Some people (all devout Christians) saw *nyvu* as a High God, whereas others (self-confessed 'pagans' or 'neo-pagans') claimed that the Wimbum did not traditionally believe in a High God, but only in the *mnyvu*. The nature of these *mnyvu* remains unclear. For some they were deities or minor gods, for others they were witches, and for yet others they were groups of ancestors or just places. My interpretation of the conversations presented here is that, basically, "nyvu" does not refer to a per-sonalistic High God, and that witches are ultimately responsible for the activities which are attributed to the *mnyvu*. A lot of con-fusion seems to have arisen from the Christian missionaries' adoption of the term "nyvu" to refer to the Christian God. This is reflected in the discussions about *yang nyvu*. In general conversa-tion the term "yang nyvu" seems to refer simply to illnesses which 'just happen' as part of the normal order of things, which 'do not have a cause', and therefore to be unrelated to the concept of God in the Christian sense. I now have the impression that it was the way I focussed on *yang nyvu* that started people thinking about the role of God in causing illness in the first place. At first they casually referred to *yang nyvu* as 'coming from god', but I doubt that they were thinking of a High God when they made these statements.

The direction that my enquiries took was determined partly by my informants' interests and partly by my own anthropological background. After discussing witchcraft and god as etiological agents the obvious next topic was the ancestors, given that the distinction illness of people/illness of god is usually supplement-ed with a category of illnesses caused by the ancestors. The mean-ings relating to "bkvubshi" constitute another range of meaning. "Bkvubshi" is as at least as indeterminate and ambiguous as "nyvu". What are *bkvubshi*? Are they deceased elders surviving in another realm as sentient beings, as they are often described in the anthropological literature? Or does the term only refer to the activities of living witches, who hide behind the names of the dead, as some people insisted? There is much disagreement, not only about the nature of the *bkvubshi,* but also on whether they cause illness. But even those like Pa Andrew, who saw the *bkvubshi* as ancestors who live in another realm, in compounds of their own, admit that witches can and do act 'through' them.

In addition to the vast scope of meaning associated with the terms I have been discussing, a number of more general themes emerge from the texts I have presented.

Tvu' is a highly ambivalent concept: people talk about *tvu'* as a disruptive, evil force and as a regulative, morally neutral force, depending on the context. When people are talking explicitly about *tvu'* they emphasise its negative side, but in conversations in which they only refer to *tvu'* indirectly, to explain the activities of *mnyvu* and *bkvubshi,* they stress its neutral side. When I asked people about the role of witchcraft in illness causation they were evasive, or simply said that they might suspect witchcraft if illnesses became chronic or followed an unexpected course. When people talked about *bfaa* they mentioned witchcraft as a possible cause of bad death, and in the discussions about *tvu'* it emerges as a more general cause of illness. Then in conversations about the role of *nyvu* and *bkvubshi* in etiology it seemed that the illnesses which were attributed to these agents are, in fact, caused by witches as well. Only in these circumstances the witches are compound elders and their motives are good.

Tvu', or witchcraft, thus emerges as prime mover, the ultimate force behind all significant illness and misfortune. The *ngaa tvu'* (witches) are all powerful: as cannibals or compound elders they cause illness and misfortune, and as diviners (*ngaa sɛng*) they are the ultimate judges who apportion moral responsibility. The ambivalence of *tvu'* is reflected in the roles of the *ngaa tvu',* who both cause disruption and uphold traditional order: the confrontation between good and evil is epitomised in the struggle between the diviners and the cannibals.

It may be argued here that *tvu'* is not the only force which is responsible for causing disruption and maintaining order. *Mcɛp* (medicine) plays a similar role. But *mcɛp,* at least the more important of its forms, are closely related to *tvu':* the compound *ncɛp* cannot cause the urban migrant to become ill if the compound elders do not intend to punish him. In other words, the *ncɛp* is a means, an instrument, through which *tvu'* can operate.[8] The same applies to the *jujus*, who receive their power through the *tvu'* of the leaders of the secret societies such as *Ngwɛrong*. It is only the more insignificant forms of *mcɛp*, pills and herbal remedies, which are not (at least explicitly) associated in some way with *tvu'*.

Both good and bad witches cause illness, in ordinary people and in each other. The good witches (*ngaa sɛng*) apportion blame. They may decide that the sick person is himself a bad witch who has visited the witch market, or that he is the innocent victim of bad witchcraft. But they may also decide that the illness has been caused by *bkvubshi* or *mnyvu* as punishment for some 'mistake'. This implies that, although witchcraft is the ultimate cause of illness, the ultimate *responsibility* often lies with the afflicted person himself. The extent to which personal responsibility for illness is emphasised varies. Lawrence insisted that traditionally *all* illness was thought to result from 'mistakes' committed by the afflicted (or by his parents or forefathers), and this was confirmed in the discussions about *mnyvu* and *bkvubshi*. Yet when people spoke about *tvu'* generally, and in particular about cannibalism and witch markets, they did not appear to think that the victims of these forms of witchcraft are responsible for their misfortunes.

When someone is incurably ill people may say that he 'knows the cause of his illness', and if someone dies a bad death people will say that he 'knew the cause of his death'. It may be that he was a witch who had gone out to do evil and had been beaten by another witch or trapped by medicines or, if a person dies of wounds which will not heal they may be interpreted as a sign that he visited the witch market and was wounded while trying to escape with a leaf package. When people say 'there must have been something...' in relation to misfortune they are referring to 'mistakes', that is to the moral responsibility of the afflicted or his kin.

In connection with the issue of personal responsibility it should also be noted that the distinction between illnesses caused by the *mnyvu* and those caused by the *bkvubshi* (ancestors) correspond to 'mistakes' or violations of customs or norms which have environmental and social consequences respectively. The *mnyvu* punish violations of the natural environment: destruction of trees, pollution of streams, etc. The *bkvubshi* punish violations of

8. According to Probst and Bühler (1990), who carried out research among the Wiya Wimbum in Ndu, people who are born with *tvu'* have to use *mcɛp* in order to develop their *tvu'*.

social norms: failing to pay the brideprice, failure to adequately celebrate the death of an elder, murder, etc.

Ultimately, however, *tvu'* emerges as prime mover. But it is ambivalent, and the interpretation of illness or misfortune therefore requires a second aspect: personal moral responsibility. These two themes bring together the moral issues of good and evil in the interpretation of illness and misfortune, and vest the diviners (viz the good witches) with the power and authority to decide on the cause and apportion personal moral responsibility. There are no fixed rules, though, and the diviners' interpretations are as flexible and ambivalent as the conceptual constellations themselves. In fact, they resemble the kind of interpretation which I see as fitting for anthropology, interpretations which 'draw their convincingness primarily from communication, rhetoric, and persuasion, and only secondarily from systemic fits or logical proofs'. They are 'more a matter of Socratic persuasion in conversation than of Platonic appeal to transcendent truths' (Fabian 1990b: 757, see also Fish 1980, Taylor 1979, Bernstein 1983).

All of this has implications for the conventional distinction between illnesses of people and illnesses of god. If the illnesses that people call *yang nyvu* are minor ailments that just happen as part of the normal order of things, so that people do not talk about them in terms of causation; if the illnesses people say come from *mnyvu* are caused by witches protecting certain areas; and if the illnesses said to be caused by the *bkvubshi*, or ancestors, are really inflicted as punishment by the living compound elders, then all illnesses which are worth talking about or acting upon, all illnesses that are *caused*, are ultimately caused by witches, that is to say by living people. This means that if we can talk about a 'Wimbum etiology' at all then it is a personalistic etiology. Indeed, the word 'etiology' would refer by definition to illnesses caused through witchcraft.

Finally, if *nyvu* is not God and *mnyvu* are not gods, and the activities attributed to *nyvu* are ultimately the activities of witches (mortals) on the one hand and the impersonal functioning of 'nature' on the other, then it seems to follow that (disregarding the influence of Christianity, if that were possible) those I spoke to were basically atheistic.

The Production of Local Knowledge

The meanings and the themes that emerge from this study are part of a world shared by my informants and myself because we produced it together (partially at any rate). But, just as I appropriated their words and meanings, interpreted them in terms of my own concerns and made them part of anthropological discourse before taking them back to confront my informants, so too they appropriated our terms and meanings into their discourse, developed them in new ways and fed them back into their dialogue with me. Translation was at the basis of this mutual appropriation, and as a result of this the multifaceted meanings and the themes I have discussed above contain Limbum, Pidgin and English terms.

Because terms are indeterminate their translation is problematic. It has become clear in the course of this book that the semantic overlap between "ngang", "bfaa" and "yang bobkɛ'", on the one hand, and "kwashiorkor" on the other, is not only very limited but also highly indeterminate. The same applies to "witchcraft" and "tvu'", "nyvu" and "god", "bkvubshi" and "ancestors", "mcɛp" and "medicine". What conclusion is it possible to reach about the relationship between vernacular terms like "bfaa", "nyvu" and "tvu'" and English terms like "kwashiorkor", "god" and "witchcraft"?

Crick (1982) has suggested that such general terms should be avoided. In his critique of the use of the concept of witchcraft in anthropology he claims that it has probably become a separate topic for anthropological study because of its role in our own history. It is a ready-made concept that can be easily applied to other cultures and leads to the translation of domains of meaning of other cultures in terms of the categories of Western cultures (Crick 1982: 346). Through the work of Evans-Pritchard the concepts of witchcraft and sorcery have 'tended to become frameworks into which ethnographers could fit their own field material instead of paying more attention to the particularity of the culture they happen to have studied' (p. 351). Concepts such as witchcraft form part of a wider conceptual field and can only be understood when they are placed in the context of the other concepts which make up that field. 'Great violence must be done to the conceptual structures of another culture in speaking of witchcraft if it lacks those environing categories which defined it in our own. Where the conceptual field is so different we could not reasonably expect to find the same phenomenon, and so the one term should not be used twice' (pp. 346–7).

Crick points out that English witchcraft was part of a culture which had such categories as 'natural philosophy' and that it was partly parasitic on Christianity (p. 346). He therefore appeals for the analytical dissolution of witchcraft, claiming that

> our understanding will advance when 'witchcraft' is analytically dis-solved into a larger frame of reference. Some still argue that our first task is to define witchcraft, and then by comparison to see what the phenomenon really is... But it is vital to locate the nature and dimensions of the field by which 'witchcraft' is constituted. Such a location can then define the phenomenon away. Studies of witchcraft – let alone comparative studies – would then appear a semantic nonsense, and the mark of our better comprehension would be a decreasingly frequent employment of the term. (p. 346)

This critique could be extended to include many of the general terms that anthropologists use to describe and analyse other cultures, and it seems to be particularly relevant to the concepts examined in this ethnography. I am generally sympathetic toward Crick's criticism of the way in which culturally specific concepts and categories are given universal status and imposed on other cultures (and this criticism is particularly applicable to such concepts as 'the medical system', which I will discuss below). However, I feel uneasy with Crick's argument: he goes too far in one respect and not far enough in another.

He seems to assume that concepts that are constituted in specific cultural contexts must remain bound to them, that because of this their adoption in other contexts is necessarily distorting, and that this distortion is something which is undesirable but can be identified and prevented. But what are we to think if it is not the anthropologist who imposes these categories on the people he studies from above, but local people themselves who actively appropriate and integrate them into their discourse, giving them new meanings and using them in novel ways? Can we then still speak of 'doing violence to their conceptual structures'? Crick's concern with not 'distorting' the people's conceptual structures seems to be just one more expression of the anthropological quest for uncontaminated data, for mirror-image representations of the other. This becomes clear when he states, in terms reminiscent of

Tedlock's depiction of analogical anthropology: 'The common language used here to recast witchcraft seeks to sink beneath cultural terms which are not safely used in anthropology to an analytical level of sufficient depth that satisfactory commensurability between cultures can be attained. Indeed, the proposed framework may be a cultural universal' (p. 347).

In the conversations presented in this study we can see the way in which biomedical conceptions are being adopted into indigenous discourse thereby producing new meanings. Women who attend health education talks are starting to refer to *yang bobkɛ'*, *ngang* and *bfaa* as kwashiorkor; medicine men refer to cases of *ngang* and *bfaa*, which bear no resemblance to the biomedically defined syndrome, as kwashiorkor, and even as malnutrition; health workers use the term "ngang" to refer to kwashiorkor, apparently oblivious to the fact that the term has a completely different meaning for the patient.

We can see how Christianity influences the production of meanings relating to "nyvu" and "bkvubshi", even though we cannot say what the terms 'traditionally' meant in pre-Christian times. Catholic priests use the term "nyvu" to preach about God and they call Satan "nyvurka'" (the being said to inhabit *ntaa tvu'*, the witch market); villagers talk about *nyvu ro* as the god of the stream, while at the same time insisting they are talking about the activities of witches who protect a water source, or are simply referring to the source itself; they use the term 'ancestors' to refer to the regulatory witchcraft of living compound elders and they refer to Abraham and Moses as *bkvubshi*.

Crick is right, of course, when he says that European witchcraft may bear little resemblance to ethnographic descriptions of witchcraft in Africa, and that each term is embedded in a unique conceptual field. And I think we can be reasonably sure that pre-Christian conceptions of *nyvu* were different to the Christian concept of God, just as we are sure that *mcɛp* is different to what is called medicine in the West. But local people have adopted terms such as "witchcraft", "god", "ancestors", "satan", "medicine" and, increasingly, "kwashiorkor" and "malnutrition", into their discourse to such an extent that we would be 'doing violence to their conceptual structures' if we now tried to eliminate them: they have become vernacular terms, (just as the Ga term "kwashiorkor" has been appropriated by Western biomedicine). Could I talk meaningfully to Tobias or Fai Gabriel about *nyvu* while excluding any semantic overlap with the Christian concept of God? Or could I discuss *ngang* with Henry, the village health worker, without evoking in him any thought of protein? I doubt it. The 'paraliterate feedback' about which Owusu is so worried is a *fait accompli*, it is, ironically, part of the very act which constitutes 'indigenous culture'. In other words, the semantic fields or indigenous conceptual structures to which Crick refers already contain the terms which he wants to abolish because they have been constituted and are continually being re-constituted in an ongoing and inter-cultural praxis, and therefore can never be revealed in their pristine form.

There was, of course, a time when the Wimbum had never heard of the terms "god", "witchcraft", "kwashiorkor", etc., but did they then have an uncontaminated conceptual system? I doubt it. The historical and linguistic evidence shows that the Wimbum as we now know them are the product of a long process of migration, integration and cultural exchange. Long before Cameroon became a German colony during the nineteenth century there had been trading and raiding, migration and contact with other peoples: there were trade routes to the Atlantic coast in the south and to Bornu in the north, there were Fulani slave raids and displacement of populations. Given this history, any description of Wimbum culture must be seen as a momentary impression of one point in this process. Culture is always syncretic and any attempt to 'reveal' it in an 'uncontaminated' form implies a denial of the other's historicity.

Discourse and Power

In this study I have been concerned with discourse, with the ways in which people talk about certain things, rather than with their behaviour, and in the last section I criticised the incursion of biomedical categories into ethnographic discourse. The concern with discourse was very much the vogue of medical anthropology in the late 1980s: there have been a number of books with the term in their titles[9] and special numbers of three leading journals were devoted to discourse in medical anthropology.[10] As Harwood points out in his introduction to one of these collections, discourse is in the anthropological air we breathe.

9. Mishler 1984, Johnson Pettinari 1988.
10. Greenwood, et al. 1988, Harwood 1988, Good, Good and Fischer 1988.

The concern with discourse is expressed in different ways. Individual studies are often concerned with communication across discourses. This may take different forms: conflicts between the management of a General Electric plant on the one hand and the workers and community on the other about the detrimental effects of PCBs (Nash and Kirsch 1988), dialogue between genetic counsellors and lay people about heredity (Rapp 1988), the interaction between a shaman and his clients in a healing session (Brown 1988), the relationship between male doctors and female patients during consultations (Davis 1988).

My own approach is related to these studies to the extent that I also emphasise discourse and the interaction between different discourses. But it differs in two significant respects. Firstly, in the studies I have just mentioned the researcher remains a passive and neutral observer/listener who records and analyses the discourse of others. In the present study I proceed from the assumption that it is no longer tenable for the ethnographer, who plays such a determining role during fieldwork, to efface himself from the final text. Secondly, in some studies it has been assumed that different groups of participants utilise distinct discourses, which can be kept separate. Though I speak of biomedical, Christian and traditional discourses this is meant as a heuristic device and, as I think I have shown, it is not easy to separate these discourses in the texts I have presented.

Another point on which I differ from such studies is in the emphasis placed on power and the attempts by the different parties to control discourse (Nash and Kirsch 1988, Brown 1988, Davis 1988). While I fully agree that power plays a role, I do not think it is a fact that can be demonstrated in any simple way. This is related to what I have said above: if different discourses are seen as discrete entities which are the property of unequally related and competing groups of people (management and worker, doctors and patients, men and women) then it is easier to make an interpretation in terms of a struggle for control convincing than when it is assumed that meanings are indeterminate and partially produced in a praxis of which the research process is part.

In my own research I initially thought that I could interpret the texts by showing the influence of Western biomedicine and Christianity on traditional discourse. I soon realised, though, that there were not simply three discrete discourses with power being exercised in one direction. Local people actively appropriated biomedical and Christian concepts and terms and altered them to suit their own purposes, thus creating new concepts, even as I spoke to them. Is the concept of *nyvu* being colonised by hegemonic Christian conceptions of God, or is God being creatively adapted and appropriated into a new local discourse? Are *ngang* and *bfaa* being reduced to biomedical kwashiorkor, or is kwashiorkor being taken over, shed of its irrelevant meanings and expanded to include phenomena which local people consider to be really important? Power is being exercised and there is a struggle for control of discourse, but it is not a simple one-way process.

Medical Systems?

I now want to briefly return to the issues raised by Fortes and Yoder with regard to the distinction between naturalistic and personalistic etiologies, and consider them in the light of my own findings. These issues can be summed up as follows: the focus on etiology, and in particular on comprehensive personalistic etiologies in the medical ethnography of Africa has led to the blurring of the distinction between the domains of medicine, magic and religion. Anthropologists have been too eager to relegate indigenous disease theory to the realms of religion and magic by describing witches or supernatural beings as the most important, or indeed the only, etiological agents recognised by Africans, who are seen as interpreting disease primarily in social and moral terms. This has led anthropologists to accept (implicitly or explicitly) that there is a fundamental dichotomy between Western biomedicine on the one hand and all other medical systems on the other. The focus on etiology accentuates the contrast between biomedicine and other medical systems. This has in turn led to the neglect of the practical, behavioural aspects of non-Western medical systems, and therefore to a neglect of medical systems *per se*. Yoder notes that more recent studies with a *broader* focus on *medical* ideas and practices presents a different picture of etiology and medical knowledge (Yoder 1982b: 13).

When Yoder claims that anthropologists have uncritically accepted biomedical definitions of what is relevant in the study of health care and medicine, he is right. But his advice has not always been heeded. Medical anthropologists who try to bridge the gap between biomedicine and other medical systems tend to make use of the very biomedical categories they explicitly reject, and the broader view that they claim to have is, in fact, narrower: they select certain elements from that continuous whole constituted by indigenous discourse and behaviour and use them to construct a *medical* system. The criteria and assumptions employed in this selection are ultimately biomedical. After all, why study medical systems? All this talk of medical systems, medical knowledge, medical behaviour, medical situations, behaviour related to health and illness (Yoder 1982b: 8) flows from a biomedically determined interest in disease and health care. That health workers focus their attention on such matters is understandable, but why should anthropological enquiry be limited to a domain defined beforehand: a medical system, consisting of disease and health care behaviour (rather than, say, witchcraft, motor accidents and crop failure)?

Not only is the object of much medical anthropology, the medical system, created as a separate domain by the very attempt to study and describe it as something discrete (though its creation is concealed by the assumption of its prior existence), it is also, and this is one of its more problematic aspects, surreptitiously created in the very image of biomedicine, from which these anthropologists explicitly distance themselves. By focussing on the 'practical', 'natural' 'empirical' and 'behavioural' aspects of disease they automatically exclude the 'supernatural' and 'ritual' aspects of illness (which Rivers and Evans-Pritchard included, even if they did consider them to be less 'real') as well as other non-illness misfortunes, and thus not only create an indigenous medical domain, but also reduce it to a somewhat inadequate version of biomedicine.

Indigenous conceptions of illness are thus narrowed down (naturalised and separated from other misfortune, their 'supernatural' aspect either being purged or socialised) and so brought into line with biomedical conceptions of disease, based ultimately on positivistic assumptions about the nature of physical reality (thus making anthropological interpretations more acceptable to biomedical experts?).

It is assumed that the 'supernatural' aspects of indigenous culture are somehow less real or less important than the 'natural' aspects. Even when witchcraft is recognised as an important part of the medical system it is socialised – transformed from a 'supernatural' phenomenon into a social phenomenon. When people refer to witchcraft as a cause of illness then this is not interpreted literally, as meaning that witchcraft 'really' causes illness, but as a metaphorical statement about social conflicts and moral issues (see for example Taussig 1980).

What are we to make of the explicit criticism of biomedical hegemony and the commitment to discovering the native's point of view when it is so subtly combined with the projection of the dominant definitions and categories of this very same hegemonic system onto indigenous culture, followed by the 'discovery' that they really do have a medical system after all and that it basically looks just like ours: naturalistic, empirical, pragmatic, disease-oriented? To what extent are medical anthropologists repeating the surreptitious appropriation of indigenous discourse that certain scholars of religion perpetrated before them, when they 'discovered' that the pagans had believed in one 'High God' all along (see Smith 1950, Parrinder 1969, Mbiti 1970)? Like kinship, religion and witchcraft, medicine has become one of the topoi of anthropological discourse (see Fabian 1983).

I should not want to be misunderstood at this point to be accusing authors such as Bibeau, Warren or Yoder of blatantly imposing biomedical categories. Indeed, their analyses are sophisticated and they are highly sensitive to indigenous interpretations and categories. Neither do I consider a biomedical approach 'wrong' in itself. I am not implying that biomedically trained health workers or medically schooled anthropologists who work in other cultures should abandon their assumptions (indeed, my argument has been that they *cannot* entirely abandon or bracket these assumptions). As Prins has argued: 'In practice, at work in a sea of infectious disease, how can western physicians in poor countries internalise any other taxonomy than their own and be able to function effectively? Should they even try?' (Prins 1981: 178). Prins points out that Gilbert Lewis, like most medical anthropologists, chooses to view diseases as objective, biological entities or conditions which can be interpreted independently of historical and cultural factors. This is necesary, Prins argues, in order to make possible a comparative study of cultural factors related to sickness in the first place. If he did not do this he would be forced to proceed from indigenous definitions and categories, and ignore 'the mass of undiagnosed but objectively present illness which Lewis, as a physician, found in the Sepik' (Prins 1981: 179).

Does this have to be a problem for the *anthropologist*, however? When we study illness, or religion for that matter, as anthropologists, is it necessary to proceed a *priori* from a distinction between the putatively objective (biology, disease) and the subjective (culture, illness)? Must we take a stance on the ontological status of the entities we study? Here I agree with Geertz.

> The thing to ask about a burlesqued wink or a mock sheep raid [or illness or witchcraft] is not what their ontological status is. It is the same as rocks on the one hand and dreams on the other – they are things of this world. The thing to ask is what their import is: what it is...that, in their occurrence and through their agency, is getting said. (Geertz 1973: 10)

The problem is not that biomedical categories are being adopted into local discourse. People are inventive and use these categories to create new meanings for themselves (as we have seen in the case of terms such as "witchcraft" and "god"). Rather, the problem is the surreptitious incursion, through ethnographic descriptions and analyses which claim to be neutral, of these historically and culturally contingent categories into *anthropological* discourse where they pose as objective and universal. This does not stem from any sinister attempt to impose biomedical categories, but from the very attempt to avoid those categories through the use of an 'emic' perspective to reveal the native's point of view more accurately, and from attempts, usually based on some form of ethnoscience methodology, to bracket out contaminating assumptions and categories. The ideology which has to be opposed here is not blatant cultural imperialism but rather liberal humanism. After all, why should we want to bridge the gap between traditional medicine and biomedicine by identifying indigenous medical systems? Attempting to show that non-Western cultures are inferior to ours because they are different is reprehensible, but is the only alternative to reduce them to variations on some universal theme in order to be able to take them seriously or treat them equally? Why can other 'medical systems' not be taken at face value and judged in their own terms?

Part of the reason may be the assumption that underlies much medical anthropology: that it must make some contribution, directly or indirectly, to 'development'. This is assumed to be a one-way process, whose outcome for non-Western societies is that they come to resemble contemporary Western society, or some variation of Western conceptions of the ideal society (industrial, socialist, parliamentary democratic or whatever). As a result, applied medical anthropology is in danger of becoming 'a secular, scientifically neutral substitute for missionising or carrying out an *oeuvre civilisatrice*' (Fabian n.d.). Scholte has also pointed to the continuity between Christian and scientific missions, which he traces back to a Judeo-Christian passion to transcend comparative history through universal categories.

> The Occidental *Weltanschauung*, however diverse its actual contents or concrete historical manifestations, is ultimately guided by universal (hence abstract) and teleological (hence judgmental) aims to be realized or realizable in history. Western theologians, scientists, and others argued *ad infinitum* about the specific nature of these ultimate aims, but the over-riding anthropological consideration is that all interested parties presuppose transcendental and prescriptive norms by means of which concrete and diverse historical societies may be described, analyzed, assessed, *and* influenced. To the non-Western 'beneficiaries' of these Occidental *idées fixes*, they must seem like so many exotic variations on an alien theme: Christ's Second Coming, the Proletarian Revolution, Rational Scientific Closure. (Scholte 1983: 261–2)

The present study can be seen in part as an attempt to limit (or perhaps more accurately to make explicit) the surreptitious incursion of biomedical categories into ethnographic discourse in the guise of objective description through a dialogical approach which emphasises the production of meaning rather than the gathering of pre-existing information. Though my research was rooted in the very biomedical assumptions I am criticising (and I think I have shown that it could not have been otherwise), I have attempted to make the process more explicit by placing it within the context of an ongoing praxis.

The result of all this is perhaps not so much that the 'medical system' is wider and more inclusive than some authors suggest, but that there is no system at all. As we have seen, no clear line can be drawn between the meanings of indigenous and biomedical (and Christian) terms, and interpretations depend largely on context. Can we still talk about Christianity and traditional religion, or traditional medicine and biomedicine? Somewhat like Murray Last's description of the 'non-system' in Malumfashi, Nigeria, the Wimbum do not have a medical system, but are confronted with a wide-ranging complex of illnesses and other misfortunes for which all the various kinds of healers, whether traditional or biomedical should, between them, have a cure (Last 1981). Medicine is seen 'not so much as a medical system but as part of the necessary cultural camouflage, like clothing and food, that enables one to survive...' (Last 1981: 389).

I have criticised Crick's argument that the use of certain general terms in ethnography distorts indigenous conceptual structures by showing that they are partially constituted by these very terms. I think, though, that his plea for the dissolution of general concepts may well apply to the object of medical anthropology: the medical system.

Epilogue

Lawrence's Departure

On my arrival in Ndu Lawrence had confidently presented himself to me as the only suitable research assistant. Employing him for more than language lessons had entailed distinct advantages and disadvantages. In Tabenken, which was not his native village and was even in a different clan area, there would be none of the obligations, conflicts, rivalries and jealousies which characterise village life, and Lawrence would be reasonably neutral. On the other hand, he would have less inside information about those local conflicts and rivalries and know nothing of kinship relations, etc. I let him convince me that the advantages outweighed the disadvantages and employed him as research assistant. It did not take much persuading. Lawrence was easy to get on with and we shared the same ironic sense of humour.

Lawrence was a born socialiser. From the day of our arrival in Tabenken he set to work with a serious intensity. Within no time he seemed to know not only everyone in the village but also all the local gossip and intrigues. His popularity never ceased to amaze me. He was both an outsider and an insider at the same time. In his own way he was already an anthropologist.

When I arranged to visit Pa Takwi on his treatment days Pius would say 'You are welcome, as long as you come with that Ndu man and not with a Tabenkenian.' He was afraid that a local would attempt to steal his father's secrets. Lawrence worked hard, was never late for our appointments and never tried to trick me. The ideal assistant. He helped me when I needed him and I helped him when he needed me. When he decided to participate in the Mount Cameroon Race, the marathon to summit of Mount Cameroon and back, I switched the project into low gear for three weeks and we drove down to Buea together so that he could train on the mountain. If I needed him on his days off he put his son in charge of his vegetable shop and came to assist me.

About halfway through the project news came that his sister was seriously ill and Lawrence made several trips, apparently to visit her. Then one day he asked me for an advance of six months' salary. He wanted to buy a herd of goats and sell them at Christmas when the price was high. It sounded like a reasonable project so I paid him. Earlier I had helped him in the purchase of carrot seeds. Nothing changed in our work routine, but I saw no evidence of the goats either. I suspected that he had invested the money in one of the subscription societies instead, but that was his business. I asked no questions and he volunteered no explanations.

Then people in the village started to complain to me about him, saying that he was no good and that I should dismiss him. When I arranged to visit Pa TaKwi Pius now started saying 'As long as you *don't* come with that Ndu man.' By the time Lawrence showed up in Tabenken with his broken leg his popularity had declined even further and he had fallen out with a number of our former friends (or rather his former friends; those concerned were still friendly to me, but could not understand what I still saw in him). After his leg had healed I hardly saw him at all, and he only came to Tabenken sporadically. When we did arrange to work together he hardly ever showed up, or if he did show up it was only the next day when it was too late. His excuses became weaker and weaker. He became lethargic. In the early days he would arrive in Tabenken only to put on his running gear and jog back to his farm, some twenty kilometres away, because he had forgotten his keys or some other insignificant object and was too impatient to wait for a bush taxi. Now he stopped training altogether and began to put on weight.

Rumours started to reach me about witchcraft accusations. People said that he had been accused of being involved in his sister's illness. I was told that he had not been beaten-up by muggers in Ndu but by his own 'brothers' and that this was related to his sister's illness. There were rumours that he had fallen out with the *fon* of Ndu, who had been his mentor. I once heard someone refer to him as 'that witchman'. Was there some truth in these rumours or was it just malicious gossip? I do not know.

By the time I reached the end of my fieldwork, I had not seen Lawrence for some months. I packed my belongings into the car, said my goodbyes and headed for Bamenda. On the way I stopped in Ndu for petrol. While I was filling up Lawrence appeared. He needed me to sign some declaration or other at the local gendarmerie affirming that he had been in my employ. We strolled over to the gendarmerie together and I confirmed that he had been working for me. A policeman, who could hardly write, attempted to fill in a form, looking up suspiciously when Lawrence said 'anthropologist–linguist' in answer to a question about his occupation. When the form had been completed and signed I left. Lawrence did not tell me what had happened between us nor did I ask. Neither did I ever find out.

During a subsequent fieldwork trip the following year I did not see him at all, but his popularity in the village had reached an all-time low. He had apparently eloped with the daughter of one of my neighbours, taking along her two children and not paying any bride price to her father. People said he had abandoned his wife and was living somewhere in Ngwa, where the witches were sometimes said to go on their nocturnal trips.

I never found out what had happened, but in the course of time I have speculated. Lawrence was a fervent traditionalist. He was opposed to Christianity and did not like missionaries. He often told me about his grandfather, who was the head of the very traditionalist family compound. Situated far from the main road, no outsiders, and in particular no White men, were admitted to any of the traditional ceremonies. He told me of the fantastic *jujus* belonging to his grandfather's *ndap ngong*. In comparison, the *jujus* of the villages along the Ring Road, such as Tabenken and Ndu, were meek and powerless and their music bland and insipid, Lawrence said. Doubtless exaggerations, I thought, until one day he brought me a recording of his grandfather's *jujus* 'singing'. When I played the strange sounds for Fai Nga Kontar and Pa Tanto Ngeh, two the leaders of *Ngwerong*, the regulatory *juju* society in Tabenken, they sat white-lipped and transfixed. Those were *very* powerful *jujus*, they assured me.

Traditionalists did not divulge secrets to outsiders, particularly White outsiders. Pa Tanto Ngeh, perhaps my best friend in Tabenken, was probably, and somewhat paradoxically, also the most stringent traditionalist in the village, which is why he does not appear in these pages, except in the acknowledgements. He visited me faithfully every single day during my whole eighteen-month stay in Tabenken, and on many days we drank palm wine together in a little hut in his palm grove. It was he who introduced me into *Ngwerong* as a member and told me much about Wimbum tradition. But there were limits. He always refused to be interviewed and never permitted informal conversations to be recorded. When we talked he would occasionally strain his head to check whether perhaps my cassette recorder was turned on. When I asked him what was wrong with recording innocent informal chat, he said that he may inadvertently divulge something which he was not supposed to. If I were just listening I would forget it again or I might not even notice, but if it was recorded then it would be revealed and he would have to bear the consequences. It would be a mistake which would then lead to illness or worse in his compound, or at least that is how I interpreted it. Pa Tanto was not happy with other traditionalists who revealed certain things to White men, and he made no secret of this to me, suggesting that they would reap what they had sown.

My speculation about Lawrence's behaviour first focussed on the possibility that he had been accused of providing his sister to a witch society, but this did not seem likely. Finally I came to the conclusion that, given his background and the stories of his grandfather, his sister's illness and his own broken leg must, in some way, have been related to his having worked with me. Old traditionalists in his compound must have known that he was working with me and suspected that he told me secrets, though I do not know whether he really did so or not. In any case the impression would have been there. Also, the 'songs' of *jujus* were not supposed to be recorded. On occasions in Tabenken when I had asked Lawrence what would happen if I recorded them secretly, he said that 'the old men would know' and would take the necessary measures. He had recorded the songs of the most terrible *jujus* and given them to me. Perhaps diviners diagnosing the cause of his sister's illness had pointed to Lawrence's collaboration with me as a cause; perhaps his broken leg had been a warning from the *bkvubshi* that he should sever his contact with me.

But maybe I have got it all wrong. Maybe I am too imbued with a Western scientific and anthropological need for explanation and systemic closure after all. Perhaps it was just one of those inexplicable quirks which transform friendship into indifference and communication into incomprehension, and for which there is, in true postmodern fashion, just no explanation at all.

Bibliography

Ardener, E., 1970, Witchcraft, Economics, and the Continuity of Belief. In M. Douglas (ed.), *Witchcraft Confessions and Accusations*. London: Tavistock, pp. 141–60

Arens, W., 1980, Taxonomy versus Dynamics Revisited: The Interpretation of Misfortune in a Polyethnic Community. In I. Karp, and C.S. Bird (eds), *Explorations in African Systems of Thought*. Bloomington: Indiana University Press, pp. 165–80

Bauman, R., 1977, *Verbal Art as Performance*. Prospect Heights. Waveland

Bayart, J.F., 1981, Le Politique par le Bas en Afrique Noir. *Politique Africaine* 1: 53–81

——, 1986, Civil Society and the State in Africa. In P. Chabal (ed.), *Political Domination in Africa*. Cambridge: Cambridge University Press, pp. 109–25

Beidelman, T.O., 1963, Witchcraft in Ukaguru. In J. Middleton and E.H. Winter (eds), *Witchcraft and Sorcery in East Africa*. London: Routledge and Kegan Paul, pp. 57–98

Bernstein, R., 1983, *Beyond Objectivism and Relativism: Science, Hermeneutics and Praxis*. Oxford: Blackwell

Berreman, G., 1972, *Hindus of the Himalayas: Ethnography and Change*. Berkeley: University of California Press

Bibeau, G., 1979, *De la maladie à la guérison. essai d'analyse systématique de la medicine des Angbandi du Zaire*. Unpublished doctoral dissertation, Laval University

——, 1981, The Circular Semantic Network in Ngbandi Disease Nosology. *Social Science and Medicine* 15B: 295–307

——, 1982, A Systems Approach to Ngbandi Medicine. In P.S. Yoder (ed.), *African Health and Healing Systems: Proceedings of a Symposium*. Los Angeles: Crossroads Press, pp. 43–84

Bloch, M. and J. Parry (eds), 1982, *Death and the Regeneration of Life*. Cambridge: Cambridge University Press

Bohannan, P., 1958, Extra-Processual Events in Tiv Political Institutions. *American Anthropologist* 60: 1–12

Bomnsa, J., 1984, A Theological Analysis of Traditional Confession among the Wimbum. Bambui (Cameroon): Major Regional Seminary

Boutin, M.E. and A.Y. Boutin, 1987, Classification of Disease Among the Baggi of Sabah. *Anthropological Linguistics* 29(2): 157–69

Brock, J.F. and M. Autret, 1952, *Kwashiorkor in Africa*. Rome: FAO

Brokensha, D., D.M. Warren and O. Werner (eds), 1980, *Indigenous Knowledge Systems and Development*. Lanham: University Press of America

Brown, M.F., 1988, Shamanism and its Discontents. *Medical Anthropology Quarterly* N.S. 2(2): 102–20

Browner, C.H., B.R. Ortiz de Montellano and A.J. Rubel, 1988, A Methodology for Cross-cultural Ethnomedical Research. *Current Anthropology* 29(5): 681–702

Buckley, A.D., 1985, The God of Smallpox: Aspects of Yoruba Religious Knowledge. *Africa* 55(2): 187–200

Carpenter, F.W., 1934a, Intelligence Report on the Nsungli Area, Bamenda Division. Buea: Buea Archives

——, 1934b, Progress Report on the Ndu, Mbwat and Tang Native Authority Areas, Formerly Known as the Nsungli Tribe of Bamenda Division. Buea: Buea Archives

Cassidy, C.M., 1982, Protein–Energy Malnutrition as a Culture-Bound Syndrome. *Culture, Medicine and Psychiatry* 6: 325–45

Chilver, E.M., 1961, Nineteenth Century Trade in the Bamenda Grassfields, Southern Cameroons. *Afrika und Ubersee* xlv(4): 233–58,

——, 1966, *Zintgraff's Explorations in Bamenda. Adamawa and the Benue Lands 1889–1892*. Buea: Ministry of Primary Education and Social Welfare and West Cameroon Antiquities Commission

——,(ed.), 1981, Dr. P.M. Kaberry's fieldnotes on Tang Mbo or Tabenken. Unpublished manuscript

Chilver, E.M. and P.M. Kaberry, 1965, Sources of Nineteenth Century Slave Trade: The Cameroon Highlands. *Journal of African History* 6(1): 117–20

——, 1967, *Traditional Bamenda: The Pre-colonial History and Ethnography of the Bamenda Grassfields*. Buea: Ministry of Primary Education and Social Welfare and West Cameroon Antiquities Commission

Clements, F.E., 1932, *Primitive Concepts of Disease*. University of California Publications in American Archeology and Ethnology 32(2): 185–252

Clifford, J., 1983, On Ethnographic Authority. *Representations* 2: 132–43

Clifford, J. and G. Marcus (eds), 1986, *Writing Culture: The Poetics and Politics of Ethnography*. Berkeley: University of California Press

Coulter, J.B.S., R.G. Hendrickse, S.M. Lamplugh and S.B.J. Macfarlane, 1986, Aflatoxins and Kwashiorkor: Clinical Studies in Sudanese Children. *Transactions of the Royal Society of Tropical Medicine and Hygiene* 80: 945–51

Crapanzano, V., 1980, *Tuhami: Portrait of a Moroccan*. Chicago: University of Chicago Press

Crick, M., 1982, Recasting Witchcraft. In M. Marwick (ed.), *Witchcraft and Sorcery*. Harmondsworth: Penguin, pp. 343–64

Davis, K., 1988, *Power Under the Microscope*. Dordrecht: Foris

Douglas, M., 1970, Introduction: Thirty Years after Witchcraft, Oracles and Magic. In M. Douglas (ed.), *Witchcraft Confessions and Accusations*. London: Tavistock, pp. xiii–xxxviii

Driberg, J.H., 1936, The Secular Aspect of Ancestor Worship in Africa. *Supplement to the Journal of the Royal African Society* 35(138)

Dwyer, K., 1982, *Moroccan Dialogues: Anthropology in Question*. Baltimore: Johns Hopkins University Press

Ebrahim, G.J., 1983, *Nutrition in Mother and Child Health*. London: Macmillan

Eisenberg, L., 1977, Disease and Illness. *Culture, Medicine and Psychiatry* 1: 9–23

Evans-Pritchard, E.E., 1937, *Witchcraft, Oracles and Magic among the Azande*. Oxford: The Clarendon Press

Fabian, J., 1983, *Time and the Other: How Anthropology Makes its Object*. New York: Colombia University Press

——, 1985, Religious Pluralism: An Ethnographic Approach. In M. Schoffeleers and W. van Binsbergen (eds), *Theoretical Approaches in the Study of African Religion*, pp. 138–63

——, 1990a, *Power and Performance. Ethnographic Explorations through Proverbial Wisdom and Theater in Shaba, Zaire*. Madison, University of Wisconsin Press

——, 1990b Presence and Representation: The Other and Anthropological Writing. *Critical Inquiry* 16: 753–72,

——, Cultural Anthropology and Research in the Non-Western World. Amsterdam, unpublished manuscript

Feinberg, R., 1990, Spiritual and Natural Etiologies on a Polynesian Outlier in Papua New Guinea. *Social Science and Medicine* 30(3): 311–23

Field, M.J., 1937, *Religion and Medicine of the Ga Peoples*. London: Oxford University Press

——, 1960, *Search for Security*. London: Faber

Firth, R., 1982(1956), Reason and Unreason in Human Belief. In M. Marwick (ed.), *Witchcraft and Sorcery*. Harmondsworth: Penguin, pp. 38–40

Fish, S., 1980, *Is There a Text in this Class?* Harvard: Harvard University Press

Fortes, M., 1976, Foreword. In J. Loudon, (ed.), *Social Anthropology and Medicine*. London: Academic Press, pp. ix–xx

Foster, G., 1976, Disease Etiologies in Non-Western Medical Systems. *American Anthropologist* 78: 773–82

Friedrich, P., 1986, *The Language Parallax. Linguistic Relativism and Poetic Indeterminacy*. Austin: University of Texas Press.

Geertz, C., 1973, *The Interpretation of Cultures*. New York: Basic Books

——, 1984, Distinguished Lecture: Anti Anti-Relativism. *American Anthropologist* 86: 263–78

Gellner, E., 1985, *Relativism and the Social Sciences.* Cambridge: Cambridge University Press

Geschiere, P., 1978, *Stamgemeenschappen onder Staatsgezag. Veranderende Verhoudingen binnen de Maka Dorpen in Zuidoost Cameroun sinds 1900.* Unpublished doctoral dissertation. Amsterdam: Free University

——, 1983, *Village Communities and the State. Changing Relations Among the Maka of South-Eastern Cameroon Since the Colonial Conquest.* London: Kegan Paul International

——, 1988, Sorcery and the State. Popular Modes of Action among the Maka of Southeast Cameroon. *Critique of Anthropology* 8(1): 35–63

Gillies, E., 1976, Causal Criteria in African Classifications of Disease. In J. Loudon, (ed.), *Social Anthropology and Medicine.* London: Academic Press, pp. 358–95

Godelier, M., 1986, *The Making of Great Men. Male Domination and Power among the New Guinea Baruya.* Cambridge: Cambridge University Press

Good, M-J., B. Good and M.J. Fischer (eds), 1988, Emotion, Illness and Healing in Middle Eastern Societies. Special issue of *Culture, Medicine and Society* 12(1)

Gopalan, C., 1968, Kwashiorkor and Marasmus. Evolution and Distinguishing Features. In R.A. McCance and E.M. Widowson (eds), *Calorie Deficiency and Protein Deficiency.* London: Churchill

Greenwood, D., S. Lindenbaum, M. Lock and A. Young (eds), 1988, Theme Issue: Medical Anthropology. *American Ethnologist* 15(1)

Hall, R.A., 1966, *Pidgin and Creole Languages.* Ithaca: Cornell University Press

Harley, G.W., 1941, *Native African Medicine: With Special Reference to its Practice in the Mano Tribe of Liberia.* Cambridge: Harvard University Press

Harwood, A., 1970, *Witchcraft, Sorcery and Social Categories among the Safwa.* Oxford: Oxford University Press

——, (ed.), 1988, Special issue of *Medical Anthropology Quarterly* N.S. 2(2)

Hawksworth, E.G., 1923, Report on the History of the Nsungli Area. Buea Archives

——, 1924, An Assessment Report on the Nsungli Clans. Buea Archives

Hendrickse, R.G., 1984, The Influence of Aflatoxins on Child Health in the Tropics with Particular Reference to Kwashiorkor. *Transactions of the Royal Society of Tropical Medicine and Hygiene* 78: 427–35

——, 1985, Kwashiorkor: 50 Years of Myth and Mystery. Do Aflatoxins Privide a Clue? Second P.H. van Thiel lecture of the Institute of Tropical Medicine, Rotterdam-Leiden, 26 September, 1985

——, 1986, Aflatoxins and Child Health in the Tropics. Stanley Davidson Lecture

Hobsbawm, E. and T. Ranger (eds), 1983, *The Invention of Tradition.* Cambridge: Cambridge University Press

Horton, R., 1962, The Kalabari World View: An Outline and Interpretation. *Africa* 32(3): 197–219

——, 1967, African Traditional Thought and Western Science, (parts I and II). *Africa* 37: 50–71, 155–87

——, 1971, African Conversion. *Africa* 40(2): 85–108

Hsu, F.L.K., 1973, Prejudice and its Intellectual Effect in American Anthropology: An Ehnographic Report. *American Anthropologist* 75(1): 1–19

Jacobson-Widding, A. and D. Westerlund (eds), 1989, *Culture, Experience and Pluralism. Essays on African Ideas of Illness and Healing.* Uppsala: Almqvist & Wiksell

Janzen, J.M., 1978, *The Quest for Therapy in Lower Zaire.* Berkeley: University of California Press

——, 1981, The Need for a Taxonomy of Health in the Study of African Therapeutics. *Social Science and Medicine* 15B: 185–94

Jeffreys, M.D.W., 1962, The Wiya Tribe (parts I and II). *African Studies* 21(2): 83–104 and 21(3–4): 174–222

Jelliffe D.B., 1959, Protein–Calorie Malnutrition in Tropical Preschool Children, a Review of Recent Knowledge. *Journal of Pediatrics* 54: 227–56

Johnson Pettinari, C., 1988, *Task, Talk and Text in the Operating Room. A Study in Medical Discourse.* Norwood: Ablex

Kellehear, A., 1990, *Dying of Cancer. The Final year of Life.* London: Harwood

Kleinman, A., 1980, *Patients and Healers in the Context of Culture.* Berkeley: University of California Press

Larner, C., 1982 (1974), Is all Witchcraft Really Witchcraft? In M. Marwick (ed.), *Witchcraft and Sorcery.* Harmondsworth: Penguin, pp. 48–53

Last, M., 1981, The Importance of Knowing about not Knowing. *Social Science and Medicine* 15B: 387–92

Loudon, J. (ed.), 1976, *Social Anthropology and Medicine.* London: Academic Press

Marcus, G.E. and D. Cushman., 1982, Ethnographies as Texts. *Annual Review of Anthropology* 11: 25–69

Marcus, G. E. and M. Fischer, 1986, *Anthropology as Cultural Critique: An Experimental Moment in the Human Sciences.* Chicago: University of Chicago Press

Marwick, M., 1982 (1964), Witchcraft as a Social Strain-Guage. In M. Marwick (ed.), *Witchcraft and Sorcery.* Harmondsworth: Penguin, pp. 300–13

Mayer, P., 1982 (1954), Witches. In M. Marwick (ed.), *Witchcraft and Sorcery.* Harmondsworth: Penguin, pp. 54–70

Mbiti, J.S., 1970, *Concepts of God in Africa.* London: S.P.C.K.

Mbunwe-Samba, P., 1989, Witchcraft, Magic and Divination. A Personal

Testimony. Bamenda, unpublished manuscript

Mburu, J.M., 1979, Witchcraft Among the Wimbum. Unpublished B.A. thesis in philosophy. Bambui (Cameroon): Regional Major Seminary

McLaren, D.S., 1974, The Great Protein Fiasco. *Lancet* 2: 93–6

Middleton, J., 1982, Lugbara Death. In M. Bloch and J. Parry (eds), *Death and the Regeneration of Life*. Cambridge: Cambridge University Press, pp.134–54

Middleton, J. and E.H. Winter (eds), 1963, *Witchcraft and Sorcery in East Africa*. London: Routledge and Kegan Paul

Mishler, E.G., 1984, *The Discourse of Medicine*. Norwood: Ablex

Morley, D.C., 1973, *Paediatric Priorities in the Developing World*. London: Butterworth

Murdock, G.P., 1980, *Theories of Illness. A World Survey*. Pittsburg: University of Pittsburg Press

Nash, J. and M Kirsch., 1988, The Discourse of Medical Science in the Construction of Consensus Between Corporation and Community. *Medical Anthropology Quarterly* N.S. 2(2): 158–71

Ngubane, H., 1976, *Body and Mind in Zulu Medicine*. London: Academic Press

Njingti, J., 1979, Witchcraft Among the Wimbum. Unpublished B.A. thesis in philosophy. Bambui (Cameroon): Regional Major Seminary

Nkwi, P.N. and J-P. Warnier, 1982, *A History of the Western Grassfields*. Yaounde: University of Yaounde

Nordstrom, C.R., 1989, Ayurveda: A Multilectic Interpretation. *Social Science and Medicine* 28(9): 963–70

Owusu, M., 1978, Ethnography of Africa: The Usefulness of the Useless. *American Anthropologist* 80: 310–34

Pacey, A. and P. Payne (eds), 1985, *Agricultural Development and Nutrition*. London: Hutchison

Parekh, B., 1974, The Spectre of Self-Consciousness. In B. Parekh (ed.), *Colour, Culture and Consciousness: Immigrant Intellectuals in Britain*. London: George Allen and Unwin, pp. 41–85

Parkin, D., 1985, Introduction. In D. Parkin (ed.), *The Anthropology of Evil*. Oxford: Basil Blackwell

——, 1986, Violence and Will. In D. Riches (ed.), *The Anthropology of Violence*. Oxford: Basil Blackwell

Parrinder, G., 1958, *Witchcraft: European and African*. London: Faber and Faber

——, 1969, African Religion. London: Penguin

Parry, J., 1982, Sacrificial Death and the Necrophagous Ascetic. In M. Bloch and J Parry (eds), *Death and the Regeneration of Life*. Cambridge: Cambridge University Press

Price Williams, D.R., 1979 (1962) A Case Study of Ideas Concerning Disease among the Tiv. In Z.A. Ademuwagun, J.A.A. Ayoade, I.E. Harrison and D.M. Warren (eds), *African Therapeutic Systems*. Los

Angeles: Crossroads Press, pp. 26–30

Prins, G., 1981, What is to be Done? Burning Questions of our Movement. *Social Science and Medicine* 15B: 175–83

Probst, P., 1989, The Letter and the Spirit. Literacy and Religious Authority in the History of the Aladura Movement of Western Nigeria. *Africa* 59: 478–95

Probst, P. and B. Bühler, 1990, Patterns of Control on Medicine, Politics, and Social Change among the Wimbum, Cameroon Grassfields. *Anthropos* 85: 447–54

Rapp, R., 1988, Chromosomes and Communication: The Discourse of Genetic Counseling. *Medical Anthropology Quarterly* N.S. 2(2): 143–57

Van Reenen, P., 1988, Bijbelvertalen in de Derde Wereld, Pidgin en Limbum in Kameroen. In K.H. van Reenen-Stein and A. Dees (eds), *Jaarboek VWF-Programma Corpus gebaseerde Woordanalyse 1987–1988*. Amsterdam: Vrije Universiteit, pp. 101–10

Rivers, W.H.R., 1924, *Medicine, Magic and Religion*. London: Kegan Paul

Rosaldo, M., 1980, *Knowledge and Passion: Ilongot Notions of Self and Social Life*. Cambridge: Cambridge University Press

Rosny, E. de, 1985, *Healers in the Night. A French Priest's Account of his Immersion in the World of an African Healer*. Maryknoll, New York: Orbis Books

Rowlands, M. and J-P. Warnier, 1988, Sorcery, Power and the Modern State in Cameroon. *Man* N.S. 23: 118–32

Scholte, B., 1983, Cultural Anthropology and the Paradigm Concept: A Brief History of Their Recent Convergence. In L. Graham, W. Lepenies and P. Weingart (eds), *Functions and Uses of Disciplinary Histories*. Dordrecht: Reidel, pp. 229–78

Shankman, P., 1984, The Thick and the Thin: On the Interpretive Theoretical Program of Clifford Geertz. *Current Anthropology* 25(3): 261–85

Smith, E.W. (ed.), 1950, *African Ideas of God: A Symposium*. London: Edinburgh House Press

Spiro, M., 1986, Cultural Relativism and the Future of Anthropology. *Cultural Anthropology* 1: 259–86

Stannus, H.S., 1935, Kwashiorkor. *Lancet* 2: 1207–8

Stallcup, K., 1980, The Linguistic Geography of the Grassfields. In L. Hyman and J. Voorhoeve (eds), *Les Classes Nominales dans le Bantou des Grassfields*. Société d'Etudes Linguistiques et Anthropologiques de France

Tanto, R., 1976, Witchcraft Among the Wimbum of Tabenken. Bambui (Cameroon): Regional Major Seminary

Taussig, M., 1980, Reification and the Consciousness of the Patient. *Social Science and Medicine* 14B(1):3–13

Taylor, C., 1979, Interpretation and the Sciences of Man. In P. Rabinow and W. M. Sullivan (eds), *Interpretive Social Science: A Reader*.

Berkeley: University of California Press, pp. 25–72

Tedlock, D., 1983, *The Spoken Word and the Work of Interpretation*. Philadelphia: University of Pennsylvania Press

——, 1987, Questions Concerning Dialogical Anthropology. *Journal of Anthropological Research* 43(4): 325–37

Todd, L., 1979, *Some Day Been Dey. West Africal Pidgin Folk Tales*. London: Routledge and Kegan Paul

Trowell, H.D., J.N. Davies and R.F.A. Dean., 1954, *Kwashiorkor*. London: Edward Arnold

Turner, V., 1967, *The Forest of Symbols. Aspects of Ndembu Ritual*. Cornell: Cornell University Press

Tyler, S., 1984, Ethnopoetics, or the Anthropologist as Coyote. Unpublished manuscript

——, 1986, Post-Modern Ethnography: From Document of the Occult to Occult Document. In J. Clifford and G. Marcus (eds), pp.122–40

——, 1987, On "Writing-Up/Off" as "Speaking-For". *Journal of Anthropological Research* 43(4): 338–42

URCNNS, 1978, *United Republic of Cameroon National Nutrition Survey*. Washington: Agency for International Development

Warren, D.M., 1974, Disease, Medicine and Religion among the Bono of Ghana: A Study in Culture Change. Unpublished doctoral dissertation, Indiana University

——, 1979a, The Role of Emic Analyses in Medical Anthropology: The Case of the Bono of Ghana. In Z.A. Ademuwagun, J.A.A. Ayoade, I.E. Harrison and D.M. Warren (eds), *African Therapeutic Systems*. Los Angeles: Crossroads Press, pp. 36–42

——, 1979b, Bono Traditional Healers. In Z.A. Ademuwagun, J.A.A. Ayoade, I.E. Harrison and D.M. Warren (eds), *African Therapeutic Systems*. Los Angeles: Crossroads Press, pp. 120–4

——, 1982, The Techiman-Bono Ethnomedical System. In P.S. Yoder, (ed.), *African Health and Healing Systems: Proceedings of a Symposium*. Los Angeles: Crossroads Press, pp. 85–106

Williams, C.D. , 1933, Nutritional Disease of Children Assiociated with a Maize Diet. *Archives of Disease in Childhood* 8: 423

——, 1935, Kwashiorkor: Nutritional Disease of Children Associated with a Maize Diet. *Lancet* 2: 1151–2

Wittgenstein, L., 1958, *Philosophical Investigations*. Oxford: Basil Blackwell

Yoder, P.S., 1981, Knowledge of Illness and Medicine among Cokwe of Zaire. *Social Science and Medicine* 15B: 237–45

——, 1982a, Introduction. In P.S. Yoder (ed.), *African Health and Healing Systems: Proceedings of a Symposium*. Los Angeles: Crossroads Press, pp.1–20

——, (ed.) , 1982b, *African Health and Healing Systems: Proceedings of a Symposium*. Los Angeles: Crossroads Press

Young, A., 1975, Magic as a Quasi-Profession: The Organization of Magic and Magical Healing Among Amhara. *Ethnology* 14: 245–65

———, 1976, Internalizing and Externalizing Medical Belief Systems: An Ethiopian Medical Example. *Social Science and Medicine* 10: 147–56

———, 1977, Order, Analogy, and Efficacy in Ethiopian Divination. *Culture, Medicine and Psychiatry* 1: 0183–99

Glossary

The English translations of some of the Limbum terms below are not exact. The terms in question are inderterminate and this study is devoted to exploring their different meanings. However, to give the reader some provisional source of reference I have given the most obvious translations in this glossary.

Throughout the book I have used my own orthography for Limbum terms. I have chosen to write the Limbum terms in such a way that they more or less conform to existing orthography (there is as yet no single generally accepted Limbum orthography), and in such a way that the average English speaking reader will pronounce them approximately as they should sound. In quoting from other authors I have adapted their orthography to bring it into line with my own.

'	after a word or in a word indicates a glottal stop, as in *tvu' bara'*
c	is pronounced as the *ch* in change
ɛ	is pronounced as the *e* in red
e	is pronounced as the *e* in be
ee	is pronounced as the *e* above but is longer
o	is pronounced as the *o* in bored
oo	is pronounced as the *o* above but is longer
i	is generally pronounced as the *i* in ink, but in a few cases it is pronounced as the *e* above for reasons of convention, such as the *li* in Limbum and the *wi* in Wimbum and Wiya.

Adjectives may take concord markers determined by the class of the noun they modify. For example, when *bibip* (= bad) is combined with the noun *rkwi* (= death) it becomes *rbibip*, as in *rwki rbibip*.

Tonal markers have only been included in the odd case in which two terms appearing together are only distinguished by tone, as in the case of *nkvùu* (farm) and *nkvúu* (chief). In most

cases it is clear from the context which term is being used.
A (p) behind a word indicates a Pidgin term.

baa	mad
bara'	things from outside, modernity
bee	people
beengir	turn into, become
bfaa	illness resembling kwashiorkor, mistake, abomination
bibip	bad
bkvubshi	ancestors
Bongabi	women's dance society
boo	children
buu	things
byir	those who are dead
chop (p)	food
fai	traditional title holder, quarter-head
fon (p)	chief, king
gee	to cause, to make
juju (p)	masked figure
kɛrni	to hang, to commit suicide
kibai	traditional title holder, sub-chief
koo	to attack, to take, to catch
kop	forest
kop bfu	forest on top of the Tabenken-Binka mountain, where a witch market is said to be situated
kubci	to fix, to repair
kubci mfar	fixing twins
kubci ncɛp	fixing medicine
kupey (p)	type of witchcraft in which victims are exchanged for money
kvu	treat?
kvu bfaa	ritual for cleansing *bfaa*
la'	compound
li	language
Limbum	language spoken by the Wimbum
lir	eye
lvur	fool
mbe buu	up in the sky, heaven
mbimnyor	side (of the body)
mcɛp	medicines, charged objects

mfar	twins
Mfu'	warrior lodge
mimbu (p)	alcoholic beverage
mnyvu	gods, deities, certain places
mo'sir	one, single
munyongo (p)	type of witchraft (in the southwest of the country)
muu	child
muu ncɛp	literally medicine child, single twin
ncɛp	charged object, medicine, juju
ncvu la'	cleansing ritual for the compound
ndap	house
ndap ngong	house of the land, where sacrifices are made for good harvests, etc.
ngaa	people
ngaa ngang	people who treat *ngang*
ngaa ye bee	people who eat people
ngaa yɛ buu	people who see things
ngaa yɛr lir	people with eyes, i.e. diviners
ngambe (p)	divination
ngang	illness resembling kwashiorkor, masked figure who seeks out harmful medicines
ngang mshong	wet *ngang*
ngang yinto'	wet *ngang*
ngang yur	dry *ngang*
ngong	earth, world, land
ngwɛɛ	person
ngwɛɛ jaja	person who is not a witch
ngwɛɛ mcɛp	medicine man
Ngwɛrong	secret/regulatory/*juju* society
ngwɛɛ sɛng	diviner
ngwɛɛ ye bee	person who eats people
ngwɛɛ yɛ buu	person who sees things
ngwɛɛ yɛr lir	person with eyes, i.e. a diviner
njangi (p)	subscription society
njee	back
njincang	witch market
nkvúu	chief, king
nkvùu	farm
ntaa bsaa	gift market, where witches go to get 'things'
ntaa tvu'	witch market
nyvúu	god, God, nature, sun

nyvu kop	god of the forest
nyvu la'	god of the compound
nyvu ngong	god of the land, world, earth
nyvurka'	inhabitant of the witch market, devil
nyvu ro	god of the stream
rbvuu	stomach
rfar mo'sir	single twin
rkwi	death
rkwi rbibip	bad death
ro	stream
Samba	men's dance society
sɛng	divination
sha	corn beer
shong	wet
Tang	one of the Wimbum clans, another name for Tabenken
tu	head
tvu'	witchcraft, mystical power, night
tvu' bara'	witchcraft of the White men, technology
War	one of the Wimbum clans
wi	people
Wimbum	people of Mbum
wi tvu'	witches
Wiya	people of Ya (Ndu), one of the Wimbum clans
yang	illness, dis-ease
yang binji	literally women's illness, gonorrhea
yang bobkɛ'	literally children's illness, resembles kwashiorkor
yang gee	illness which is made/caused (by people, i.e. witches)
yang nyvu	illness which is natural or comes from god
ye	eat
ye bee	eat people, cannibalism
yɛ	see
yinto'	wet [?]
yur	dry, to itch

Index